International Ethics

International Ethics

Concepts, Theories, and Cases in Global Politics

Mark R. Amstutz

ROWMAN & LITTLEFIELD PUBLISHERS, INC.
Lanham • Boulder • New York • Oxford

WMAN & LITTLEFIELD PUBLISHERS, INC.

Published in the United States of America
by Rowman & Littlefield Publishers, Inc.
4720 Boston Way, Lanham, Maryland 20706

12 Hid's Copse Road
Cumnor Hill, Oxford OX2 9JJ, England

British Library Cataloguing in Publication Information Available

Library of Congress Cataloging-in-Publication Data

Amstutz, Mark R.
    International ethics : concepts, theories, and cases in global
politics / Mark R. Amstutz.
        p. cm.
    Includes bibliographical references and index.
    ISBN 0-8476-9152-7 (cloth : alk. paper).—ISBN 0-8476-9153-5
(paper : alk. paper)
    1. International relations—Moral and ethical aspects.   I. Title.
JZ1306.A48   1999
172'.4—dc21
                                                                98-43537
                                                                CIP

Printed in the United States of America

♾ ™ The paper used in this publication meets the minimum
requirements of American National Standard for Information
Sciences—Permanence of Paper for Printed Library Materials, ANSI/
NISO Z39.48–1992.

CONTENTS

TABLES AND FIGURES

CASE STUDIES

INTRODUCTION

A fundamental aim of this study is to demonstrate, through arguments and illustrations, that moral values are an essential element of international relations and that international ethics are foundational to global politics. Although international relations scholars have increasingly recognized the importance of moral values and ethical reasoning in international affairs, political realism continues to serve as the dominant paradigm in international relations; and, although realism does not deny international ethics, it allows little room for moral reasoning, focusing instead on the quest for national security and the promotion of economic and social well-being.

In this book, I argue that the realist notion that international politics is fundamentally a quest for political power and economic interests is false and untenable. Instead, I suggest that international politics is rooted in ethics and that states and other nonstate actors share a basic moral vocabulary that influences the individual and collective choices of states. To be sure, the ethical analysis of foreign policies and global structures is fraught with significant epistemological and methodological challenges. However, the difficulty of applying ethical principles to concrete issues and problems does not invalidate the possibility of or the responsibility for morally assessing political actions and institutional structures.

Realists assert that international society is a realm of power and necessity, not morality and choice. Because no common authority exists in the international system to protect states and to resolve disputes, some political thinkers have suggested that states' overriding interests are national security and material well-being. These interests, it is suggested, automatically displace morality. George Kennan, for example, argues that because a statesman's primary duty is to secure the vital interests of the state, foreign affairs are essentially amoral. He writes,

> Government is an agent, not a principal. Its primary obligation is to the inter-
> ests of the national society it represents . . . its military security, the integrity
> of its political life and the well-being of its people. These needs have no
> moral quality. They are the unavoidable necessities of national existence and
> therefore are subject to classification as neither "good" nor "bad."[1]

Kennan thinks that because interests such as security, political independence, and national well-being are essential to the survival and economic
viability of states, they have no moral quality. But why should vital interests be amoral? Are not human wants and interests rooted partly in morality? And does not the pursuit of foreign policy goals involve moral judgment? As Arnold Wolfers has wisely observed, international relations are
not beyond the scope of morality but are themselves based on moral
norms.[2]

A brief perusal of contemporary international developments illustrates
the pervasive and significant role of moral values and ethical judgments.
Consider the following events, each of them involving important moral
norms:

1. In the aftermath of the post-Cold War disintegration of Yugoslavia,
a major war broke out among Muslim, Serb, and Croat peoples, focusing
mainly on the multinational state of Bosnia-Herzegovina. Prior to the October 1995 cease-fire, which provided the basis for the subsequent Dayton
Peace Accord, the war had claimed more than a half million casualties,
including 250,000 deaths, and had resulted in more than one million refugees.[3] One of the most evil aspects of the Bosnian war was the gross violation of human rights, the most grotesque of which was "ethnic cleansing,"
that is, the detention, forced removal, or killing of persons because of their
ethnicity and religion. Although all three warring parties were guilty of
these atrocities, the main offenders were the Bosnian Serbs, who forced
the evacuation of tens of thousands of Muslims from their towns and villages. When the media published photos of emaciated Muslim men in
overcrowded, inhumane detention camps, there was universal moral condemnation for this evil behavior.

In light of this senseless war, should Western powers have intervened to
halt the killing and the human rights abuses? Are major European powers
partly responsible for failing to prevent ethnic genocide? Should the
United States have used its superior military power to punish the Serbs,
thereby deterring future aggression? Moreover, should the United States
have lifted its military embargo against Bosnia in order to allow the Bosnian government to acquire military arms to better defend itself, even
though such action would have undoubtedly intensified the military conflict?

2. In 1994, a major civil war erupted in Rwanda, resulting in some 800,000 deaths and more than two million refugees. Whereas France carried out a limited military intervention, the international community did little to halt the killing, save providing humanitarian relief. Should Western powers have intervened to restore order when civil war first broke out, thereby preventing genocide?

3. In September 1991, Haitian President Jean-Bertrand Aristide was overthrown in a military coup. To pressure Haiti's military to reinstate Aristide, economic sanctions were imposed, first a trade ban by the Organization of American States and then an oil embargo by the UN Security Council. When these measures failed to alter the Haitian military government, the United States, backed by Security Council authority, prepared for military intervention. Although the crisis eased after military rulers agreed to reinstate democracy in October 1994, some of the moral issues raised by this conflict persisted. Some of these issues included the following: Did the United States have a right (or an obligation) to help reinstate Aristide, the democratically elected president? Were U.S. military actions justified by the restoration of a democratically elected president? Were the economic sanctions imposed on Haiti morally legitimate, especially when they resulted in significant suffering by civilians? When thousands of Haitian refugees ("boat people") sought to flee Haiti to the United States in 1992 and 1993, was the U.S. refusal to accept them a morally legitimate response?

4. In December 1994, the Mexican government devalued its currency (the peso) to stimulate exports and decrease imports. This action unexpectedly led to a loss of confidence in the Mexican economy, resulting in a dramatic (40 percent) fall in the peso's exchange rate. Subsequently, the United States, supported by the International Monetary Fund (IMF), provided loan guarantees to help the Mexican economy recover, a decision deeply criticized by some American political leaders. Was the U.S. action morally legitimate, especially in view of its many domestic needs?

Two years later, in a similar development, foreign investors began losing confidence in the East and South Asian economies, especially those of Indonesia, Malaysia, South Korea, and Thailand. As a result, their economies contracted sharply as currencies lost from 30 to 50 percent of their value. To help restore financial confidence in these countries, the IMF provided tens of billions of dollars of credit to the region, including more than $40 billion for South Korea alone. Although most countries adjusted to the increased economic austerity, Indonesia experienced significant civil unrest in the spring of 1998, forcing President Suharto to resign. As with the Mexican crisis, these severe financial dislocations raise significant moral questions about the growing role of international capital markets in global society. Is increased economic interdependence a salutary development for

Third World states? More fundamentally, is the neoliberal international economic order, which allowed speculative market forces to severely weaken the Mexican and East Asian economies, itself a morally problematic system?

5. In a 1994 state referendum, voters in California overwhelmingly approved Proposition 187, which called for an end to state health, social, economic, and educational benefits for all illegal residents. Although courts have declared this action unconstitutional, the issue of legal and illegal immigration raises profound moral concerns for the United States and other Western industrial countries. How restrictive should immigration policies be? Which peoples should be given priority? Should countries provide equal treatment to legal and illegal immigrants? Is it morally legitimate to halt "boat people" (migrants fleeing their homeland by sea) and return them to their country of origin?

6. In light of egregious international economic inequalities, how much foreign economic assistance should developed countries give to the poor states? Are developed nations morally obligated to assist the economic development of low-income states? If countries are morally responsible for alleviating Third World poverty, to whom should the aid be given: to governments themselves for infrastructure development and welfare programs or to nongovernmental humanitarian organizations?

7. Finally, in May 1998, India carried out five nuclear tests, thereby demonstrating its nuclear capabilities to the international community. Shortly thereafter, Pakistan, India's neighbor and enemy, also carried out five nuclear tests, thereby also signaling its nuclear capabilities. Because these tests violated both the nonproliferation regime as well as the Comprehensive Test Ban Treaty, President Bill Clinton, as required by U.S. foreign policy statutes on nuclear nonproliferation, immediately imposed economic sanctions on both states.[4] The mutual nuclear testing by both India and Pakistan is clearly a dangerous international development because it creates a potential arms race between the two countries and increases regional instability and insecurity. From a moral perspective, the nuclear tests raise numerous issues. For example, is the existing nonproliferation regime—a regime that allows nuclear powers to keep their weapons of mass destruction while disallowing other states from gaining them—morally legitimate? Is the expansion of the nuclear "club" beneficial or harmful to world order? Given the poverty of both Pakistan and India, are their weapons development programs morally justified?

As these multilateral issues suggest, contemporary international relations involve fundamental moral choices. Although not all international relations issues involve moral values, most foreign policy decisions are based in part on ethical judgment. Moreover, the development of the international community's rules, procedures, and structures will similarly depend on values and norms that are partly moral.

This study explores two distinct dimensions of international political morality: the role of moral values in foreign policy and the ethical foundation of the rules and structures of global society. It is frequently suggested that moral values have no place in foreign policy because each sovereign state is entitled to its own cultural, behavioral, legal, and moral norms; and, because of the international community's cultural diversity, some theorists have argued that there is and can be no common morality in global society. However, this conclusion is untenable for two reasons. First, although cultural diversity is a feature of global society, state and nonstate actors share a common moral vocabulary that influences international relations. These shared basic norms provide the basis for moral claims on issues such as self-determination, human rights, the use of force, and humanitarian relief. Second, and more significant, despite the reality of cultural pluralism, there is no necessary or logical connection between the empirical fact of cultural pluralism and the normative belief that there is no morality in global society. The normative belief in moral relativism does not and cannot follow necessarily and logically from the fact of cultural diversity. Morality, after all, is based not on consensus but on perceived moral obligations.

This is a study in applied international political ethics. Although I address important philosophic issues, such as the epistemological and substantive challenges posed by cultural pluralism, the major aim of this book is to describe and assess the nature, role, and impact of international political morality on the individual and collective conduct of foreign relations. This task is undertaken by examining the nature and legitimacy of moral values and the role of ethical strategies and traditions in applying moral values to specific issue-areas such as human rights, war, and foreign intervention.

This study also examines the ethical nature of the rules, structures, and informal patterns of the international system itself. Whereas the morality of foreign policy focuses on the role of moral norms in international relations, international ethics is concerned with the justice of global society, including the moral legitimacy of the nation-state and the structures and dominant patterns of the international community. For example, are territorial boundaries morally significant? Is the norm of nonintervention a principal ethical rule of international society? If it is, can the norm be violated to protect other moral norms, such as basic human rights? Is humanitarian intervention morally defensible? Are the egregious economic and political disparities among states morally acceptable, and do high-income states have a moral obligation to admit a large number of refugees?

This book comprises two distinct dimensions. The first part, chapters 1 through 3, analyzes conceptual and theoretical issues. Chapter 1 defines the nature of morality and ethics and the role of political morality in foreign policy, illuminating the limits and possibilities of a moral foreign policy. Chapter 2 examines different methodologies for applying moral reasoning to political action, focusing on rule-based analysis (often defined as deontological, or Kantian, ethics) and ends-based analysis (often defined as consequentialism). Chapter 3 describes the nature of ethical traditions and their role in structuring moral analysis. Although many different ethical traditions are utilized in international ethics, this study focuses on the two traditions that have had greatest influence in the United States in the postwar era: realism and idealism. The remainder of the book, chapters 4 through 8, focuses on five important problems in global politics: human rights, military force, foreign intervention, economic statecraft, and global political justice.

Throughout this study, I use case studies to illuminate and apply moral norms to specific international relations issues and problems. To encourage ethical analysis, each case study concludes with a brief discussion of relevant moral questions and concerns raised by a particular conflict or problem. Because the test of political morality is whether it contributes to a more just global society, the challenge in international ethics is not simply to identify appropriate moral values but to apply them to global issues and problems. The aim of this study is thus to encourage ethical reflection that fosters better, more just political judgments.

*   *   *

In preparing this study, I have benefited from the assistance and encouragement of numerous persons. First, I thank my parents, Mahlon and Ruth Amstutz, for teaching me as a young boy the value of personal integrity and the importance of moral reflection. Second, I thank the students of my ethics and foreign policy course for encouraging and challenging my thinking on many of the issues examined in this book. Third, I am grateful to Wheaton College for giving me an Aldeen Development Grant, which allowed me to get this project underway during the summer of 1996. Fourth, I thank my teaching assistants, Megan Holst, Jana Morgan, and Janet Rosenblad, for providing invaluable research and editorial support. Fifth, I am grateful to Stephen Smith and Jonathan Eastvold, two Wheaton College students, for carefully reading the manuscript and offering helpful comments. Finally, I thank Jennifer Knerr, executive editor of Rowman & Littlefield, for providing invaluable substantive and organizational suggestions. She and her colleagues, especially Lynn Gemmell, the production editor, helped to make the book much better than it would have been otherwise.

CHAPTER ONE

MORALITY AND FOREIGN POLICY

The "necessities" in international politics, and for that matter in all spheres of life, do not push decision and action beyond the realm of moral judgment; they rest on moral choice themselves.

Arnold Wolfers[1]

Man's moral sense is not a strong beacon light, radiating outward to illuminate in sharp outline all that it touches. It is, rather, a small candle flame, casting vague and multiple shadows, flickering and sputtering in the strong winds of power and passion, greed and ideology. But brought close to the heart and cupped in one's hands, it dispels the darkness and warms the soul.

James Q. Wilson[2]

There does not exist such a thing as international morality.

Sir Harold Nicolson[3]

What passes for ethical standards for governmental policies in foreign affairs is a collection of moralisms, maxims, and slogans, which neither help nor guide, but only confuse, decision.

Dean Acheson[4]

This chapter examines the nature and role of moral values and ethical reasoning in international relations. It begins by identifying distinctive features of the terms *morality* and *ethics* and then explores the nature and bases of international political morality, addressing the challenge posed by

1

cultural pluralism to the conceptualization and application of such morality in global society. It then examines the role of moral norms in foreign policy, giving special emphasis to the goals, methods, and problems of applying international morality. The chapter illustrates the role of international political morality with two case studies: the 1994 U.S. intervention in Haiti to restore to power the constitutionally elected president, Jean-Bertrand Aristide, and the moral debate precipitated by President Ronald Reagan's 1985 visit to the military cemetery in Bitburg, Germany.

Morality and Ethics

The word *morality* derives from the Latin *mores*, meaning custom, habit, and way of life. It typically describes what is good, right, or proper. These concepts, in turn, are often associated with such notions as virtue, integrity, goodness, righteousness, and justice. The term *ethics* is rooted in the Greek *ethos*, meaning custom or common practice. Because its root meaning is similar to that of *morality*, the two concepts are often used interchangeably. Strictly speaking, however, the two terms represent distinct elements of normative analysis: *morality* referring to values and beliefs about what is right and wrong, good and bad, just and unjust and *ethics* referring to the examination, justification, and critical analysis of morality. Because of the significance of these elements in international ethics, I explore each of them more fully below.

The Nature of Morality

Moral values have at least three important distinguishing features: they command universal allegiance, they demand impartiality, and they are largely self-enforcing.

The claims of universality mean that moral norms are binding on all peoples. Immanuel Kant articulated this requirement in his famous *categorical imperative,* which calls on persons to treat others as having intrinsic value and to act in accordance with principles that are valid for others.[5] As one scholar has explained, universalization means that if "I ought to do X, then I am committed to maintaining that morally anyone else ought to do X unless there are relevant differences between the other person and myself and/or between his situation and mine."[6]

The second dimension of morality—the impartiality of norms—helps to ensure that morality is not simply a means to clothe and advance self-interest. Because of the propensity for human selfishness, philosophers have emphasized the need for dispassion and disinterest. As a result, they have argued that morality must be defined and applied in terms of the perspectives and interests other than those of the actor. For example, in his classic work *A Theory of Justice*, John Rawls argues that moral principles should be based on impartiality by requiring that they be selected through a "veil of ignorance," that is, defining and selecting norms without knowledge of who will benefit from them.[7]

A third important feature of morality is its self-enforcing quality. Unlike law, which is enforced by government, morality is applied mainly through the voluntary actions of persons. The decision to abide by moral obligations is rooted in the beliefs and values that people hold. In a short article titled "Law and Manners," which was published in 1924 in *The Atlantic Monthly,* English jurist John Fletcher Moulton defined the moral domain as "obedience to the unenforceable." According to Moulton, human affairs involve actions in three different realms: legal, moral, and voluntary. In the domain of the law, persons fulfill the legal norms because of government's capacity to enforce its norms. In the third domain, the realm of free choice, persons are free to do as they wish. Between these two realms is the area of morality, or what Moulton termed "manners," by which people behave in accord with "consciousness of duty" rather than the coercive rules of public authority. Moulton describes this domain as follows: "[I]t is the domain of obedience to the unenforceable. That obedience is the obedience of a man to that which he cannot be forced to obey. He is the enforcer of the law himself."[8] Morality, whether private or public, individual or collective, involves a duty to obey moral precepts that are accepted as inherently binding because of their claims to rightness or justice.

Although morality is pervasive in human life, it is concerned mainly with a particular dimension of human affairs, namely, individual and collective judgments involving moral values. It is not concerned with choices and actions in the nonmoral realm.[9] Because government policies have a society-wide impact, most political affairs, whether domestic or international, involve some level of moral judgment. For some decisions, such as military intervention to halt genocide or the development of a weapon of mass destruction, moral considerations are primary; for others, such as selecting the UN secretary-general or determining the level of foreign economic assistance to a particular country, the role of moral norms will be limited. However, regardless of the issues, foreign policy will generally involve moral values.

The Nature of Ethics

Fundamentally, ethics involves choosing or doing what is right and good and refraining from choosing or doing what is bad or evil. From an ethical perspective, the good is realized by the application of appropriate moral

norms to private and public affairs. This is no easy task, especially in domestic and international politics, in which government decisions do not
lend themselves to simple moral verdicts. This difficulty is partly due to
the complexity of public affairs as well as to overlapping and even competing moral values that are often involved in specific political issues and policy dilemmas. As a result, decision makers must select the most desirable
action from a number of available alternatives, each involving moral limitations. Thus, if political decisions are to be developed and implemented
on the basis of morality, *ethical reasoning* will be required. At a minimum,
this process will entail identifying the moral dimensions of issues (a process sometimes called moral imagination), selecting relevant moral norms,
critically assessing the issue or problem in the light of morality, applying
morality to the potential alternatives, and then implementing the preferred
policy. Thus, ethical reasoning in international relations will involve the
identification, illumination, and application of relevant moral norms to the
conduct of states' foreign relations.

Another important dimension of international ethics involves the assessment of rules, practices, and institutions of global society in light of
relevant moral norms. In effect, international ethics is concerned with the
moral architecture of the international system, that is, the moral legitimacy
of the patterns and structures of global society. For example, international
ethics addresses such issues as the fairness of the existing international
economic order, the justice of global institutions, and the justice of international regimes (rules and semi-institutionalized patterns of decision
making in specific issue areas) in such areas of common concern as refugees, energy, biodiversity, and waste disposal. The aim of such moral reflection is to assess the justice of the existing world system. In addition,
international ethics is concerned with the implementation of the rules and
structures of global society. Are the rules applied fairly and impartially?
For example, are the international rules governing fishing and pollution
applied equitably? Are the judgments of the International Court of Justice
fair and consistent?

In this chapter and the next, I examine two dimensions of political morality in world politics. Here I examine the nature and sources of international political morality and then analyze the relationship of moral norms
to the development and implementation of foreign policy. In doing so, I
specifically assess some of the major aims, methods, and problems involved in explicitly integrating moral norms with the foreign policies of
states. In chapter 2, I examine alternative strategies for applying international political morality. That is, I identify and assess three different methodologies for carrying out ethical decision making.

The Nature and Bases of Political Morality

Personal morality is frequently identified with political morality. Although the two are related, they are not identical. Individual morality consists of moral values and norms (i.e., principles, rules, prohibitions and duties) that are applicable to the conduct of persons in their personal or private relations. The Ten Commandments, the admonition to "love your neighbor as yourself," and obligation to truth telling are examples of personal morality. Political morality, by contrast, consists of moral values and norms that are applicable to the political life of communities, including neighborhoods, cities, states, and the international community itself. Examples of political morality include such norms as the equality of persons, freedom of conscience, equal treatment under the law, the right of self-defense and nonintervention. Although political morality is rooted in personal morality, the former differs from the latter both in the nature of its norms and in the sphere in which moral norms are applied. Whereas individual morality governs the actions of individuals, political morality applies to the public decisions of political or government officials acting on behalf of public institutions.

Fundamentally, a political community is one in which a government exists with the authority to make society-wide decisions. It is a society based on a hierarchical distribution of power, with rulers and subjects having different levels of authority and thus different types of political responsibilities. It is a mistake to assume that the responsibilities of citizens and rulers are identical; individual and political moralities are not symmetrical. Although citizens and government officials share similar moral obligations as human beings, their different roles in political society place different moral obligations on them. As Lea Brilmayer observes, "The prohibitions found in interpersonal morality cannot be mechanically transplanted into a code of conduct for public officials."[10] Political morality may allow some actions that are prohibited by personal morality. For example, a soldier may kill in wartime, or a state may carry out capital punishment, but such actions are not synonymous with murder. Similarly, a state may tax its citizens, but an individual may not steal or extort resources from another person. Political morality thus provides norms for the just and effective use of legitimate power in political society. Although it is beyond the scope of this study to describe the nature and bases of legitimate political authority, it is significant, for our purposes, that political morality not only helps justify government authority but also provides norms for judging political action.[11]

Domestic and international politics are qualitatively different. Although scholars differ in their explanations of these differences, one widely accepted comparison characterizes domestic politics as a hierarchical system in which sovereign authority exists to make society-wide decisions and international politics as a nonhierarchical system without common authority to make and enforce decisions. Domestic society is the realm of authority, whereas international society is the realm of anarchy (i.e., no authority to impose order). In view of the structural differences in domestic and international politics, some scholars argue that the political moralities of domestic and international communities are also qualitatively different.

Some realists, for example, argue that in domestic society moral judgments are possible because typically cultural and moral values are widely shared, whereas in global politics, in which cultural and moral pluralism is prevalent, few moral judgments are possible. According to this perspective, whereas domestic society provides a rich and substantive political morality, international society provides a limited moral menu. Indeed, for some realists the only morality is that which promotes and protects the territorial security and economic well-being of a state. However, other scholars argue that differences between domestic and international politics have been greatly exaggerated and that moral values are far more significant in global society than realists suggest.

This group is represented by two types of thinkers: communitarians, who believe that states are significant moral actors in global society, and cosmopolitans, who regard the individual, not the state, as the major moral actor. Michael Walzer, a communitarian, gives a prominent place to international political morality by deriving states' international obligations from the "domestic analogy," that is, by arguing that states have rights and duties in global society analogous to the rights and duties of individuals in domestic political society.[12] For Walzer, international political morality entails such norms as the prohibition against aggression, the right of political sovereignty and the corollary right of self-defense, the duty of nonintervention in other states' domestic affairs, the protection of human rights, and the duty to settle disputes peacefully. By contrast, Charles Beitz, a cosmopolitanist, develops a global morality based on the rights and well-being of persons, challenging the morality of the existing Westphalian political order of sovereign states.[13] Because territorial boundaries are not morally significant in his cosmopolitan ethic, the autonomy of states can be qualified by the moral claims of individuals. In effect, the rights of states ultimately depend on the rights of persons.

In assessing the role of political morality in foreign policy, scholars have periodically made two errors. First, some have simply denied the relevance of morality to international affairs. For them, although moral norms might be relevant to interpersonal relations or even to domestic political affairs, they have little to do with interstate political affairs. Global politics is the realm of necessity, and there can be no right and wrong when the survival of the state is at stake. However, as Arnold Wolfers noted at the outset of this chapter, the fundamental choices of statesmen are rooted in moral values. Thus, international politics is not divorced from ethical judgment but rests on morality.

The second error, frequently related to the first, is the tendency to deny the existence of political morality altogether. Here, morality consists solely of norms governing individual private behavior. George Kennan illustrates both of these errors in the following passage:

> Moral principles have their place in the heart of the individual and in the shaping of his own conduct, whether as a citizen or as a government official. . . . But when the individual's behavior passes through the machinery of political organization and merges with that of millions of other individuals to find its expression in the actions of a government, then it undergoes a general transmutation, and the same moral concepts are no longer relevant to it. A government is an agent, not a principal; and no more than any other agent may it attempt to be the conscience of its principal. In particular, it may not subject itself to those supreme laws of renunciation and self-sacrifice that represent the culmination of individual moral growth.[14]

Although Kennan is correct in his claim that personal morality should not govern the behavior of diplomats, his failure to recognize that political morality is an essential element of all normative decision making in global politics is a serious error. To be sure, the political morality applicable to interstate relations is not the same as personal morality. Thus, the challenge in bringing moral norms to bear on global political relations is to first identify and then apply relevant norms of international political morality.

Before exploring the role of morality in foreign affairs, it will be helpful to briefly address the validity of political morality. Because of the growing influence of postmodern subjectivism, there has been a growing skepticism in the contemporary world about the legitimacy of moral claims in public life. This has been the case especially for political morality in global society, in which cultural pluralism is much more pronounced than in domestic society.

Sources of Political Morality

Because philosophers hold a number of theories about the source of moral values, political theorists have offered a variety of justifications for political morality. Three of the most important theories include foundationalism, constructivism, and consensualism. The foundationalist approach assumes that international morality is rooted in universal, unchanging first principles that are apprehended by reason. The constructivist approach, by contrast, derives moral values from general conceptions of justice (or the common good) through deductive arguments based on hypothetical cases. Finally, the consensual approach derives political morality from existing agreements among member states.

The foundationalist perspective assumes that transcendent moral norms exist and that such universal standards can be apprehended by rational reflection. Foundationalist thinkers such as Thomas Aquinas, John Locke, and Kant believed that morality was valid and true not because it made the world better or more humane (pragmatism) or because it increased the happiness and well-being of persons (utilitarianism) but because it was divinely ordained by a transcendent Creator. An example of international morality from a foundationalist perspective is the belief that universal human rights exist and that they are rooted in a transcendent moral law (natural law) that is universal and unchanging. Another illustration is the just-war doctrine, which provides moral principles for defining when and how force can be utilized in pursuing just international relations. Foundationalists recognize that the international community is comprised of a large number of nations, each with its own cultural norms and social patterns; and, although such cultural and social diversity results in different value systems, there is nonetheless substantial consensus among moral value systems at a foundational level.

The constructivist thesis assumes that moral values are derived from hypothetical arguments. Whereas foundationalists assert that the basis of morality consists of transcendent norms whose truth and validity are inherent in the created order, constructivists ground morality in instrumental, deductive reasoning. For example, constructivists might deduce moral values from political and normative premises (e.g., political liberalism, justice as fairness, or some related normative proposition) through hypothetical arguments guided by logic and impartiality. Rawls illustrates this moral theory in an important essay titled "The Law of Peoples," in which he seeks to extend his domestic theory of justice to international society.[15] Rawls imagines an "original position," in which representatives from different societies gather to impartially develop norms of international justice. He argues that a just "law of peoples" can be developed only if the societies themselves have achieved a minimal level of justice. Rawls specifies three minimal conditions for well-ordered societies, whether liberal or not: They must be peaceful, they must be perceived as legitimate by their own people, and they must honor basic human rights. Rawls assumes that when representatives from liberal and nonliberal societies meet to develop a just "law of peoples," they will be able to define minimal norms that will advance justice within international society. Some of these rights and duties of "peoples" include a right to freedom and independence, the equality of peoples, the right of self-defense, the duty of nonintervention, the obligation to fulfill treaties, and the responsibility to honor human rights.[16]

A third view of political morality is consensual theory, sometimes called ethical positivism.[17] According to this approach, political morality is rooted in binding norms expressed by the formal and informal rules of domestic society, whereas international political morality is rooted in the shared norms embodied in the conventions, informal agreements, and declarations that states accept as obligatory in their international relations. These shared norms are obligatory because they are part of international law and morally obligatory because they specify norms conducive to order, justice, or the perceived common good. Some thinkers have argued that, because it is impossible to derive "ought" from "is," it is similarly impossible to derive international ethical obligations from existing interstate legal conventions. However, scholars such as Terry Nardin have convincingly demonstrated that to the extent that law establishes binding obligations on individuals, groups, and states, it fulfills the criteria of an ethical framework.[18] In her seminal study on twentieth-century international legal and political ethics, Dorothy Jones has illuminated how international law has produced an authoritative and widely accepted framework, or "code," of international peace. This framework, she argues, is a normative system because it prescribes behavior that is conducive to global order and international harmony. Jones's study thus reinforces the claim that international morality can be based on consensual norms and multilateral declarations.[19]

It is significant that international law has established a category of law that is binding apart from the consent of states, thereby recognizing the limitations of consent as a basis of political morality. This type of international law—known as the *jus cogens*—refers to peremptory norms that are authoritative because the norms are inherently valid. Such norms, rooted in the values and practices of civilized society, include prohibitions against piracy, slavery, terrorism, and genocide. To some extent, the Tokyo and Nuremburg tribunals that prosecuted Japanese and German military officials for crimes against peace and humanity were based in part on this tradition of international law.

Although moral intuition, rational construction, and consent can each contribute to the development and articulation of international political morality, political morality must ultimately be grounded in norms that transcend human experience. Thus, this study proceeds from the belief that political morality, however it is justified, is based on normative principles of right and wrong, justice and injustice.

The Challenge of Cultural Pluralism

One of the significant challenges in defending international political morality is the absence of a shared, universal morality. Because the international system is comprised of many different nation-states, each with its own social patterns and values, cultural pluralism is a prevalent feature of the international community. Moreover, not only do peoples from different cultures hold different political moralities, but their moral systems have also evolved over time. Because of the evident variability and pluralism of global morality, some thinkers have concluded that there is no universal morality applicable to the international community. In their view, the only morals in international society are the subjective, relativistic values associated with each society. This perspective, known as the doctrine of *cultural relativism*, holds that because notions of right and wrong, justice and injustice, are rooted in each society's cultural mores, there is no universal moral code.

Although competing and conflicting moralities can inhibit the development of moral consensus and call into question the role of moral values in international politics, they do not necessarily substantiate the cynic's conviction that morality is nothing more than the subjective preferences of the powerful. To begin with, morality is concerned with what "ought" to be, not with what "is." Because the diversity of cultural norms and social practices is a manifestation of what "is," the existence of cultural pluralism does not threaten the notion of moral obligation. Moreover, it is important to emphasize that cultural and social pluralism is generally concerned with secondary norms, not basic principles. Although peoples from different cultures do not normally share particular beliefs about women's rights, government structures, and policies of distributive justice, there is generally widespread commitment to such notions as truth and justice as well as agreement about such fundamental norms as the dignity of human persons, freedom from torture, impartial application of the law, and freedom of conscience. Walzer calls this shared morality "minimal" to differentiate it from the particular, more developed "maximal" moralities found in each society.[20] Moral minimalism is a "thin" morality not because it is unimportant or makes few claims on human beings but because its claims, although general and diffuse, are expressed universally. Because of this shared minimal morality, human beings from different societies "can acknowledge each other's different ways, respond to each other's cries for help, learn from each other and march (sometimes) in each other's parades."[21]

In light of the distinction between minimal and maximal moralities, the claim that all morality is subjective and relative is not empirically sustainable. Although maximal norms vary significantly from culture to culture, there is also a high level of global consensus about thin morality, namely, those norms that are essential to social and political life. Thus, although humans often disagree about many issues and social and economic values, there is also significant agreement about foundational norms, such as truth telling, beneficence, promise keeping, courage, self-control, and justice.[22] A. J. M. Milne has argued that moral diversity in global society cannot be total because some moral principles are necessary to sustain social life. According to him, the international community's common morality includes such norms as: respect for human life, pursuit of justice, fellowship, social responsibility, freedom from arbitrary interference, honorable treatment, and civility.[23]

One way of illustrating the existence of common morality is to imagine the likely response to the arbitrary denial of property in different cultures. For example, if a number of persons were to visit various remote regions of the world and, on arriving in these distant, isolated areas, were to walk up to strangers and take some of their possessions, how would these strangers respond? What would mothers do if the visitors were to take their children from their arms? In all likelihood, they would oppose the arbitrary deprivation of their property and, most assuredly, resist the removal of their children. In addition, they would do so because of the universality of social values regarding friendship, family bonding, self-control, and property.

The pervasiveness of political morality has been convincingly demonstrated by Walzer's study of the ethics of war, *Just and Unjust Wars*, in which he argues that throughout history human judgments and arguments in wartime have been guided by a moral structure. This structure is revealed, says Walzer, not by the fact that soldiers and statesmen come to the same conclusions but by the fact that they acknowledge common difficulties, face similar problems, and talk the same language. "The clearest evidence for the stability of our values over time," writes Walzer, "is the unchanging character of the lies soldiers and statesmen tell. They lie in order to justify themselves, and so they describe for us the lineaments of justice."[24]

In the final analysis, cultural relativism is a wholly unacceptable ethical theory because it is impossible to live with the doctrine's severe consequences. If there are no standards, everything is possible, and if everything is possible, torture, forced expulsion, systematic violation of human rights, denial of freedom, and religious persecution are not wrong. Although moral values and cultural patterns vary across societies, there is significant agreement among primary norms. For example, most human beings have a basic moral intuition that gross violations against other human beings are wrong. Thus, it does not follow, as cultural relativists assert, that there are no universal norms. Despite the existence of moral and cultural pluralism among secondary and tertiary norms, most thinkers reject cultural relativism. They do so, as Thomas Donaldson has noted, not because of compelling evidence for moral absolutism (i.e., the notion that eternal, universal ethical norms exist and are applicable to human actions) but because relativism is itself intellectually indefensible.[25]

The Development of a Moral Foreign Policy

What role do moral principles play in the conduct of foreign relations? First, morality helps define the goals and purposes of states and other actors. Moral norms do not provide policy directives, but they can offer a general vision and broad direction and provide the moral norms by which to illuminate and define a country's vital interests. As the late theologian John C. Bennett noted, moral values contribute to public policy debates on foreign policy goals by providing "ultimate perspectives, broad criteria, motives, inspirations, sensitivities, warnings, moral limits."[26] In effect, moral norms can establish the boundaries for policy deliberation and execution.

Moral norms also provide a basis for judgment. Without standards, evaluation is impossible. Moral norms thus provide an ethical foundation for assessing the foreign policies of states as well as for judging the rules and structures of international society. For example, the widely accepted norms of international human rights provided the basis for the widespread condemnation of Serb "ethnic cleansing" carried out against the Bosnian Muslims in 1992 and 1993. Moreover, the growing recognition of ecological interdependence has resulted in an increasing international acceptance of principles and practices that protect the earth's environment. Thus, when Saddam Hussein deliberately sought to destroy Kuwait's environment during the Persian Gulf War (by dumping oil into the sea and setting hundreds of oil wells on fire), these actions were condemned throughout the world.

Finally, moral norms provide the inspiration and motivation for policy development and implementation. Morality, in effect, provides the "fuel" for the government "engine." For example, the U.S. government's decision to intervene in Somalia in December 1992 to permit humanitarian relief was inspired in great measure by the humane concerns of leaders to alleviate starvation and keep hundreds of thousands of people from dying. In his important study of foreign aid, David Lumsdaine shows that the principal motivation for Western countries' substantial postwar foreign economic assistance to poor nations was morality. Although many factors and motivations influenced the giving of economic aid, the major inspiration and motivation was donor countries' "sense of justice and compassion."[27] Lumsdaine argues that international political morality, or what he terms "moral vision," shapes international relations. Contrary to realist claims that global politics is simply a realm of necessity, he claims that international relations involve freedom of action based on moral choice. As a result, international politics is an environment in which "conceptions of fairness and compassion, human dignity and human sympathy, justice and mercy" can be applied to the reform of global society.[28]

As will be made clear in chapter 2, there is no simple, easy method of applying political morality to foreign policy. One reason that international political action is generally morally ambiguous is that foreign policy issues and problems typically involve multiple and frequently conflicting moral norms. Thus, the process of moral reasoning must identify and apply the relevant moral criteria and, where moral conflict occurs, make the necessary trade-offs among the relevant criteria. Moreover, developing a moral foreign policy is a challenging task because an ethical decision-making strategy requires that morality be applied to the goals, means, and results of political action. However, because moral norms rarely result in ethical action at all three levels, trade-offs among the goals, means, and potential outcomes are generally inevitable.

Methods

How are moral norms applied in global politics? Among the different ways that moral norms influence international relations, three instruments are especially noteworthy: (1) the conscience of decision makers, (2) the influence of domestic public opinion, and (3) the influence of international reputation.[29] William Wilberforce, the early nineteenth-century British parliamentarian, illustrates the first approach. After becoming a Christian, Wilberforce concluded that slavery was immoral and contrary to the will of God. For nearly four decades he led the fight in the House of Commons against this inhuman practice, first seeking to abolish the slave trade and then attempting to abolish slavery altogether.[30] President Jimmy Carter also demonstrates the significant influence of a leader's moral values. As a result of his strong convictions about human rights, his administration pursued an activist human rights policy, leading U.S. officials to publicly condemn repression and the abuse of basic rights and to halt foreign assistance to repressive military regimes.

The role of domestic public opinion in foreign relations—the second method by which morality is applied to foreign policy—is applicable only in democratic societies, in which a government's continuing authority and influence depend on its perceived legitimacy. To be sure, public opinion is not an automatic by-product of the thinking and analysis of the masses. Rather, public opinion is developed, organized, and mobilized by elites, including the media, interest groups, professional associations, and political parties. The important role of public opinion in foreign affairs in democratic societies is illustrated by the inability of the government of the

Netherlands to accept deployment of NATO nuclear missiles in the early 1980s. Although the Dutch government was committed to such a deployment, the mass opposition to such action delayed the Netherlands' acceptance of cruise missiles for several years. In the United States, the role of mobilized public opinion was especially influential in the imposition of economic sanctions against South Africa. As a result of mass mobilization against South Africa's apartheid policies, many corporations halted their operations in South Africa, and universities and local and state governments adopted policies requiring divestment of stock for companies continuing their South African operations. The growing public opposition to apartheid also resulted in government action. In 1985 congressional debate forced the Reagan administration to adopt modest sanctions, and a year later Congress imposed, over presidential objections, much more substantial sanctions.

Finally, the application of international political morality is influenced by global public opinion. Because public opinion is comparatively weak in the international community, its impact on government decision making is limited. Still, dominant international perceptions of power and morality do affect the foreign policy behavior of states. Just as an individual's reputation is based on other people's perceptions, so too the reputation of states is derived largely from people's perception of international actions. For example, the growing perception in the United States and other industrial powers in 1997 and 1998 that the Swiss government failed to return financial assets to Jewish people at the end of World War II has significantly tarnished Switzerland's financial reputation.

Foreign policy behavior can contribute to a state's reputation as a reliable, credible, and moral actor, or it can damage such a reputation. Because a state's influence is rooted to a great extent in public perceptions, governments continuously assess the impact of their decisions on global public opinion. For example, during the Cuban missile crisis of 1962, U.S. officials considered numerous options in responding to the Soviet Union's installation of medium-range ballistic missiles. According to Robert Kennedy, the main reason that direct military intervention was deemed unacceptable is that it would have harmed the international reputation of the United States.[31] Moreover, although some military officials advocated the limited use of nuclear arms in the Vietnam War, this action was never seriously contemplated by government leaders, in part because of the loss of prestige and influence that the United States would have suffered from such action.

Problems

Scholars and statesmen have called attention to a number of important challenges to the effective integration of morality into the fabric of foreign relations. One of the most common criticisms of international ethics is the belief that the decentralized structure of global society allows little room for moral judgment. Although the decentralized, anarchic structure of global society places a premium on national security and the promotion of national well-being, the priority of national interest does not obliterate the moral claims of other actors in the international community. Politics, after all, is the means by which actors pursue the common good in light of competing and conflicting individual and group interests. If actors pursued only self-interest in domestic or international politics, there would be no place for moral action. However, international politics, like domestic politics, involves the quest for order and justice based on the cooperative actions of actors.

Scholars and statesmen have also questioned the role of morality in foreign affairs because moral norms have been repeatedly misused in global politics. Rather than guiding and judging policies, morality has been used to clothe and justify national interests, resulting in rigid, moralistic foreign policies. In addition, rather than contributing to the process of moral reflection, morality has been used as an ideological and moralistic instrument, fashioning a self-righteous and hypocritical policy that has contributed to cynicism rather than public justice. In effect, morality has not contributed to justice because of the absence of impartiality.

The dangers of moralism are clearly illustrated in American history, especially during the late nineteenth and early twentieth centuries, when political leaders sought to define and justify U.S. foreign policy through morality. For example, President William McKinley supposedly relied on divine guidance in using military force to end Spanish colonial rule in Cuba and the Philippines, and when President Woodrow Wilson intervened in Veracruz, Mexico, he did so on the basis of the moral conviction that such action would foster greater democracy in Mexico. More recently, the Carter administration used foreign aid to reward states that improved human rights and to punish those that violated basic human rights. Because the use of moral language in foreign policy has often led to moralism, fanaticism, inflexibility, and utopianism—qualities that are inimical to orderly international relations—some scholars, including historian Arthur Schlesinger, Jr., and diplomatic historian George F. Kennan, argue that foreign policy should be based on national interests, not morality. Schlesinger writes, "Saints can be pure, but statesmen must be responsible. As trustees for others, they must defend interests and compromise principles. In politics, practical and prudential judgment must have priority over moral verdicts."[32] Both Schlesinger and Kennan note that when moral values dictate foreign policy, foreign policy becomes inflexible, simplistic, utopian, and fanatical, perverting, if not eliminating, the process of ethical reasoning.

Although the misuse of morality can lead to cynicism and the denial of moral values, moral duplicity and hypocrisy do not justify the removal of moral values from international politics. Indeed, because human choices involve morality, domestic and international politics are inescapably moral enterprises. At the same time, it is essential to recognize that the integration of morality into the fabric of decision making and judgment poses dangers. For example, because political action is partly an exercise in self-interest, public officials frequently apply moral norms to the conduct of foreign relations with partiality, thereby encouraging an arrogant and moralistic foreign policy. Moreover, because most political conduct typically involves multiple moral norms, moral action will inevitably involve trade-offs among relevant competing norms. Because no public actions are ever completely right and just, the application of political morality should always be undertaken with humility and self-criticism. This is why Stanley Hoffmann has observed that an essential norm of the international system is the virtue of moderation, or what he calls "the morality of self-restraint."[33]

In the following, I illustrate the role of moral values in two case studies. In the first, I explore the role of political morality in U.S. foreign policy initiatives to restore to power Haiti's first democratic government in the early 1990s. In the second, I examine President Reagan's 1985 visit to Bitburg, Germany, exploring and assessing the potential role of repentance and forgiveness in foreign relations.

A principal motivation of the Clinton administration's Haitian foreign policy was its moral commitment to supporting democratic rule, especially in the Western Hemisphere. Although other factors, including the growing exodus of Haitian refugees, influenced U.S. foreign policy actions, political morality provided a dominant motive for restoring civilian rule in Haiti. Although sovereignty allows states to determine their own government, military coups do not automatically ensure international legitimacy. Thus, when the United States urged the international community to isolate and eventually overthrow an illegal military regime, it received widespread international support, largely because of the growing moral legitimacy of consent as the sole basis of political power.

CASE NO. 1-1
U.S. INTERVENTION IN HAITI

Background

Haiti, located some 600 miles south of the Florida coast, is the poorest and most densely populated country in the Western Hemisphere. Although Haiti achieved political independence from France early in the nineteenth century, the nearly two centuries of political self-rule had not resulted in the country's political and economic development. Rather, it had led to cultural decay, economic stagnation, and political oppression. Indeed, because of the country's corruption, political instability, and authoritarianism, conditions in Haiti were, in the words of Thomas Hobbes, "nasty, brutish and short."

In December 1990, Haiti held its first democratic elections, resulting in the overwhelming election of the Reverend Jean-Bertrand Aristide as president. Because the elections were supported by the international community and monitored by foreign officials, many observers were optimistic that the new regime would strengthen democratic institutions and promote human rights while halting the instability, violence, and oppression that had characterized Haitian political life throughout much of the nation's history. However, a year and a half after assuming office, Aristide was overthrown in a military coup and forced to flee the country. The international community strongly condemned the military's action while states in the Western Hemisphere took more forceful action by imposing a regional trade ban. When these sanctions failed to reinstate Aristide, the UN Security Council imposed a worldwide oil and arms embargo on Haiti, an action that led to immediate oil shortages and forced military leaders back to the negotiating table. Moreover, because of increased economic hardship imposed by sanctions, a growing number of citizens sought to escape the adversity and oppression by seeking illegal entry into the United States. As the number of "boat people" rose, the U.S. government was faced with the difficult moral dilemma of responding to Haiti's rapidly expanding human needs by either sending refugees to a detention camp at the U.S. Naval Base in Guantanamo, Cuba, or returning them to Haiti itself.

As international pressures increased on the Haitian regime, President Aristide and General Raoul Cedras, the head of Haiti's military, met at Governors Island, New York, and concluded an agreement calling for the creation of an interim government, amnesty for military officers involved in the coup, and the return of Aristide as president. Although parts of the agreement were implemented, the military ultimately refused to relinquish power, leading the Security Council to renew the oil embargo. The United States also decided to impose stricter sanctions, including the halting of all commercial air traffic between the United States and Haiti and the banning of all financial transactions between the two countries.

Despite the growing economic adversity within Haiti, the military regime refused to give up power. As a result, in July 1994 the Security Council adopted a resolution authorizing the use of force to reinstate Aristide. Armed with this collective legitimation of force, President Bill Clinton authorized an invasion plan to force compliance with the Governors Island Agreement. However, he also sent a team, headed by former President Jimmy Carter, to seek to convince the Haitian military to comply with the international community's demands. Just as U.S. military forces were about to invade Haiti, General Cedras and the Carter negotiating team reached an accord that averted bloodshed. The agreement required the transfer of political power from the military government to civilian authorities by October 15. Immediately thereafter, a 20,000-member U.S. peacekeeping force began landing in Haiti to ensure the safe return of President Aristide and the peaceful transfer of power. As required by the negotiated agreement, General Cedras resigned on October 10, opening the way for Aristide to return to Haiti to serve out his remaining term as president.

Ethics and the Restoration of Democracy

After President Aristide was removed from office in 1991, the United States and other leading powers strongly condemned the military's overthrow of the first freely elected government of Haiti. However, after making public declarations and endorsing a number of economic sanctions designed to punish the new regime, they faced the harsh reality of what other actions, if any, should be taken. In the United States, the Haitian imbroglio resulted in two distinct debates, one political and the other moral.

The first debate focused on the relative significance of the political and economic developments within Haiti in light of other competing foreign policy interests. Was the restoration of Haitian democracy of vital significance to the United States, or was the promotion of human dignity and constitutional government merely a secondary interest? If the former case, the U.S. government needed to use its considerable political and economic power to restore the former government and to do so in a timely manner. If the latter case, the U.S. government could pursue its interests in the Caribbean region without urgency or military force.

The second debate focused on international ethics and in particular on what additional actions, including the possible use of military force, should be utilized to restore Aristide to power. Fundamentally, the United States and other members of the international community faced a moral dilemma about how to respond to the new Haitian regime: On the one hand, the United States could view the coup as a domestic political development, protected by the norm of political sovereignty; on the other hand, U.S. government officials could regard the coup as a violation of widely shared moral norms, including human rights and participatory democracy, thereby justifying the use of individual and collective military force to restore the constitutional government of President Aristide. The ethical debate thus involved the two moral polarities: national sovereignty on the one hand and human rights and democratic rule on the other.

In devising U.S. foreign policy toward Haiti, administration officials were deeply influenced by the norms of human rights and democratic rule. For the administration, the restoration of democracy was significant because it offered the most promising way of overcoming the legacy of tyranny and oppression that had characterized much of Haiti's history. Moreover, the persistent oppression in Haiti would have continued to cause thousands of refugees to flee the island, resulting in large numbers of asylees (persons who request asylum after they have successfully arrived in a foreign country) and massive refugee dislocations. In short, the determination to restore democratic rule, even if it involved military force, was rooted in a strong moral commitment to the protection and enhancement of Haitians' human dignity.

Moral Reflections

This brief case study raises numerous important ethical issues about international moral obligations toward nations suffering from oppressive regimes, human rights abuses, and unconstitutional domestic political change.

- When Third World states such as Haiti suffer from poverty, political oppression, and human rights abuses, which moral values should influence the foreign policies of major states? Which international norm is more important: sovereignty or human rights?
- Do gross human rights violations justify foreign (unilateral or multilateral) intervention? Does international political morality require the removal of illegal military regimes and the restoration of democracy?
- More particularly, did the United States, as the dominant power in the Western Hemisphere, bear special moral obligations to Haiti in the aftermath of the coup that toppled Aristide from power? If so, what were those obligations?
- Although the United Nations legally approved the U.S. intervention, was it moral?
- Given the continued suffering and political instability in the years following the U.S. intervention, was the retoration of Aristide to power morally justified?

The second case—President Reagan's visit to Bitburg—is important because it illuminates the potential role of contrition, forgiveness, and reconciliation in overcoming past injustices. Because this case involves the lingering effects of the Nazi holocaust, it raises difficult issues about the extent to which past gross evils can be overcome, even after governments have admitted culpability, provided some restitution, and sought reconciliation through forgiveness.

Hannah Arendt once observed that the only way to overcome past wrongs, or what she termed the "predicament of irreversibility," is through forgiveness, a doctrine that she regarded as Jesus' greatest contribution to political thought.[34] Like justice, forgiveness entails accepting and admitting the wrongs of the past, but unlike justice, it seeks to overcome the legacy of past wrongs through repentance and reconciliation. Forgiveness does not solve the injustice of the past, but it does create the possibility for a new, more just, and more peaceful political order through the restoration of relationships. Because forgiveness offers the possibility of reconciliation among enemies, a growing number of scholars have called attention to its potentially significant role in international affairs. Patrick

Glynn, for example, writes, "Nations may cling to the angry past or embrace the hopeful future. But the path to peace and prosperity for all nations today lies through the gate of forgiveness."[35]

Because forgiveness is seldom applied to domestic politics and even more rarely to international politics, it will be helpful to first explore its nature and role in interpersonal relations. In common usage, forgiveness implies, first, the cancellation of a debt or the pardoning of a past wrong and, second, the restoration of a relationship. Theologians commonly define the process of interpersonal reconciliation through confession and pardon as involving four distinct but interrelated elements. First, the wrongdoer confesses the evil committed, openly admitting personal culpability. Second, after acknowledging personal guilt, the wrongdoer apologizes for the injury committed, frequently demonstrating the authenticity of contrition through acts of restitution. Third, in response to the wrongdoer's contrition, the victim declines vengeance and instead pursues restoration through forgiveness. Finally, on the basis of the mutual interactions between the wrongdoer and the victim, the parties move toward reconciliation, creating a new relationship based on a restored moral foundation.

Repentance and forgiveness are often difficult to apply in personal life. This is so because unjust human actions frequently result in significant bitterness and anger, encouraging a desire for vengeance and restitution. Additionally, practicing forgiveness is difficult because the moral virtues on which it depends—such as the courage to confront the past, the humility to repent, the self-control to limit anger and oppose vengeance, and the magnanimity to pursue reconciliation—are rarely cultivated in society.

However, if forgiveness is challenging in interpersonal relations, it is much more difficult in public life.[36] This is true for two reasons: first, because political morality, as noted earlier, is not identical with personal morality and, second, because responsibility for political action is frequently elusive and difficult to assign. For example, who is responsible for the Vietnam War? For South Africa's apartheid? For Rwanda's genocide? To be sure, although political leaders and government officials bear primary responsibility for policies such as these, they do not assume sole responsibility. Indeed, all members of a political community also bear some responsibility through their actions or inactions.

Forgiveness in public life is similar to individual forgiveness. Following the interpersonal model sketched previously, we can conceive of international political forgiveness as entailing four elements. First, forgiveness requires complete truth telling—a full accounting of past communal wrongs. This means that a past aggressive war or other international injustice requires that a state acknowledge its collective responsibility for the pain, evil, or injury that it might have brought about to other peoples. This truth telling must be public so that knowledge of the past evil becomes part of the collective conscience of society. Second, leaders must acknowledge past wrongs and express public contrition for the injury committed. If the apology is to be genuine, the expiation needs to be specific, concrete, and public, involving in some instances acts of restitution. Third, forgiveness requires that the group or state that has been victimized acknowledge the contrition and repentance of the wrongdoers and not pursue vengeance or seek retribution. Rather than attempting to rectify past wrongs, the victims pursue the restoration of political relationships based on the renewal of trust and the cancellation of debts. Finally, the forgiveness process culminates with reconciliation, that is, with the restoration of just political relationships. The renewal of right relationships, in which enemies learn to live and work with each other, occurs with the creation of a new moral foundation based on trust.

It is important to emphasize that political forgiveness does not negate the possibility of restitution. Authentic forgiveness will seek to rectify and restore past wrongs as much as possible. However, whereas justice requires restitution (repayment for past wrongs), forgiveness simply allows for the possibility of restitution, as wrongdoers manifest their contrition through tangible actions.

CASE NO. 1-2
POLITICAL FORGIVENESS AND THE BITBURG DILEMMA

Background

In January 1985, the White House announced that President Ronald Reagan would visit West Germany to commemorate the fortieth anniversary of the defeat of the Axis powers. Subsequently, the White House announced that President Reagan would lay a wreath at the German military cemetery at Bitburg as a gesture of German-American reconciliation and at the Bergen-Belsen concentration camp as a commemoration for the many Jews who died there and in other concentration camps. Soon after the planned visit to Bitburg was announced, it was discovered that forty-nine members of the Waffen SS, the Nazi movement's elite police force, were among the 2,000 German soldiers' graves.

The decision to visit Bitburg precipitated much criticism from American Jewish groups, war veterans, and the media. Within one week of the announced visit, fifty-three senators signed a letter urging President Reagan to call off his Bitburg visit; subsequently, the U.S. Senate decisively passed a resolution recommending that President Reagan "reassess his planned itinerary." In addition, some 257 members of the House of Representatives wrote to West German Chancellor Helmut Kohl urging that he release President Reagan from his Bitburg commitment. However, the most potent moral criticism of the planned trip was from Nobel Laureate Elie Wiesel, a survivor of the holocaust. In a brief address at a White House ceremony honoring his selection for the Congressional Gold Medal of Achievement, Congress's highest award, Wiesel observed,

> I belong to a traumatized generation. And to us, as to you, symbols are important. And furthermore, following our ancient tradition—and we are speaking about Jewish heritage—our tradition commands us "to speak truth to power." . . . I am convinced, as you have told us earlier when we spoke that you were not aware of the presence of SS graves in the Bitburg cemetery. Of course, you didn't know. But now we all are aware. May I, Mr. President, if it's possible at all, implore you to do something else, to find another way, another site. That place, Mr. President, is not your place. Your place is with the victims of the SS.[37]

After the discovery of the SS troops' graves and the ensuing political opposition to the planned trip, the Reagan administration faced a foreign policy dilemma. The dilemma was fundamentally rooted in morality, including the responsibilities involved in acknowledging, accepting, and overcoming the historic evil of the Holocaust. White House officials were aware of the great evil that the Nazis had committed against the Jewish people, but they were also aware that West German officials had frequently expressed sorrow and regret for the evil perpetuated by the Nazi regime and had tangibly acknowledged this evil by prosecuting more than 91,000 Germans who were involved in "crimes against humanity" and by providing modest financial restitution to the families of Holocaust victims. Most important, West Germany had developed strong democratic institutions and had become one of the strongest postwar allies of the United States in confronting the evil of totalitarian communism. Nonetheless, West Germany continued to bear the scars from the terrible evil inflicted by Nazis on all of humanity but especially on Jewish peoples. As one commentator observed at the time of the Bitburg conflict, the Third Reich "was the greatest failure of civilization on the planet."[38]

The Ethics of Bitburg

From a narrowly defined perspective, the issue facing President Reagan was whether to participate in a ceremony of bilateral American-German reconciliation in a cemetery with symbols of evil. For Elie Wiesel and other opponents of the Bitburg visit, the issue was not politics but "good and evil."[39] Associating even indirectly with Nazi symbols was morally unacceptable. This was a time for protecting and proclaiming the truth, or what Wiesel termed the necessity of speaking "truth to power." While recognizing the development of strong bilateral ties between West Germany and the United States, Bitburg critics argued that such reconciliation must always be rooted in the memory of the past, and in this case, it was imperative to honor the historical record of the Holocaust and recognize anew the great evil committed by Nazi officials against the Jewish people. In Wiesel's words,

Mr. President, I know and I understand . . . that you seek reconciliation. So do I. So do we. And I, too, wish to attain true reconciliation with the German people. I do not believe in collective guilt, nor in collective responsibility, only the killers were guilty. Their sons and daughters are not. And I believe, Mr. President, that we can and we must work together with them and with all people. And we must work to bring peace and understanding to a tormented world that, as you know, is still awaiting redemption."[40]

In short, critics argued that because remembering is more important than reconciliation and history is more significant than forgiving, President Reagan should have altered his plans and not have gone to Bitburg. Laying a wreath at the Kolmeshöhe military cemetery was wrong, in their view, because it involved an unnecessary association with evil symbols, namely, the burial sites of soldiers who had participated in the Jewish genocide.

From a broadly defined perspective, the issue for President Reagan was whether memory would always define the future or whether it was possible for nations to overcome their evil legacies. Although the Reagan administration never fully explained its moral reasoning behind its actions, it was clear that President Reagan was strongly motivated by the desire to commemorate Germany's moral rehabilitation and U.S.-German reconciliation rather than to dwell on the legacies of history. Those who defended the planned trip emphasized two anticipated outcomes. First, because the visit to Bitburg had been developed cooperatively by U.S. and German government officials, the cancellation of the Bitburg ceremony would undoubtedly jeopardize official relations between the two countries. Second, because the ceremony was regarded by many Germans as a symbol of reconciliation between the two former enemy states as well as an expression of Germany's increased acceptance into the international community, some analysts argued that canceling the trip would be psychologically injurious to German political leadership.

After weighing the pros and cons of the Bitburg dilemma, President Reagan decided to follow the original plan and participate in a brief ceremony at the Bitburg cemetery. "I think it is morally right to do what I'm doing," he said, "and I'm not going to change my mind about that." In justifying his decision, President Reagan relied on consequentialist logic:

But this all came about out of a very sincere desire of Chancellor Kohl and myself to recognize this 40th anniversary of the war's end—and incidentally, it's the 30th anniversary of our relationship as allies in NATO—that shouldn't we look at this and recognize that the unusual thing that has happened, that in these 40 years since the end of that war, the end of that tragedy of the Holocaust we have become the friends that we are, and use this occasion to make it plain that never again must we find ourselves enemies, and never again must there be anything like the Holocaust. And if that is what we can bring out of these observances and the trip that has been planned, then I think everything we're doing is very worthwhile.[41]

One of the ironies of the presidential dilemma over the Bitburg ceremony was that it greatly increased historical awareness of the Holocaust, fostering greater human sensitivity to the psychological pain rooted in the Nazi genocide committed four decades earlier. According to columnist William Safire, Reagan's blunders in dealing with this dilemma turned out to be a blessing in disguise, because it made millions of people aware of the costs of reconciliation in a way that no other process could have accomplished. "In seeking at first to sidestep the smoldering resentments," Safires writes, "the President brought on a firestorm 40 years after a Holocaust, which in turn forced a forgetful world through a most necessary grief."[42]

Moral Reflections

The Bitburg case study raises a number of general and specific issues about the nature and role of moral values in overcoming past wrongs.

- Can nations that have abused power and committed great evils against other peoples be restored into the family of nations? Can a state overcome its evil past, or must its citizens bear continuing shame and guilt?
- If the bitter, angry past can be overcome, what actions must states take to atone for past evils to achieve international political rehabilitation and bring about the preconditions for reconciliation?
- Can political forgiveness contribute to international reconciliation? If so, how?
- In a major speech to the Bundestag on May 8, 1985, West German president Richard von Weizsäcker observed that "whoever closes his eyes to the past becomes blind to the present."[43] In light of this claim, how can memory be sustained to honor past suffering while also encouraging reconciliation and the establishment of new political relationships?
- Has Germany atoned sufficiently for the atrocities of World War II? Given West Germany's postwar history and more particularly the political solidarity and close ties that emerged between the United States and West Germany during the Cold War, was it wrong for President Reagan to visit the German military cemetery at Bitburg? Why or why not?
- In view of the existence of forty-nine SS graves at this cemetery, will the Kolmeshöhe military cemetery always remain a symbol of evil?

Summary

In this chapter I have suggested that moral values and ethical reasoning are essential elements of foreign policy decision making. Although government officials did not explicitly attribute U.S. policies toward the restoration of Haitian democracy and the Bitburg visit to moral values, the two case studies clearly demonstrate that moral norms provided the fundamental direction and inspiration for the official actions taken by the U.S. government. Moreover, both cases show the morally ambiguous nature of foreign policy decision making because in each case numerous competing moral norms justified alternative courses of action. In the Haiti case, it would have been morally appropriate to respect the autonomy of Haiti; to encourage the Haitian people themselves to resolve the problem of political legitimacy; and, because American vital interests were not at stake, to avoid threatening the use of force. In the Bitburg case, there also were morally compelling reasons to justify alternative actions to the planned cemetery visit. Such alternatives would have reinforced the legacy of pain and suffering by Holocaust victims and would have called into question the complete moral rehabilitation of West Germany.

CHAPTER TWO

STRATEGIES OF ETHICAL DECISION MAKING

When it comes to politics, we get no moral Brownie points for good intentions; we will be judged by the results.

Peter Berger[1]

Moral politics is an art of execution: principles unaccompanied by practical means or by an awareness of possible trade-offs remind one of Peguy's famous comment about Kant—his hands were pure, but he had no hands.

Stanley Hoffmann[2]

In the previous chapter, ethics was defined as a moral reasoning process involving the identification, interpretation, and application of moral principles to specific issues or problems. In carrying out this task in the political sphere, statesmen and political thinkers rely on distinct strategies and traditions. *Ethical strategies* provide alternative decision-making methodologies based on different emphases being given to goals, means, and consequences. *Ethical traditions*, by contrast, provide substantive systems that structure moral reasoning and action. Unlike ethical strategies, which are mainly methodological tools, ethical traditions provide a normative structure of rules and principles that are regarded as authoritative. Both ethical strategies and ethical traditions are important in international ethics because they provide the tools and instruments by which moral values are applied to issues and problems of global society.

In this chapter, I examine the nature and role of two dominant strategies of ethical decision making: ends-based action and rule-based action. These two strategies are illustrated with case studies on nuclear deterrence and famine relief. In addition, I describe and assess a third approach, a tri-dimensional ethical model, that judges international political ethics by its comprehensive emphasis on goals, means, and results. This approach is illustrated with a case study on the the Reagan administration's Strategic Defense Initiative (SDI), a program that explored the feasibility of developing a protective shield from strategic nuclear attack. In the next chapter, I examine the nature and role of ethical traditions in international affairs.

Ends-Based Action

This approach, generally defined by philosophers as *consequentialism* or *teleological ethics* (from the Greek *teleos*, meaning "end" or "issue"), assumes that the morality of an action must be ultimately judged by the good results that are realized. In contrast to rule-based action, which assumes that the morality of a decision should be judged by the faithfulness with which moral rules are applied, consequentialism believes that the most important moral criterion is the overall outcome. Political actions typically involve three distinct elements: goals or intentions, means, and results. Although all three elements are incorporated into ends-based thinking, the consequences of human choices are given priority. According to this view, the moral legitimacy of an action, as noted by Peter Berger at the outset of this chapter, ultimately depends on its consequences.

Thus, for the consequentialist, the goals and means of political actions must be morally justified by the results of such actions. Policies involving questionable intentions and means might be morally permissible if sufficient good is achieved by those policies. To illustrate, an ends-based analysis of nuclear deterrence might regard the possession and threat of nuclear weapons (generally considered to be evil) as a morally legitimate strategy in helping to prevent nuclear aggression and to promote world order (considered good). Although the failure of deterrence could result in a nuclear war (an evil), the probability of such a conflict occurring has been considered so small that nuclear deterrence, although itself partly evil, has been considered a conditionally moral policy. In short, most ends-based analyses of nuclear strategy have assumed that preventing nuclear aggression through limited, credible threats (deterrence) is a morally legitimate strategy.

One of the major philosophical expressions of ends-based thinking is *utilitarianism*, a doctrine that assumes that individual and collective actions should be judged mainly by their "utility" or results. As Jeremy Bentham (1748–1832), the founder of this movement argued, "Nature has placed mankind under the governance of two sovereign masters, pain and pleasure."[3] The task of government is thus to establish policies that maximize collective pleasure and minimize collective pain. He proposed that policy making should be judged by the principle of *utility*, which he defined as the "greatest good for the greatest number." Because Bentham was concerned with increasing the scientific basis of policy making, he developed a number of quantitative norms for measuring societal pleasure and pain. Subsequently, his disciple and friend, John Stuart Mill (1806–1873), sought to further refine utilitarianism by distinguishing between desirable and less desirable pleasures.

More recently, political philosophers have distinguished between two types of utilitarianism: *rule utilitarianism* and *act utilitarianism*. The former applies the principle of utility to rules and procedures, holding that such norms derive their ethical legitimacy from their "procedural utility," that is, their perceived fairness and expected contribution to the common good. In global politics, such utilitarianism applies to the norms and structures of the international community's political, economic, and legal systems, and the validity of such norms and structures depend on their overall effect on individual and global welfare. The moral legitimacy of a basic rule, such as nonintervention, is thus judged in terms of its contribution to global order and international peace as well as its impact on the welfare and security of individual countries. Rule utilitarianism, in short, judges the inherent "usefulness" of policies and structures in terms of their consequences.

Act utilitarianism, by contrast, applies the utility criterion to particular actions, holding that the moral legitimacy of decisions must be based on the extent to which overall good (i.e., utility) is maximized in each specific circumstance. Political actions based on act utilitarianism are thus judged in terms of their anticipated results. For example, the decision of whether the United States should assist a country or region facing a major financial crisis (as was the case with Mexico in December 1994 and with East Asia in 1997–98) would be determined by the anticipated short-term and long-term consequences of such aid.

Ends-based thinking is an influential ethical strategy in domestic and international politics in great part because government decisions are judged generally in terms of results rather than intentions. As a result, political ethics, whether domestic or international, tend to be consequentialist. However, the widespread support for ends-based action in public life should not obscure the strategy's significant limitations. One of these is decision makers' inability to fully determine or predict policy outcomes. Because policy making is at best a probabilistic science in which outcomes depend on many factors over which decision makers have little or no control, government initiatives frequently fail to promote desired goals. For example, although economic sanctions are often imposed to foster behavioral reforms, economic penalties seldom lead to desired behavioral outcomes. Similarly, foreign aid is often given to promote democracy and economic prosperity even though such aid sometimes fails to advance desirable outcomes and can even undermine the goals being pursued. Given the indeterminacy of public policies the moral assessment of political action from an ends-based strategy is thus likely to involve significant uncertainties and ambiguities.

A second and more important limitation is the inability of ends-based thinking to provide an authoritative ethical standard by which to evaluate action. Bentham, who defined the principle of utility as the greatest good for the greatest number, provided a number of general norms by which to judge this principle. However, his conceptualization of outcomes, like that of other consequentialist political thinkers, provides no clear, unambiguous standard by which to define and judge results. Whether the end is defined as stability, pleasure, happiness, fairness, human rights, or economic and social well-being, there is no widely accepted framework by which to assess political outcomes. In short, although an ends-based perspective needs to be incorporated in political ethics, consequentialism alone does not provide a fully satisfactory ethical methodology for applying morality in international affairs.

Because politics is fundamentally about the art of the possible, political action is generally judged primarily by its results. As noted previously, ends-based analysis is the dominant ethical methodology in politics. The following case study illustrates the nature and role of this methodology in terms of the ethics of nuclear deterrence.

CASE NO. 2–1
THE ETHICS OF NUCLEAR DETERRENCE

Background

Historically, military force has been viewed as a morally legitimate means to protect and defend vital interests and to deter aggression. Theologians and strategists have developed an elaborate moral theory of military force, known as "just war," that specifies when a state may resort to war and how such a war should be conducted. After nuclear weapons were invented in 1945, it was clear that the new weapons could not easily be encompassed by existing conceptions of military force. In particular, traditional just-war norms designed to help determine whether, when, and how force should be used in settling global conflicts no longer applied to nuclear weapons because of their extraordinary destructive power. Typically, atomic (nuclear) bombs were many thousand times more powerful than conventional arms, and hydrogen (thermonuclear) bombs were many million times more powerful than conventional weapons. As a result, a war between two nuclear powers could threaten not only the mutual destruction of the two combatants but also, in the words of Jonathan Schell, "the extinction of the species." "To say that we and all future generations are threatened with extinction by the nuclear peril," Schell wrote in 1982 in *The Fate of the Earth*, his influential and popular account of the nuclear dilemma, "is to describe only half of our situation. The other half is that we are the authors of that extinction."[4]

The development of nuclear arms thus posed profound moral issues. Was it morally permissible to possess such weapons? If so, could a state threaten their use? In addition, if the threat failed to deter action, could nuclear arms be used? After atomic bombs were used in Hiroshima and Nagasaki, it became evident that nuclear arms could not be encompassed by conventional strategic thought. The power of these new weapons was so overwhelming that they could no longer be regarded as instruments of warfare. Nuclear and thermonuclear weapons provided a nation with military power but not with usable force to compel a foreign state to alter its behavior. One of the first thinkers to recognize the moral and strategic problem posed by the nuclear invention was Bernard Brodie, who in 1946 observed, "Thus far the chief purpose of our military establishment has been to win wars. From now on its chief purpose must be to avert them."[5] Subsequently, strategists continued to emphasize the strategic significance of nuclear arms while calling into question the military utility of such weapons. Henry Kissinger, for example, describes the radical challenge posed by nuclear arms to traditional strategic thought:

In the past the military establishment was asked to prepare for war. Its test was combat; its vindication, victory. In the nuclear age, however, victory has lost its traditional significance. The outbreak of war is increasingly considered the worst catastrophe. Henceforth, the adequacy of the military establishment will be tested by its ability to preserve peace.[6]

Fundamentally, nuclear weapons pose two major moral problems. First, because their destructive power is based not only on blast but also on heat and radiation, nuclear weapons can inflict greater and longer-term destruction, involving both immediate human suffering from severe burns and long-term genetic deformities. Second, because of their extraordinary power, nuclear weapons are indiscriminate instruments of mass destruction. As a result, they cannot be regarded as war-fighting instruments that give states another means of implementing policy. Because of the qualitative differences between nuclear and conventional arms, the former do not, like the latter, provide usable force to compel an enemy. "A weapon," writes George Kennan, "is something that is supposed to serve some rational end—a hideous end, as a rule, but one related to some serious objective of governmental policy, one supposed to promote the interests of society which employs it. The nuclear device seems to me not to respond to that description."[7] Although nuclear arms are not useful war-fighting instruments, they are a vital element of the national security of some states. Their usefulness, however, does not lie in their ability to compel through force but in their ability to prevent aggression. Indeed, because of their extraordinary power, nuclear arms are history's most formidable instruments of deterrence.

Given the significant qualitative differences between conventional and nuclear arms, the traditional prudential and moral analysis of war is not immediately applicable to nuclear power. Michael Walzer, for example, argues that nuclear weapons "are the first of mankind's technological innovations that are simply not encompassable within the familiar moral world."[8] Indeed, he suggests that they "explode" the theory of just war.

Because nuclear weapons are the most powerful weapons ever devised by human beings, a nuclear military capability can provide a state with a dramatic expansion in perceived national power. At the same time, because nuclear weapons are instruments of indiscriminate destruction, they do not provide a state with usable military force, especially if an enemy state also has such weapons. This is the situation that developed between the United States and the Soviet Union in the late 1940s after the latter became a nuclear power. Moreover, as both states expanded their nuclear arsenals in the 1950s, they became mutually vulnerable to each other's nuclear power. By the early 1960s, both superpowers had achieved arsenals sufficiently large and invulnerable that a condition of mutual assured destruction (MAD) emerged, a condition by which neither state could win a major war but both could lose. MAD was not a policy; rather, it was a condition reflecting a nuclear "balance of terror" by which each rival could destroy the other, even after being subjected to a nuclear surprise attack.

Because nuclear arms imposed mutual vulnerability on the superpowers, the American challenge in devising a moral strategic policy was to reconcile the demands for national security with the demands for global order without increasing the risks of nuclear war. Not surprisingly, nuclear deterrence, that is, prevention by threat, emerged as the principal American strategic doctrine. As articulated by U.S. strategists, nuclear deterrence would help keep peace by inhibiting aggression through the implicit threat of unacceptable nuclear retaliation. According to deterrence theory, as long as U.S. nuclear forces could carry out unacceptable punishment, no rational state would risk major aggression. Moreover, the credibility and stability of deterrence were assumed to rest on two essential conditions. First, societies needed to be vulnerable (there could be no effective strategic defense). Second, nuclear forces needed to be sufficiently invulnerable to carry out nuclear retaliation involving unacceptable damage. As a result, deterrence did not rest so much on the number, quality, or size of strategic weapons as on their invulnerability to attack. As long as a significant part of a state's nuclear arsenal could be used to retaliate following a major nuclear attack, deterrence would remain credible.

The Moral Justification of Deterrence

War is evil. It is evil because it results in death and destruction. Despite its evil effects, war can be morally justified when certain moral conditions are fulfilled.[9] However, from an ends-based, or consequentialist, approach, which is the perspective I am seeking to illuminate here, war can be morally justified when the good outcomes of war outweigh the evil undertaken in war. Thus, when the anticipated results justify the means—when a war results, for example, in the restoration of a just peace without excessive destruction—a war can be morally justified by a consequentialist ethic.

However, if conventional war can be morally justified under some circumstances, this is not the case for nuclear war. Michael Mandelbaum, for example, writes, "In the sense that the term 'war' connotes some proportion between damage done and political goals sought, an all-out nuclear conflict would not be a war at all."[10] Similarly, the U.S. Catholic bishops, in their influential 1983 pastoral letter on nuclear strategy, argue that a nuclear war is morally unacceptable and that every effort must be taken to ensure that nuclear arms are never used in resolving international disputes. As a result, the bishops argue that the church should emphasize not the morality of war fighting but the avoidance of nuclear war altogether. The letter observes, "Traditionally, the church's moral teaching sought first to prevent war and then to limit its consequences if it occurred. Today the possibilities for placing political and moral limits on nuclear war are so minimal that the moral task . . . is prevention."[11] In sum, strategic thinkers and ethicists have generally agreed that nuclear war is morally wrong because the political goals could not legitimize the society-wide destruction resulting from a major nuclear conflict.

Like nuclear war, nuclear deterrence is evil. It is evil because it threatens to do what is morally impermissible, namely, to carry out mass destruction. Although threats and actions are not morally identical, nuclear deterrence bears some of the evil of nuclear war because the credibility of deterrence rests partly on the fact that nuclear weapons might be used. In assessing the morality of nuclear deterrence from an ends-based perspective, the issue comes to this: Can the implicit or explicit threat of nuclear retaliation be morally justified by the policy's alleged contributions to peace and security? Because the answer will depend on the good that is achieved in light of the evil involved in the threat, I briefly examine various costs and benefits, evils and goods, involved in nuclear deterrence.

In assessing the evil involved in nuclear deterrence, numerous factors need to be considered. First, the aim of deterrence is not to inflict destruction but to prevent unwanted behavior through the promise of unacceptable punishment. Thus, deterrence does not intend evil; rather, it seeks to do good (e.g., prevent aggression, or foster peace) by threatening evil (retaliation). Second, the extent of evil involved in explicit or implicit nuclear threats is difficult to ascertain, in great part because of the infinite number of degrees of intention involved, varying from a bluff (a threat without a commitment to fulfill it) to assured retaliation (certain punishment in response to aggression). Third, although scholars hold different views on the moral effect of intentions and actions, ethicists generally concur that intentions do not bear the same moral consequences as actions. As a result, because the threat of force is normally considered to involve less evil than the use of force itself, nuclear deterrence is likewise not considered to be morally commensurate with nuclear war. Finally, not all nuclear strategies are morally equivalent. Because a major aim of deterrence is to achieve political goals without resorting to nuclear war, strategies that maintain a robust "firebreak," or gap, between conventional and nuclear arms (thereby maintaining a low risk of nuclear conflict) will be judged more acceptable morally than those strategies that undermine the firebreak.[12] Thus, nuclear strategies that inhibit resort to war (e.g., countervalue strategies based on massive nuclear retaliation) will be deemed more morally preferable than those that encourage limited nuclear war-fighting strategies (e.g., counterforce strategies based on small, accurate, flexible threats).[13]

Despite the evil involved in relying on nuclear arms, such weapons contribute to the well-being of global society in a number of ways. First, nuclear deterrence can inhibit aggression. Because of the enormous power of nuclear arms, nuclear or conventional attack is virtually unthinkable. John Mearsheimer writes, "The more horrible the prospect of war, the less likely war is. Deterrence is more robust when conquest is more difficult. Potential aggressor states are given pause by the patent futility of attempts at expansion."[14] Second, nuclear deterrence can promote international stability and foster world peace. It does so because deterrence helps preserve the status quo. In international politics, nuclear deterrence fosters global stability because it prevents aggression and forcible changes in global cartography. A number of scholars have argued that despite significant conflict between the United States and the Soviet Union during the Cold War, the existence of a nuclear balance between them and their respective allies resulted in a "long peace," unprecedented in modern history. In writing about the postwar peace, strategist Thomas Schelling observes, "Those 40 years of living with nuclear weapons without warfare are not only evidence that war can be avoided but are themselves part of the reason why it can be."[15] Finally, nuclear weapons can provide security at a comparatively low cost, thereby conserving scarce national resources. For example, in extending the nuclear shield to Western Europe during the Cold War, the United States was able to deter potential aggression from the much larger conventional Warsaw Pact forces by maintaining a defense strategy of "flexible response" based in part on nuclear arms.

From a consequentialist, or ends-based, perspective, nuclear deterrence is considered morally legitimate when the strategy's beneficial outcomes (e.g., the prevention of aggression, the fostering of regional peace, and the maintenance of global order) outweigh its evils (e.g., the threat to carry out massive nuclear retaliation). This is the conclusion of many strategists and ethicists who have examined this extraordinarily complex moral problem. Walzer, for example, argues that in conditions of supreme emergency—when the existence of a state is threatened by potential aggression—nuclear deterrence can provide a morally defensible strategy. In defending nuclear deterrence, he writes that "we threaten evil in order not to do it, and the doing of it would be so terrible that the threat seems in comparison to be morally defensible."[16] Following a similar consequentialist logic, the U.S. Catholic bishops conclude their pastoral letter on nuclear strategy by conditionally endorsing deterrence. Deterrence, they suggest, can be justified only temporarily while states seek to reduce political tensions and carry out arms control and disarmament. They conditionally defend such a strategy in light of geopolitical realities because they believe that it contributes to "peace of a sort."[17]

From an ends-based perspective, nuclear deterrence is morally permissible only if deterrence succeeds in keeping peace and nuclear retaliation is unnecessary. However, how is strategic success to be ascertained? For example, numerous scholars have argued that the general global peace achieved during the Cold War was a result of the existence of nuclear weapons and the implicit strategy of nuclear deterrence. Historian John Lewis Gaddis has argued that the "long peace" of the second half of the twentieth century was due in part to the superpowers' nuclear arsenals, which made major war between them unthinkable.[18] Schelling also attributes the unprecedented Cold War order to nuclear weapons.[19] Others, however, have argued that nuclear weapons and the threats they pose have been largely irrelevant to global order.[20] Because the efficacy of deterrence can be proved ultimately only by its failure, it is impossible to either confirm or disprove the claim that nuclear weapons contributed to the Cold War's long peace. Still, there can be little doubt that the existence of major nuclear stockpiles contributed to fear of nuclear war, which in turn inhibited major military conflict between superpowers.

Moral Reflections

This case study raises several important issues about the strategy of nuclear deterrence as well as the ends-based ethical reasoning used to justify it.

- Given the extraordinary destructiveness of nuclear armaments, are such weapons fundamentally immoral? Because nuclear arms "explode" the just-war doctrine, is it moral for states to possess and threaten to use them?
- Although it is evident that war and the threat of war are both evil, is the threat of war less evil than war itself? As suggested previously, is nuclear deterrence more moral than nuclear war?
- Because deterrence might fail, does the possibility of carrying out nuclear retaliation undermine the moral justification of deterrence? More particularly, is it immoral to declare a policy of deterrence if there is no intention of ever fulfilling the threat? In effect, is a policy of deceit morally permissible if it contributes to global order and inhibits aggression?
- Is the resort to nuclear war, however limited, ever morally permissible? If deterrence fails, is it morally permissible to carry out the promised nuclear punishment?
- Is the proliferation of nuclear weapons contrary to the order and well-being of the international system? In mid-1998, both India and Paki-

stan, sworn mutual enemies that have fought three wars in the postwar era, each carried out five nuclear tests. Western nations, especially the United States, strongly condemned these nuclear tests, implying that the attempt to acquire nuclear weapons was contrary not only to the nonproliferation norms but also to international morality. Is the development of nuclear capabilities by India and Pakistan contrary to international ethics?

- Is an ends-based ethic an adequate methodology for judging nuclear deterrence? Is it an adequate ethical strategy for assessing and implementing a moral foreign policy?

Rule-Based Action

Rule-based analysis, known as *deontological thinking* (from the Greek word *deon*, meaning "duty" or "obligation"), denies what consequentialist analysis asserts, namely, that an action is good or bad, depending on the goodness or badness of its consequences. Deontologists assert that actions should be judged by their inherent rightness and validity, not by the goodness or badness of policy outcomes. Because deontological thinking places a premium on duty and right intention, rule-based analysis is agent centered, emphasizing duties and obligations of actors, not the results of decisions. Thus, this approach or methodology appeals to the goodness of policies themselves, not to their effects. As a result, ethical decision making is determined mainly by the morality of goals and intentions. Decisions that disregard moral obligations or utilize morally questionable means are themselves immoral, even if desirable outcomes are achieved. For example, from a deontological perspective, the firebombing of Dresden and Tokyo, carried out by the allies to defeat Germany and Japan, is regarded as immoral because civilians were part of the intended targets of those raids. Because reliance on evil means can never be condoned, even if it results in good outcomes, the use of evil means (intentionally killing civilians) cannot be justified by good intentions (defeating the Axis powers).

However, how can a statesman or political decision maker know what his or her ethical duties are? How are goals and methods to be determined to ensure ethical action? Immanuel Kant, the eighteenth-century German philosopher and father of rule-based analysis, argues that the rightness of a rule or action should be based on the *categorical imperative*. This principle has two key dimensions: First, persons should be treated as having value themselves (i.e., persons are always ends, never a means to an end). Second, individuals should act in accordance with principles or maxims that can be universalized.[21] Kant defines the universalizability norm as follows: "Act only on the maxim through which you can at the same time will that it should become a universal law." In other words, ethical decision making should be judged on the basis of the extent to which a principle should be applied to others. It is important to emphasize that in Kantian ethics moral obligations should be fulfilled not because they are more effective in creating a better, more just world but because that is what moral action requires. "An action done from duty has its moral worth," Kant observed, "not in the purpose to be attained by it, but in the maxim in accordance with which it is to be decided upon." Finally, how can persons discover which moral principles should guide their behavior? According to Kant, reason is the faculty by which norms can be discovered and applied.

A deontological approach contributes important perspectives about the development of ethical behavior, especially its emphasis on good intentions and the inherent value of persons. A Kantian perspective is important because it guards against the relativism of consequentialism. However, critics of rule-based analysis have suggested that deontological ethics is overly rigid in requiring universal or absolutist morality. In view of the vagaries and contingencies of life, some critics argue that principles need to be adapted to the specific cultural environment and particular circumstances in which actions are carried out. Lying is wrong, but under some circumstances, so goes the argument, it might be morally permissible, such as to protect a child from a madman or to threaten massive destruction to prevent aggression. Moreover, critics argue that Kantianism is unduly optimistic in at least two respects. First, it assumes that human beings have the capacity to rationally identify appropriate moral rules. Second, it assumes that human beings will behave in accordance with known moral obligations.

Although political actions based solely on moral obligations are rare, rule-based action is nonetheless undertaken periodically in global society by states and other international nonstate actors in fulfillment of perceived moral duties. For example, throughout the Cold War era, Western democratic countries provided significant economic assistance to developing nations, in great part because of the conviction that economically prosperous states had a moral obligation to assist poor peoples. In his study of postwar foreign aid, David Lumsdaine found that the strongest source of support for assisting poor countries was "the sense of justice and compassion."[22] Similarly, countries have often responded to the great human suffering perpetrated by civil war by allowing refugees to temporarily settle within their borders, and government and nongovernment actors have frequently provided massive food aid to alleviate hunger and starvation. Additionally, beginning in 1997, the United States provided foodstuffs to North Korea, a communist enemy state, to relieve starvation in that land.

To illustrate rule-based action, I next examine the humanitarian assistance that the United States provided Soviet Russia in 1921–23.

CASE NO. 2–2
FAMINE RELIEF FOR SOVIET RUSSIA

Background

In 1921, a massive famine developed in Soviet Russia, threatening the lives of some thirty million persons. Seven years of civil and international wars had devastated agricultural production, and when drought hit the Volga valley in the southwestern region of the Soviet Union, it resulted in a disastrous crop failure, leading to unprecedented mass starvation. Hundreds of thousands of Russian peasants fled their rural communities in search of food, flooding major cities and further aggravating famine-related epidemics, especially typhus and smallpox. The Bolshevik revolutionary rulers recognized that the famine threatened not only the lives of tens of millions of Russians but also the new Marxist regime itself. In light of Soviet Russia's famine, the Russian author Maxim Gorky was authorized to make a public appeal for humanitarian assistance.

At the time of the famine, U.S. foreign relations with the Soviet Union were bitterly strained. After communists had forcefully taken control of the Russian regime in 1918, President Woodrow Wilson refused to recognize the new regime or to establish diplomatic relations with it, preferring instead to isolate the Soviet government in the hope that it would be overthrown. In the aftermath of the Bolshevik Revolution, U.S.-Soviet trade came to a virtual halt, with the Wilson administration refusing to accept Russian gold for U.S. imports because it regarded such gold as "stolen." Three issues in particular had contributed to poor relations between the West and the new Soviet government. First, the revolutionary regime had resorted to propaganda to destabilize Western governments. Second, the Soviet government had repudiated prerevolutionary foreign debts. Third, the Soviet government had expropriated foreign holdings without providing compensation, as required by international law.[23] Although U.S. investment in Russia was comparatively small, the U.S. government regarded the Soviet communist policies as contrary to international law and a threat to peaceful global political relations. Not surprisingly, when Warren Harding became president in 1921, he reaffirmed the policies that his predecessor had instituted. The United States would not attempt to overthrow the Soviet regime but would seek to weaken it politically and commercially through isolation.

The Soviet appeal for famine relief presented U.S. policy makers with a moral dilemma. On the one hand, the famine offered an opportunity to further undermine the communist government. For some, the Russian famine of 1921 appeared to be "divine retribution for Bolshevist crimes,"[24] whereas others regarded the human suffering as another instrument by which to undermine the power of the new Soviet state. At the Tenth Party Congress in March 1921, V. I. Lenin, the Bolshevik head of government, had warned his communist comrades that a major crop failure would weaken his regime and could possibly lead to the toppling of the government and the end of Soviet communism. Thus, when the crop failure became even more severe than first anticipated, the famine appeared to provide a means to advance the very goals being officially pursued by the U.S. government.

On the other hand, the severe famine offered people of goodwill an opportunity to respond to human needs—to fulfill the "good Samaritan" principle of caring for human beings in need, regardless of their race, gender, or nationality. During the nineteenth century, international humanitarian relief had been increasingly accepted as a legitimate moral obligation of peoples and states, so that by the early twentieth century famine relief was a widely accepted moral norm within the international community. For example, in the aftermath of World War I, the American people had established the American Relief Association (ARA), a nongovernment humanitarian relief organization, to coordinate famine relief in war-torn Europe. Internationally, humanitarianism had been explicitly recognized by the League of Nations, the international government system established in the aftermath of World War I. According to the League's charter (Article 25), member states were expected to provide humanitarian relief in times of crises. Other evidence of the further acceptance of global society's commitment to humanitarian relief was the establishment of the International Red Cross in 1921 to strengthen coordination of international humanitarian aid.

American Humanitarian Assistance

The American response to Gorky's appeal was initiated, developed, and implemented largely by Herbert Hoover, President Harding's secretary of commerce.[25] Hoover had played a key leadership role in developing and guiding the U.S. humanitarian relief effort in Central Europe in the aftermath of World War I; and, although he was a cabinet officer, Hoover continued as head of the ARA, the principal nongovernment humanitarian relief organization in the United States. Hoover's background and moral sensibilities made him especially well equipped to address the Russian appeal for famine relief.

Fundamentally, there were two alternative policies that Hoover and other leading U.S. officials could pursue: provide assistance and thereby help alleviate human suffering or disregard the appeal and thereby reinforce the isolationist strategy of U.S. diplomacy. Hoover, along with other government leaders, decided immediately that the first moral obligation of the American people was to alleviate human suffering. Hoover recommended to Secretary of State Charles Evans Hughes that the United States provide famine relief through the ARA, but only if four preconditions were met. First, the Soviet government had to release all Americans confined in Russian prisons. Second, the Soviet government needed to officially declare a need for relief. Third, relief workers needed to have complete freedom of movement without Soviet interference. Fourth, the Soviet government needed to provide free transportation and housing for American personnel. The ARA, for its part, would provide relief impartially to all persons in need and would carry out its work in a nonpolitical manner.[26] After brief consultations, the Soviet government agreed to these terms.

Although the ARA served as the major organization for collecting and distributing relief supplies, the U.S. government provided substantial assistance in supporting and funding the effort. At President Harding's request, in December 1921 Congress approved a humanitarian relief request of $24 million ($20 million for grain purchases and $4 million for medical supplies), a sum that was about 1 percent of the total 1921 U.S. government budget. By early 1922, the ARA had established some 35,000 distribution centers in Russia and was regularly feeding more than 10 million persons at the height of the famine in mid-1922. By mid-1923, most regions in Soviet Russia had regained agricultural self-sufficiency, resulting in the termination of the American relief effort by the end of the year. It has been estimated that the American relief effort, which involved the transfer of some 540,000 tons of food, or about 90 percent of the total, was responsible for saving at least 10.5 million lives. As Benjamin Weissman notes, the major effect of the American relief mission was "the defeat" of the worst famine in the history of modern Europe.[27]

The Ethics of U.S. Famine Relief

The U.S. government's decision to permit and then directly support humanitarian relief illustrates rule-based ethical analysis, as the dominant motive in undertaking the relief mission was to respond to humanitarian needs regardless of how such aid might impact the political system. Although the U.S. government was embarked on a campaign to isolate and weaken the Communist government, and although famine provided a natural means by which to undermine the regime, American leaders and citizens believed that it was their moral duty to relieve starvation. American officials made the commitment to humanitarian relief rather than to realpolitik because they recognized that international morality "obliges nations with food surpluses to aid famine-stricken countries regardless of their political regime."[28]

From an ethical perspective, the American policy was moral in its goals and methods but morally problematic in its overall consequences. Famine relief saved the lives of millions of peasants, but it also unwittingly helped keep in power a despotic, revolutionary regime. Although scholars differ on the impact of the humanitarian relief program on the stability of the Soviet regime, some argue that the assistance helped stabilize and strengthen the communist regime. George Kennan, for example, argues that the Soviet government was "importantly aided, not just in its economic undertakings, but in its political prestige and capacity for survival" by the American humanitarian assistance.[29] Regardless of how much ARA's relief program contributed to the stabilization of the Soviet communist regime, it is evident that American benevolence directly contradicted its official policy of undermining the Bolshevik regime.

Moral Reflections

This case study suggests a number of important moral issues about both famine relief and the ethical methodology employed in developing the aid policy.

- Since the U.S. decision to offer famine relief to Russia was influenced in part by the reliance on a rule-based ethical methodology, did U.S. policy succeed in fulfilling the humanitarian norm?
- If U.S. leaders had applied a consequentialist methodology, what might have been the response to Gorky's appeal for food?
- In view of the great human suffering and political oppression imposed domestically by the totalitarian communist regime in the decades following the famine—suffering that led to more than thirty million deaths and untold human rights abuses—would the denial of food aid have been a morally appropriate response? In other words, would efforts to undermine the existing communist regime through the denial of food aid have been a moral response?
- In view of the differences between rule-based and ends-based analysis, how should policy makers determine which ethical methodology is appropriate in making foreign policy? Is a rule-based strategy morally superior to an ends-based strategy, as most ethicists contend?

Tridimensional Ethics

The two ethical strategies sketched previously emphasize different ways of applying moral norms to international relations. Moreover, the alternative methodologies apply moral values and judgments to different elements of ethical decision making. Ends-based analysis judges the morality of acts mainly on the basis of their consequences, whereas rule-based analysis judges the morality of acts mainly on the basis of goals and intentions. Philosophers typically identify with the latter approach, whereas decision makers typically rely on the former. Although both the consequentialist and the deontological viewpoints offer important perspectives in developing ethical decision making, neither approach is sufficient. Indeed, both are essential in developing morally prudent foreign policies and just global political relations. Stanley Hoffmann has written,

> I repeat that morality is not merely a matter of ends or intentions, and that the likely consequences of acts must be taken into account . . . a morality that relies exclusively on expected, calculated outcomes is not acceptable either: no statesman can be sure of all effects, and confident that he will be able to avoid perverse ones altogether. Neither pure conviction nor unbridled "consequentialism" will do.[30]

As noted previously, ethical actions typically involve three distinct elements: motives, means, and results. Whereas political actions are commonly judged in terms of one or possibly two of these dimensions, a sound ethical strategy must assess action in terms of each of these dimensions.

Table 2–1: Three Dimensions of Moral Judgment

	Motives	*Means*	*Consequences*
Scenario 1	Good	Good	Good
Scenario 2	Good	Good	Bad
Scenario 3	Good	Bad	Good
Scenario 4	Good	Bad	Bad
Scenario 5	Bad	Bad	Good
Scenario 6	Bad	Good	Bad
Scenario 7	Bad	Good	Good
Scenario 8	Bad	Bad	Bad

Source: Adapted from Joseph S. Nye, Jr., *Nuclear Ethics* (New York: Free Press, 1986), 22.

Political ethics, in effect, should be tridimensional. Table 2–1 identifies eight different decision-making scenarios based on this tridimensional framework. From the eight possible options, the most desirable policy is clearly scenario 1 and the least desirable is scenario 8. To the extent that good intentions are important in decision making, scenarios 5, 6, and 7 are morally problematic, although scenarios 5 and 7 have some legitimacy since good ends are realized despite the evil intentions. Moreover, it is clear that scenarios 5 and 7 are morally preferable to scenarios 2 and 4, both of which have bad outcomes.

Because few public policy issues are totally evil (scenario 8) or totally good (scenario 1), most issues and problems in global politics are likely to involve a mixture of justice and injustice. When confronted with choices among different decision-making issues, such as between scenarios 2 and 3, how should the statesman decide? One possible approach is to rely on a particular ethical strategy, choosing actions that are consistent with either an ends-based or a rule-based methodology. All that is required is to select a consequentialist or deontological methodology and to apply it as consistently as possible.

Another preferable approach is to make the necessary trade-offs between means and results, translating ethical intentions and purposes into actions that will maximize morally desirable outcomes. This approach is essentially the practice of *prudence*, or practical wisdom. From an ideal, tridimensional perspective, prudence is best implemented in public affairs by the pursuit of moral goals through morally legitimate means that result in good outcomes (scenario 1). Decision makers pursue prudence when they seek to implement the common good by weighing different alternatives and then choosing the best one in light of relevant moral criteria.

According to Alberto Coll, the prudence tradition, as exemplified by

Aristotle, Thomas Aquinas, and Edmund Burke, has two distinctive features. First, while acknowledging the evil of human affairs, prudence insists on the ultimate authority of morality over circumstances, of "ought" over "is." Second, prudence regards human virtue and personal character rather than religion, ideology, or worldview, as the major determinants of moral statecraft.[31] A well-developed moral philosophy, although important, is not sufficient to ensure moral action in the political world. Moral leadership thus depends not on technical competence but on character and personal integrity.

However, because prudential decision making provides no fixed norms to guide the process of trade-offs among relevant norms, decision making in foreign affairs can quickly succumb to consequentialism. To protect the tridimensional system from becoming simply a tool of ends-based thinking, decision makers need to follow norms that contribute to moral accountability. One useful set of rules has been developed by Nye, who argues that ethical decision making is encouraged when it is guided by the following five norms: (1) clear, logical, and consistent standards; (2) impartiality (i.e., respect for others' interests); (3) a presumption in favor of rules: (4) procedures that protect impartiality; and (5) prudence in calculating results.[32] In short, a tridimensional ethical framework can contribute to moral action provided that decision makers rely on norms that protect the moral reasoning process from consequentialism.

To explore the nature and role of the tridimensional strategy, I next explore the morality of President Reagan's Strategic Defense Initiative (SDI).

CASE NO. 2–3
THE ETHICS OF SDI

Background

In the early 1980s, President Ronald Reagan called on the U.S. scientific community to investigate the possibility of developing a defensive system against ballistic nuclear missiles. In his famous "star wars" speech, delivered on March 23, 1983, the president suggested that because it was preferable "to save lives than to avenge them," the United States should explore the feasibility of shifting its nuclear strategy from offense to defense. Thus, he proposed that the U.S. scientific community explore the technological feasibility of developing a comprehensive defense system against ballistic missiles. As perceived by President Reagan and some of his advisers, the short-term aim of the initiative was to provide limited protection from deliberate or accidental attack; the long-term aim would be to render strategic nuclear arms "impotent and obsolete."[33]

As envisioned by some scientists, the idea of SDI involved a multilayered defensive system. Because the trajectory of a ballistic missile typically involves several stages, strategic defense would attempt to destroy enemy missiles and warheads in each of them, but especially in the first (boost) and last (terminal) phases. Scientists acknowledged that the most important phase in which to destroy a missile was in its first phase, when the missile was flying more slowly and all its warheads were still together. Once the missile entered space and launched its warheads, tracking and destroying the nuclear warheads would be much more difficult. The other critical phase for SDI was the terminal stage, when warheads were reentering the atmosphere. According to SDI reasoning, if it were possible to destroy 50 percent of all enemy missiles and warheads in each of the four major missile phases, then only 6 or 7 warheads out of 100 launched would reach their targets. Although a success rate of 93 percent or 94 percent would still allow for mass destruction, SDI advocates argued that an increased defensive capability would greatly contribute to national security from deliberate or accidental attack.

From 1984 until 1990, the U.S. government devoted more than $20 billion to SDI research. When the program was launched, some defense analysts estimated that a modest strategic defense system would cost as much as $150 billion and that a comprehensive system might cost more than $1 trillion.[34] However, the most damaging criticism of SDI came from the scientific community, which argued that a comprehensive shield was technologically unfeasible in the near future. In an important article in 1985, four influential thinkers argued that there was no prospect that science and technology could in the near future "make nuclear weapons 'impotent and obsolete.'"[35]

The SDI also raised profound issues about shifting the national security paradigm from strategic offense to strategic defense. Would a shift from mutual assured destruction (MAD) towards mutual assured security (MAS) foster peace and world order? If military conflict among superpowers were to occur, would the existence of SDI reduce wartime destruction? In the final analysis, was SDI morally desirable? In exploring the morality of SDI here, I assess the proposed initiative using a tridimensional framework that emphasizes moral judgment based on intentions, means, and outcomes.

Tridimensional Assessment

The fundamental aim of SDI was to defend a country from ballistic missile attack. Because the initiative's basic goal was to develop and deploy a ballistic missile defense system that would protect society from nuclear aggression, the intentions of SDI were morally unassailable. Thus, at the level of *intentions*, SDI was wholly ethical.

At the level of *means*, SDI sought to develop a system of satellites, missiles, laser beams, and other instruments that would protect society from deliberate or accidental nuclear attack. Whereas the existing offensive nuclear policy also sought to protect society, SDI's method was radically different. Whereas MAD inhibited nuclear aggression by threatening unacceptable nuclear retaliation (deterrence), SDI aimed to protect society by destroying nuclear missiles. In promoting SDI, Reagan administration officials emphasized the moral superiority of SDI over MAD by noting that the former would destroy weapons only, whereas MAD would destroy cities. Of course, Reagan's comparison was disingenuous, as SDI was not an unambiguous defense system. As Leon Wieseltier observed at the time, "The notion that SDI is a purely defensive system is an insult to intelligence. If a laser beam can hit a missile that has been launched, it can hit a missile that has not been launched, too. Between offense and defense, these systems are essentially ambiguous."[36] Although SDI proponents viewed the space-based defense initiative as purely defensive, SDI critics argued that such a system could also be offensive, increasing a state's overall strategic nuclear capabilities. Thus, given SDI's uncertain role involving both defensive and offensive capabilities, the means of SDI were necessarily morally ambiguous.

At the level of *likely consequences*, SDI presented even greater challenges. On the basis of three widely accepted arms control goals (war avoidance, the minimization of destruction in war, and the reduction in weapons expenditures), national security policy can be regarded as moral to the extent that it reduces the risk of war, decreases the potential for wartime destruction, and reduces the cost of military defense. In terms of the war-avoidance standard, SDI was unlikely to be as effective as MAD because the latter policy sought to keep the peace through the threat of nuclear retaliation, whereas the former aimed to protect society from nuclear attack by destroying nuclear missiles and warheads. As noted earlier in this chapter (see Case No. 2–1), it is widely assumed that nuclear deterrence contributed to global order and stability during the Cold War. Given the record attributed to nuclear deterrence, most strategists doubted that a shift in strategy from nuclear offense to nuclear defense would strengthen international peace.

Minimizing the destruction and violence of war—the second standard— could of course be realized much more effectively by SDI than strategic offense. Because SDI sought to protect society from missile attack, SDI was clearly more effective than strategic offense in limiting wartime damage. Thus, SDI was morally superior to MAD in fulfilling this arms control norm.

Finally, although policy advocates differed greatly on the anticipated cost of developing and deploying a comprehensive strategic defense system, it was clear that deploying even a modest strategic defense system would be exceptionally expensive, costing as much as $500 billion. Although the replacement of MAD with a MAS system could potentially reduce long-term national security expenditures, the transition from strategic offense to strategic defense was expected to be difficult, unpredictable, and very costly. Clearly, from a short- and medium-term budgetary perspective, maintaining the existing strategic nuclear system was preferable to undertaking the expensive and uncertain transition to a MAS security.

Thus, although SDI was morally impeccable at the level of intentions, the program's means and likely outcomes raised profound moral questions. To be sure, SDI was morally troubling because of its inordinate costs. However, SDI's more serious shortcomings were doctrinal. Because SDI tended to undermine deterrence, some SDI critics argued that the shift from MAD, a predictable and stable global order based on strategic offense, to MAS, an uncertain and elusive global order based on an unpredictable strategic defense, might lead to greater global turmoil and conflict and to a decline in security.

Moral Reflections

When President Reagan was seeking support for his initiative, he claimed that SDI was a more moral system than nuclear deterrence because the former was defensive, whereas the latter was offensive.

- Assuming that a comprehensive strategic defense system could have been developed, was President Reagan's judgment about the moral superiority of MAS over MAD justified? Was the evil involved in nuclear deterrence reduced by the adoption of an SDI strategy?
- In Case No. 2–3, it was suggested that from a tridimensional perspective SDI was morally ambiguous. Do you agree with this assessment? Why or why not?
- If decision makers had assessed SDI on the basis of an ends-based strategy, how would the initiative have been assessed morally? What would have been the moral judgment of SDI from a rule-based strategy?

Summary

International political action can be undertaken using a variety of ethical strategies. The three major types of decision-making strategies are ends-based analysis, rule-based analysis, and tridimensional analysis. Each of these approaches is distinguished by different emphases given to intentions, goals, and outcomes. Although each of these ethical methodologies can contribute to the moral basis of a sound foreign policy, I have suggested that a comprehensive, tridimensional strategy might offer the most effective approach to integrating morality with international political action.

CHAPTER 3

THE ROLE OF ETHICAL TRADITIONS

[T]here is a truth in realism that ought not be to be lost sight of: In the hands of public officials, moral principle is too easily transformed into crusading doctrine, which invites misperception, rhetorical manipulation, and public hypocrisy.

Charles Beitz[1]

It is the easiest thing in the world to proclaim a good. The hard part is to think through ways by which this good can be realized without exorbitant costs and without consequences that negate the good. That is why an ethic of responsibility must be cautious, calculating a perennially uncertain mass of means, costs and consequences.

Peter Berger[2]

Most human actions are based on moral presuppositions. Whether or not persons recognize such moral predispositions explicitly, human decision making will be based, of necessity, on moral assumptions. The moral assumptions that influence human choices are not random but tend to be a part of general ethical paradigms or traditions. Although these ethical perspectives vary greatly in terms of their nature and relevance in global politics, they play an influential role in the conduct of foreign relations, providing ethical road maps to decision makers. Thus, when statesmen develop and implement foreign policies, they utilize particular ethical frameworks that establish the parameters within which issues are debated and decided.

For example, Otto von Bismarck, Germany's chancellor from 1870 to 1890, pursued domestic and international policies that were profoundly influenced by his realist Christian worldview—a dualistic Lutheran perspective emphasizing a radical distinction between the temporal and spiritual realms. As a devout believer, Bismarck pursued a life of personal piety, but as a statesman he believed that he was responsible for using political power to bring about political order, even if it entailed power politics and war. By contrast, William E. Gladstone, a British prime minister in the late nineteenth century, sought to carry out his political responsibilities as a Christian idealist—a believer who, unlike Bismarck, assumed that there was no radical discontinuity between personal and political morality, between individual obligations and government duties. In examining the leadership styles of these two prominent European statesmen, it is clear that different religious and ethical perspectives influenced the nature and style of their leadership.[3]

As noted earlier, when political leaders and government officials apply moral values to public policy decisions, they use ethical strategies that guide the process of ethical reasoning and moral judgment. In the previous chapter, I described two major ethical methodologies that linked good and bad, right and wrong, to substantive moral rules (rule-based action) and to consequences (ends-based action). In this chapter, I explore a related but different dimension of ethical decision making, namely, the nature and role of ethical traditions in the making, implementation, and interpretation of foreign policy. Whereas ethical strategies provide procedures and methodologies for applying moral norms to political decisions, ethical traditions provide the framework for structuring the process of moral decision making. Thus, whereas ethical strategies influence how moral values are applied in public life, ethical traditions provide the substantive norms and principles for judging political decisions and public policies.

This chapter begins by sketching the nature and role of ethical traditions in foreign affairs. It then examines realism and idealism, two of the most influential ethical traditions in twentieth-century American foreign relations, and illuminates their role with two case studies: one ancient (the Peloponnesian War) and the other modern (President Jimmy Carter's human rights policy).

The Nature and Role of Ethical Traditions

Terry Nardin defines a tradition as "the thing handed down, the belief or custom transmitted from one generation to another."[4] As utilized here, an ethical tradition refers to a system of substantive moral rules and normative principles that have been passed along from generation to generation and that have been recognized as imposing binding obligations, achieving, as one scholar notes, authority that is something equivalent to "the force of law."[5] Although traditions are based on a variety of sources, including religion, political consent, law, and culture, widespread customary practice is essential in the development of a tradition. Indeed, a tradition's authority is a direct by-product of the extent to which its values, practices, and customs have been institutionalized.

A number of different ethical traditions influence the conduct of contemporary international relations. Indeed, in their study *Traditions of International Ethics*, Terry Nardin and David Mapel identify twelve major ethical traditions, including international law, realism, natural law, Judeo-Christianity, Marxism, Kantianism, utilitarianism, liberalism, and human rights.[6] Some of these traditions utilize ends-based analysis (e.g., realism, utilitarianism, and Marxism), whereas others rely on rule-based analysis (e.g., natural law, Kantianism, liberalism, and human rights). Although all these traditions have influenced modern international politics, the analysis here focuses on only two of these: *idealism* and *realism*. These two traditions are important because they have served, and continue to serve, as the dominant twentieth-century U.S. foreign policy paradigms.

Before analyzing idealism and realism, it is important to call attention to one problem posed by competing ethical traditions. Although traditions provide the moral architecture to identify and apply morality to the conduct of foreign relations, the existence of competing and conflicting moral traditions poses a serious challenge to the universal demands of moral obligation. Because statesmen and political officials from a given country often rely on alternative traditions, the ethical deliberations that they undertake are likely to result in different emphases, if not different policy conclusions. Moreover, because statesmen from different countries are even more likely to apply diverse ethical traditions, the challenge in reconciling conflicting moral claims is even greater in international diplomacy. For example, Dutch political leaders applying Kantian, realist, and legal traditions are likely to draw different policy conclusions about genocide in Rwanda or about peacemaking within Bosnia. However, French, Indian, Russian, and Japanese diplomats, representing not only divergent ethical traditions but also divergent political cultures, are likely to draw policy conclusions even more disparate than officials from a single country.

David Welch observes that, because policy conclusions drawn from a particular tradition are likely to be accepted only by adherents to that tradition, the existence of a plurality of traditions poses a major challenge, namely, how to select the most desirable one.[7] However, if a tradition is to be adopted on moral grounds, ethical criteria extrinsic to any particular tradition will be required to select the most desirable one. Because such criteria do not exist, Welch concludes that there is no authoritative ethical method of selecting a preferable tradition. Thus, Welch suggests that, rather than relying on an ethical tradition, one should apply ethics based on moral consensus, or what he terms "conventionalism." According to such a system, right and wrong, justice and injustice, are defined by consent among the relevant parties. Whatever they agree to regard as just or legitimate is just or legitimate.[8]

Although an ethical system rooted in agreement might be more palatable in confronting the problem of cultural pluralism noted in chapter 1, consensus does not provide a satisfactory basis for morality. As English philosopher David Hume observed long ago, consent provides no adequate basis for morality because it is impossible to develop a theory of moral obligation from existing facts, that is, to derive "ought" from "is."[9] To be sure, identifying shared moral norms among different societies can contribute to the development of authoritative moral regimes. For example, postwar efforts by the United Nations and its related agencies to define human rights have resulted in a more robust doctrine of rights. Notwithstanding significant differences in human rights conceptions, transnational discussion and deliberation have contributed to the internationalization of rights. However, the proliferation of global human rights discourse has not necessarily strengthened the ethical foundation of international rights claims. Indeed, as contemporary history has demonstrated, regimes not only have frequently pursued policies involving gross human rights violations but also have sought to justify such actions.

Despite the challenges posed by competing ethical traditions, there is no need to jettison them. Although a plurality of traditions can make authoritative ethical judgments more difficult, it need not paralyze ethical reasoning. Indeed, the existence of multiple traditions can provide alternative systems for judging moral action, thereby strengthening moral analysis.

Realism

Realism, arguably the oldest ethical tradition relevant to international relations, dates from the origins of political thought in the ancient Greek civilization. The historian Thucydides, author of the classic *History of the Peloponnesian War*, is often regarded as the father of realism. Other ancient and modern political thinkers who contributed decisively to the development of this tradition include St. Augustine, Niccolò Machiavelli, and Thomas Hobbes. In the twentieth century, scholars such as Herbert Butterfield, E. H. Carr, Robert Gilpin, Hans Morgenthau, George Kennan, and Reinhold Niebuhr have contributed to the further development and application of realism in modern international relations.

Like most traditions, political realism is not easily defined, in part because it is a living, dynamic tradition that is continuously evolving and also because it is a pluralistic movement comprised of distinct strands. For example, the Christian realist strand emphasizes the role of human nature in the development and maintenance of political order, whereas classical realism emphasizes the nature, role, and distribution of power in the development of political order, whether domestic or international. Moreover, *structural realism*, sometimes called *neorealism*, focuses on the nature and implications of political structures of global society. Such an approach differs from classical realism in that it disregards human nature and political morality and focuses exclusively on structural patterns and behavioral norms that explain the political behavior of states in the anarchic international environment.

Characteristics

Despite significant disparities among its different schools, the ethical tradition of realism is a coherent and powerful political worldview, deeply influencing the nature of decision making in the international community. Some of the tradition's most important elements include a pessimistic view of human nature, the priority of power in developing and maintaining political order, the primacy of the state in global politics, the anarchic character of international society, and the priority of consequences in making ethical judgments. I now briefly examine each of these norms.

First, realists assume that human nature is motivated mainly by self-interest. Because individuals and groups tend to seek their own interests first, often in disregard for or at the expense of the interests of others, the establishment of a peaceful and just order is a difficult and never-ending task. In developing political order, realists believe that political action should always be guided by how human beings are likely to behave rather than on how they ought to behave. Although realists hold a pessimistic view of human nature, they believe that the development of order and justice in the anarchic global community can be advanced through policies based on power. Because realists assume that peace is a by-product of an international balance of power, they believe that the management of power is a central requirement in pursuing a moral foreign policy. Only by balancing and counterbalancing the power of other states can a state contribute to global order and thereby help establish the precondition for international justice.

Second, realism emphasizes power. In fact, Hans Morgenthau, arguably the most influential postwar international relations realist, views politics, whether domestic or international, as essentially a struggle for power.[10] This struggle is more pronounced in global society because there is no central authority to moderate and resolve interstate disputes. Not surprisingly, Morgenthau views statesmen as officials who "think and act in terms of interest defined as power."[11] Moreover, because there is no central authority to ensure the existence of nation-states and the promotion of their national interests, Morgenthau argues that if statesmen disregard power, they will become the victims of those who have learned to acquire and use it.

Third, realism is characterized by its state-centric approach. It assumes that, although many actors participate in global politics (e.g., international organizations, nongovernmental organizations, multinational corporations, religious movements, and individuals), the main actor is the nation-state. The dominance of nation-states is rooted in the fact that they are sovereign, that is, independent, self-governing political communities not subject to any higher authority. Because power is the principal determinant of a state's capacity to act independently in the world community, the degree of a state's self-government will depend greatly on its own political, military, and economic resources. However, a state's capabilities will also be due in great measure to the capabilities of other states, which can challenge other states' power. Nation-states are a relatively recent development, dating from the mid-seventeenth century, and although they might someday be replaced by other structures, such as a global federal government or regional political unions, realists assume that nation-states will remain the principal actors in global politics in the foreseeable future.

Fourth, realism assumes that the international community is a decentralized, anarchic environment—a self-help system. According to Kenneth Waltz, such a system is one "in which those who do not help themselves, or who do so less effectively than others, will fail to prosper, will lay themselves open to dangers, will suffer."[12] Because there is no common authority in the world, each state's survival and well-being ultimately depends on its own capabilities and resources. Moreover, because the survival of states is not ensured, the most fundamental national interest is assumed to be survival. Although there are a variety of means by which states can promote their interests in the international community, realists assume that military force is the most important. Because the protection of vital interests ultimately depends on the capacity to punish aggression, states continuously seek to deter aggression by expanding their military resources and establishing alliances.

Finally, realism is characterized by its reliance on consequential ethics. Realism is often critiqued as being an amoral approach to international politics because power is regarded as the main instrument of foreign policy and national security as its principal end. One scholar, for example, argues that realism's excessive concern with national security "dissolves moral duties."[13] Another suggests that the realist tradition simply excludes morality altogether from foreign policy.[14] Perhaps the most extreme realist perspective about international ethics is taken by traditional theorists such as Machiavelli and Hobbes and modern scholars such as George F. Kennan, who argue that politics is essentially an amoral activity. Kennan writes,

> Government is an agent, not a principal. Its primary obligation is to the interests of the national society it represents . . . its military security, the integrity of its political life and the well-being of its people. These needs have no moral quality. They are the unavoidable necessities of national existence and therefore are subject to classification neither as "good" or "bad."[15]

However, most realists do not deny morality. Indeed, they assume with Aristotle that politics is rooted in ethics. As Morgenthau has noted, "Realism is aware of the moral significance of political action."[16] Thus, realism, is distinguished not by its amorality or immorality but by a morality of a different sort, one that differentiates political ethics from personal ethics and judges action in terms of consequences. Because of the radically different nature of individual and political obligations, realists assume that individual morality, such as the Sermon on the Mount, is not directly applicable to political action. Moreover, they believe that basing policy decisions on abstract moral principles is harmful to the conduct of foreign relations because it undermines the national interest and makes compromise more difficult. Rather than relying on isolated, detached moral norms, realists believe that decision making should be guided by the virtue of *prudence*, that is, rational decision making that seeks the greatest good from among relevant, morally acceptable alternatives. The aim is not to ensure compliance with particular moral rules and norms but to ensure the most effective realization of goals. Fundamentally, then, realism is a consequentialist-based tradition.

To illuminate some of realism's norms, I next examine Thucydides' classic exposition of the Peloponnesian War.

CASE NO. 3–1
THE PELOPONNESIAN WAR

Background

During the fifth century B.C., Greece was comprised of numerous independent and largely self-sufficient city-states. Because each city-state was responsible for its own security and economic welfare, ancient Greece was similar to the contemporary international system—a decentralized, anarchic political system lacking a central governing authority. States promoted their economic and security interests through military alliances and commercial trade, with two city-states dominating the interstate relations of the region: Athens, a democratic, commercial, and outward-looking regime, and Sparta, an oligarchic, agricultural, and inward-looking regime.

Early in the fifth century, the Persians tried to extend their empire into

Greece but were successfully repulsed, in great measure because of the military collaboration between Athens and Sparta. After defeating the Persians, the Spartans retreated to the Greek peninsula south of Athens (the area known as Peloponnese) and throughout the remainder of the century confined their influence largely to this region. Although Sparta had a mighty army, it limited its influence largely to the Peloponnesian peninsula, fearing that its large helot slave population might rebel if the army were away conquering new territories. As a result, Sparta's military alliance system, known as the Peloponnesian League, was confined mainly to the surrounding region. The Athenians, by contrast, attempted to deter future Persian threats by increasing their naval power and extending their economic influence throughout the Aegean Sea. Moreover, Athens institutionalized its influence in the region by establishing the Delian League, a widespread defensive alliance system comprised of some 200 city-states.

In the mid-fifth century, relations between Athens and Sparta began to deteriorate, resulting in a war (sometimes called the First Peloponnesian War), lasting from 460 to 445 B.C. This conflict ended with a negotiated settlement based on Sparta's recognition of Athens' regional influence in exchange for Athens' surrender of land acquired during the war. Although the truce was supposed to last for thirty years, within ten years tensions between the two regional powers had resumed, eventually resulting in a second war: the Great Peloponnesian War (431–404 B.C.).

Origins of War

Three developments contributed to the origins of the Great Peloponnesian War. First, a conflict developed between Corinth, a Spartan-aligned city-state at the mouth of the Peloponnesian peninsula, and Athens. The dispute arose when a civil war broke out in Epidamnus, a former colony of Corcyra (modern-day Corfu) located on the northwestern coast of Greece. The democratic forces of Epidamnus, after appealing unsuccessfully to Corcyra for help, requested assistance from Corinth, which decided to help. However, this pledge of Corinthian assistance angered Corcyra, which then dispatched a naval force to regain control of its former colony. En route, the Corcyrans engaged and defeated Corinthian naval forces. Fearing a counterattack from Corinth, Corcyra asked Athens for help. After carefully deliberating the pros and cons of involving itself in this conflict, Athens decided to provide modest assistance to Corcyra. Its decision was based partly on its fear that failure to support Corcyra would result in the latter's becoming aligned with Sparta. Because Corcyra had the second-largest navy in the region, its alliance with Sparta would shift the regional balance of power toward Sparta. Such a development was unacceptable to Pericles, the main military and political strategist of Athens.

A second factor contributing to the outbreak of war was a revolt at Potidaea, a former Corinthian colony on the northern Aegean coast. Because Potidaea was part of the Delian League, Athens feared that Potidaea, in response to Corinthian prodding, might revolt against Athens. Thus, it demanded that Potidaea tear down its fortifications, send away its Corinthian magistrates, and free its hostages. These actions, Athens assumed, would place Potidaea at its mercy and thereby deter rebellion. The Athenian's suspicion about Potidaea turned out to be justified, as Potidaeans had sent envoys to Sparta to request help in their rebellion.

The third development precipitating war was Athens' imposition of a limited economic embargo on Megara, a Spartan-aligned city-state located just west of Athens. The Athenian decree barred Megarians from harbors of the Athenian Empire, thereby harming the commercial sectors of Megara. Because Megara had helped Corinth in its conflict with Corcyra, Athens issued the decree to punish Megara and thereby, it was hoped, to deter other city-states from assisting Corinth.

In his *History of the Peloponnesian War,* Thucydides argues that the roots of war were sown in the growing imbalance of power between Athens and Sparta. In his words: "[W]hat made the war inevitable was the growth of Athenian power and the fear that this caused in Sparta."[17] However, Donald Kagan argues that Athenian power was not growing in the aftermath of the Thirty Years' Peace. Indeed, the only growth in Athenian power resulted from the Corinthian initiative against Corcyra in 433, some twelve years after the end of the first war.[18] Thus, for Kagan, the origins of the war are rooted not in the bipolar (Athens-Sparta) hegemonic system, which had resulted in some regional stability, but in the crises in Corcyra, Potidaea, and Megara. Although none of these developments alone would have been decisive in starting a war, taken together they fostered growing distrust and insecurity, rooted in great part in the shifting perceptions in the balance of power. For example, after Athens became aligned with Corcyra, Corinth threatened to join the Athenian alliance if Sparta failed to support its claims. As a result, Sparta felt compelled to assist Corinth. Athens, too, felt constrained by potential shifts in the regional balance of power. For example, its decision to help Corcyra was driven by fear that Corcyra, with the second-largest naval fleet, might become aligned with the Spartan league if it did not provide military support. Because a Corcyra-Corinthian-Spartan alliance would have radically altered the regional balance of power, Athens felt compelled to aid Corcyra. In addition, once Athens imposed the Megarian Decree to deter other city-states from helping Corinth, it refused to alter or withdraw the order, believing that modifying the decree would only invite other demands.

The War

The war itself lasted from 431 to 404 B.C. During the first ten years there was a stalemate between Athens and Sparta, but after a temporary truce of six years, military power began to shift in favor of Sparta, in great measure because of Athens' imperial overextension. In 416, Athens decided to invade Sicily, most of whose city-states were aligned with Sparta. Despite its superior naval forces, Athens was unsuccessful in gaining control of the island. Indeed, when its forces were defeated at Syracuse, Athenian morale broke, and its military and economic power never recovered. Although Athens continued fighting for another decade, its military and economic power continued to wane. By the beginning of the fifth century, the Athenian Empire had all but collapsed, and in 404 Sparta compelled Athens to level its city walls.

Realism and the War

The contemporary interest in this ancient war between Sparta and Athens is due in great measure to Thucydides' masterful account of the war, a history that not only describes the nature and historical evolution of the war but, more important, illuminates profound insights about the human condition and political life. Written from a realist perspective, Thucydides' study not only reveals important norms of the tradition of political realism but also applies those norms to the interpretation of events. In effect, Thucydides' history illuminates principles that can be conducive to order and security within a decentralized global community. One scholar has suggested that Thucydides' analysis of international relations is so insightful that there is little that is now known about global politics that was not revealed by Thucydides long ago.[19] I next briefly examine some of the most important norms illuminated by Thucydides' study.

The first realist principle illustrated by the Peloponnesian War is the importance of power in interstate relations. Because in ancient Greece, as in the modern world, there was no central authority to regulate interstate relations, the security and well-being of city-states was ultimately in the hands of each state. Thus, when Persia attempted to conquer Greece, the joint military cooperation of the two leading Greek city-states, Sparta and Athens, helped defeat Persian aggression.

Thucydides' realism also illustrates the importance of a balance of power in fostering stability in an anarchic, decentralized system. Realists believe that, in the absence of government, the only effective way of developing and maintaining global order is through the maintenance of a fundamental equilibrium of power. Such a balance can be established and maintained locally, regionally, and internationally through the parties themselves and through alliances with other states. Because the only effective deterrent against aggression is countervailing power, realists assume that states need to have sufficient power to inhibit aggression and, in the event of war, to defeat an enemy state militarily. Thus, when a state increases its military and economic power, the opposing state must seek to counterbalance such changes by increasing its own power. During the Peloponnesian conflict, Spartan and Athenian officials were especially sensitive to developments that might alter the fundamental balance of power that existed in the region. Indeed, Thucydides suggests that Sparta's decision to go to war was rooted in its belief that the Athenian Empire had become too powerful and that the failure to challenge the perceived imbalance would result in even greater future suffering.

A third realist principle illuminated by the war is the importance of alliances in interstate relations. Alliances are significant because they facilitate and institutionalize economic, political, and military cooperation among states. They provide, in effect, a means to increase power. For example, Athens' establishment of the Delian League, a political and economic alliance with some 200 other Aegean city-states, contributed immeasurably to its economic prosperity and military security. However, alliances can also result in entangling relationships that can initiate and exacerbate conflict. In fact, the outbreak of the Peloponnesian War can be directly attributed to allies of Athens and Sparta. As Thucydides' account suggests, alliances can contribute to a balance of power but they can also serve as instruments of entanglement, compelling major actors into conflicts in which they have no direct, vital interests. For example, in the Peloponnesian War Sparta had no direct interests in defending Corinth, except in maintaining a regional balance of power. Similarly, Athens had no direct, vital interests in the events in Corcyra. However, because the failure of either Sparta or Athens to respond to its allies might alter the regional balance of power, each hegemon felt compelled to get involved, thereby expanding the nature and scope of the conflict. Alliances, in short, can help keep peace through the equilibrium of power, but they can also expand the scope and intensity of conflict.

A final realist norm illuminated by Thucydides is a pessimistic view of the morality of individual and collective behavior. It is a pessimistic account because human nature is assumed to be motivated mainly by self-interest, power, and fear. For Thucydides, the natural human condition is not peace, prosperity, and justice but competition, conflict, uncertainty, fear, and injustice. In light of such assumptions about human nature, political behavior within domestic societies (city-states) is regarded as competitive, conflictual, and fearful; however, it is also influenced by "honor," which involves defending and advancing the interests of the political community to which citizens belong. Notwithstanding the limitations of human nature, Thucydides views the city as a moral community, because the governing authorities have the potential of advancing justice through rational deliberation. However, this is not the case in the anarchic interstate system, in which relations among city-states are governed by rivalry, conflict, and fear; and, because there is no authoritative way to reconcile interests and to promote the common good, there can be little hope for justice. The best that can be hoped for is a stable, peaceful interstate environment resulting from a balanced constellation of power.

This pessimistic view of interstate political relations is most graphically illustrated in the famous debate preceding Athens' conquest of the island of Melos. In the famous Melian dialogue, the Athenians make clear that, given their status as a dominant power, they have a right to rule Melos. Thucydides describes the Athenian perspective as follows: "[T]he standard of justice depends on the equality of power to compel and that in fact the strong do what they have the power to do and the weak accept what they have to accept."[20] Thus, the Melians can either accept Athenian rule on the basis of their dominant power or suffer defeat and annihilation. To the extent that a common good exists in the interstate system, it is to be determined and implemented by the powerful. The Melians reply that because they value political independence more highly than safety, they would prefer to fight than become Athenian slaves. After warning the Melians to surrender, the Athenians conquer the island, killing its soldiers and making slaves of women and children.

Moral Reflections

Thucydides' account of the Peloponnesian War is part history and part political theory. By relying on a realist conception of politics, Thucydides describes and interprets events from a particular perspective, thereby illustrating the profound impact of ethical traditions on political analysis and political action.

- Given the significant influence of the realist paradigm on Thucydides' writing, does the realist perspective distort history? Does the tradition impair the development of an objective account of the Athenian-Spartan war?
- The Peloponnesian War also raises several critical issues regarding the analysis of international relations. First, is power as important as realism alleges in ensuring the security of states and in fostering a stable world order?
- Is it true, as realism claims, that states are naturally inclined to counter hegemonic power by pursuing a balance of power?
- Is classical realism's pessimistic account of human nature valid, and does it explain the conflict and uncertainty in international political society?
- Does realism provide an adequate account of the role of morality in international affairs? Is it true that the anarchic international system is governed mainly by the quest for security, thereby allowing little freedom for moral action?

Idealism

Like realism, political idealism is a tradition rooted in ancient thought, although its application to politics, especially international relations, is comparatively recent. Two early thinkers who contributed to its early development were Thomas Aquinas, a thirteenth-century Catholic theologian, and Dante Alighieri, a fourteenth-century Italian scholar. Aquinas believed that reason could help define and establish a just political order. Despite human sinfulness, natural law could be apprehended by reason, thereby providing a basis for political justice. Dante, too, contributed to the development of the idealist tradition by emphasizing the vital role of international governmental institutions in promoting world order. In *Of Monarchy,* he argued that centralized political authority was essential for resolving interstate disputes. More particularly, he suggested that a world government ruled by a monarch was the most effective way of promoting global peace.

The most important elements of political idealism emerged in the eighteenth and nineteenth centuries with the contractarian theories of John Locke and Jean-Jacques Rousseau and the liberal philosophies of thinkers such as Adam Smith, Jeremy Bentham, and John Stuart Mill. The former theories are significant because they emphasized consent as a basis of legitimate political authority, whereas the latter are important because they emphasize individual rights, especially freedom. Another significant strand of idealism emerged in the nineteenth century with the writings of the German philosopher Immanuel Kant. His analysis is important because it calls attention to the major role of domestic and international structures in promoting global order. In *On Perpetual Peace*, Kant argued that peace among nation-states is best maintained through an informal federation of republican regimes. Although Kant thought that some centralization of global power was necessary in global society, international structures alone were insufficient to ensure international peace. In addition, states themselves had to be governed responsibly, and this could occur only if regimes were based on limited, constitutional authority.

Twentieth-century statesmen and thinkers have also contributed to the further development of political idealism. For example, President Woodrow Wilson, generally considered the father of the League of Nations, developed and popularized the belief that global order could best be realized through international law and global institutions rather than realist power politics. Wilson had so much confidence in the human capacity to establish peaceful and just human communities that he espoused self-determination as a basis of world order. According to this notion, peoples sharing a common nationality and culture had a right to political self-rule. Although this claim contributed to the decolonization movement of the mid-twentieth century, it has also contributed to significant political turmoil in the post-Cold War era, as no common definition exists to determine which peoples are entitled to self-determination. President Jimmy Carter also contributed to the resurgence of political idealism in the late twentieth century with his optimistic conception of international relations and his Wilsonian confidence in law and human rights.

The idealist tradition has been expressed historically through three distinct strands: classical idealism, political liberalism, and internationalism.[21] *Classical idealism*, represented by thinkers such as Locke, Bentham, Mill, and Richard Cobden, is characterized by a belief that relations among individuals, groups, and states are fundamentally harmonious and by an emphasis on law and constitutionalism in promoting human dignity domestically and peace internationally. In the nineteenth century, idealists expressed their optimism about the cooperative and harmonious nature of human interrelationships by espousing "commercial pacifism," the belief that international trade was conducive to global peace.[22] Thus, classical idealism's distinctive feature was its optimism about the establishment and maintenance of community life, whether at the familial, local, national, or international level.

Political liberalism, the second type of idealism, is concerned with the establishment of government structures that best secure and protect human rights, especially individual liberty, the most fundamental right. Liberal theorists, such as Thomas Jefferson and James Madison, believed that because the major impediment historically to human freedom had been tyranny, the protection of individual rights required a limited, constitutional regime—one that was based on dispersed power and accountable to people through periodic elections. Although theorists have historically defined human freedom in a variety of ways, liberals have emphasized two types of liberties: basic and political-civil. Basic liberties, sometimes termed "negative freedoms," are concerned with the protection of individuals from arbitrary authority and include such rights as the freedom of conscience, the freedom of speech, the freedom of assembly, and the freedom from arbitrary imprisonment (habeas corpus) as well as the freedom to own property. Political and civil rights are those individual freedoms that are necessary to maintain a participatory, constitutional government. Political liberalism thus celebrates individual freedom and the imperative of limited, constitutional government.

The third expression of idealism is *internationalism*, an approach that emphasizes the important role of domestic structures in determining the nature of global relations. According to Kant, the father of this approach, the most effective way of promoting global peace was through the development of a "pacific federation" of liberal states. Although international institutions were important in facilitating conflict resolution and in promoting harmonious global relations, the essential precondition for world peace was the proliferation of "republics," that is, liberal regimes based on limited, constitutional authority.[23]

In the twentieth century, other practitioners and scholars have further developed internationalism. President Wilson, for example, was especially influential in propagating this approach with his call for a different type of global politics, one rooted in public opinion, open participation, and law. With the establishment of the United Nations and the growing number and influence of nongovernmental organizations in the mid-twentieth century, a more robust and formalized internationalism emerged. Known as *liberal internationalism*, this approach was based on several core assumptions, including the following: (1) nonstate actors are increasingly important in global politics; (2) states are not unitary-rational actors; (3) national security is important, but it is not the sole or necessarily the most important state interest; (4) international institutions participate as independent actors in global society; and (5) significant international cooperation is possible both through direct initiatives of states and through international institutions.[24] Additionally, whereas classical idealism and political liberalism emphasize human nature and political morality, liberal institutionalism is mainly concerned with structural factors that contribute to global cooperation. Moreover, modern internationalism is concerned mainly with whether structures promote global cooperation, not with the effectiveness of law and institutions in global society.[25]

Characteristics

Notwithstanding the continuing evolution of political idealism and the development of differing doctrines, this tradition has remained grounded in several core assumptions. These include an optimistic view of human nature and community life, the primacy of morality over power politics, the priority of human rights and constitutional government, and the important role of law and international institutions in building political order.[26] I next examine each of these four core assumptions.

Political idealism is characterized first by an optimistic view of the establishment and maintenance of a just political order. For most idealists, this optimistic view of international affairs is rooted in a benign view of human nature. Idealists have faith in the long-term beneficence and benevolence of human nature, believing, as Michael Smith has noted, that human nature "will eventually express its true interests in peace and a thoroughly reformed international system."[27] Because human beings are fundamentally good, the evil and injustice in the world is due largely to the unjust and imperfect political and economic structures of global society. Idealists also base their optimistic political assessment on the effectiveness of human reason in developing norms and facilitating international coordination and cooperation. For them, the ability to promote international peace and tranquillity is rooted in human enlightenment and rational communication and negotiation. Still other liberals view international peace and tranquillity as an automatic by-product of the utopian conviction that the vital interests of states are fundamentally complementary. This notion, which historian E. H. Carr defines as the "doctrine of harmony of interests,"[28] was expressed in a variety of ways in nineteenth-century international relations but especially in the belief that free trade encouraged international peace.

Although idealists, especially liberal institutionalists, deemphasize human nature and political morality, it is clear that idealists share an optimistic view of international political life. They believe that global harmony is possible and that states, although motivated to maximize national gains, can work cooperatively toward the common good. Although idealists might not attribute their optimistic assessment of global relations to political morality, it is clear that their assumptions about international relations are rooted in an optimistic view of individual and collective behavior.

A second distinctive feature of idealism is the important role assigned to moral values in defining foreign policy interests and strategies. Whereas realism's struggle for power leaves little room for moral judgment in foreign affairs, idealism emphasizes moral norms in developing and implementing foreign policy. Moreover, to the extent that realists make room for ethical judgment in international relations, they do so through a consequentialist strategy. Idealists, by contrast, emphasize rule-based ethics, seeking to ensure that the goals, intentions, and outcomes are consistent with common morality. However, it is important to emphasize that modern international relations scholarship has disregarded the impact of human nature on global politics while deemphasizing the role of political morality. As noted previously, liberal internationalism stresses structures and institutions, paying little attention to the role of ethics and moral values in structuring analysis of foreign policy and international politics. For example, for contemporary neoliberal scholars global social and economic cooperation is to be explained largely by structural conditions, rather than moral values. Despite the modern predilection to emphasize empirical analysis, the tradition of idealism is nonetheless grounded in political ethics.

The third distinctive feature of idealism is the priority given to human rights and to the constitutional structures essential to protecting these rights. This dimension of the idealist tradition is rooted in the doctrine of political liberalism, which developed during the seventeeth, eighteenth, and nineteeth centuries. Liberal political thinkers, such as Locke, Rousseau, Bentham, and Mill, developed theories that asserted the priority of individual rights and the responsibility of government in securing and protecting such rights. Because government oppression was thought to have been a major barrier historically to individual rights, liberal theorists argued that a primary task of government was to secure and protect such rights by establishing limited constitutional regimes. While liberal theorists devised a variety of procedures and institutions to this end, an essential feature of liberal thought was the need for periodic elections and shared government authority to ensure limited government and to inhibit tyranny.

Because the idealist tradition is rooted in liberalism, individual rights, human dignity, and political freedom are primary. Because the tradition is confident that procedures and institutions can be established to foster and protect basic rights, idealists are fundamentally optimistic about the expansion of human dignity and the promotion of communal justice.

Moreover, the idealist tradition assumes that because interstate conflicts and wars are often the result of autocratic, illegitimate regimes, the spread of constitutional, democratic governments can help foster peace and global order. For example, President Wilson, who contributed significantly to the establishment of the League of Nations, believed that making governments and international diplomacy more responsive to public opinion would lead to a more stable, just international order. In fact, Wilson, along with other idealists of his era, had so much faith in the general public that he believed that secret diplomacy was counterproductive to global order. Indeed, this conviction became a rallying cry of the League of Nations' principle of "open covenants openly arrived at."

A final distinctive feature of idealism is the priority of international law and transnational organizations. Whereas realism emphasizes the balance of power in promoting international order, idealists believe that law and international structures—especially regimes and international governmental and nongovernmental organizations—contribute decisively to the development of global cooperation and world order. As noted earlier, the modern idealism expressed in the early part of the twentieth century gave special emphasis to international law and organization, whereas liberal institutionalism, the more recent expression of idealism, has emphasized state and nonstate actors that contribute to transnational cooperation and to the development of international regimes.

To illustrate the role and impact of the idealist tradition on foreign policy, I next explore President Jimmy Carter's human rights policy.

CASE NO. 3–2
PRESIDENT CARTER'S HUMAN RIGHTS POLICY

Background

During the 1977 presidential campaign, Democratic Party candidate Jimmy Carter emphasized repeatedly that if elected he would make the promotion of human rights a foreign policy priority. According to Zbigniew Brzezinski, his national security advisor, Carter's commitment to human rights reflected his own religious convictions as well as his political acumen. Brzezinski writes, "He deeply believed in human rights and that commitment remained constant during his Administration. At the same time, he sensed, I think, that the issue was an appealing one, for it drew a sharp contrast between himself and the policies of Nixon and Kissinger."[29]

The idea that human rights should be an integral element of U.S. foreign policy did not originate with Carter. Indeed, throughout the twentieth century, statesmen and leaders, beginning with Wilson, had periodically sought to promote human rights abroad. For Wilson and other idealists, the myth of American exceptionalism had convinced them that the world would be a better place if other countries were to adopt America's traditions of individual rights and implemented its institutions of representative government. Moreover, other recent administrations had emphasized human rights, albeit through quiet diplomacy. However, as R. J. Vincent has observed, what was different about Carter's human rights policy was the adoption of human rights both "as a standard by which to judge the conduct of others and as a set of principles that was to guide its own foreign policy."[30]

It needs to be emphasized, too, that before Carter assumed the presidency, a number of developments were underway within Congress that greatly reinforced Carter's human rights initiatives. Two of the most significant of these legislative actions were the hearings and legislative proposals of the House of Representatives Subcommittee on International Organizations and the passage of the 1975 Jackson-Vanik amendment, which linked most-favored-nation (MFN) status to compliance with human rights norms.

Beginning in 1973, Congressman Donald Fraser, chairman of the House Subcommittee on International Organizations (later renamed Human Rights and International Organizations), began holding hearings on human rights. After initial hearings, in 1974 the subcommittee issued a report calling on the U.S. government to more effectively defend human rights around the world. By the time the Fraser subcommittee ended its work in 1978, it had held some 150 hearings and was responsible for several important changes in U.S. foreign policy statutes. One of the most significant of these—the amending of Section 502B of the 1961 Foreign Assistance Act—required "that, except in extraordinary circumstances, the President shall substantially reduce or terminate security assistance to any government which engages in a consistent pattern of gross violations of internationally recognized human rights." Thus, when Carter began his presidency in 1977, Congress had already established a number of major human rights initiatives making foreign security assistance and MFN status conditional on human rights.[31]

It is important to emphasize that the principal inspiration for the development and implementation of human rights initiatives was the president himself. In fact, his idealistic worldview not only provided an optimistic outlook on international affairs but also contributed to the importance of human rights. In his inaugural address, Carter called attention to the priority of human rights and especially individual liberty. "Because we are free," Carter said, "we can never be indifferent to the fate of freedom elsewhere." Several months later, the president set forth his conception of human rights and political democracy in an important speech at the University of Notre Dame. In that address, Carter described his idealistic political worldview as follows:

> Because we know that democracy works, we can reject the arguments of those rulers who deny human rights to their people. We are confident that democracy's example will be compelling. . . . We are confident that democratic methods are the most effective, and so we are not tempted to employ improper tactics here at home or abroad. . . . Being confident of our own future, we are now free of the inordinate fear of Communism which once led us to embrace any dictator who joined us

in that fear. I am glad that that is being changed. . . . We can no longer separate the traditional issues of war and peace from the new global questions of justice, equity and human rights.[32]

After describing major elements of his worldview, Carter outlined several foreign policy initiatives that expressed his core convictions. Not surprisingly, his first policy initiative was human rights, not international peacekeeping, U.S.-Soviet relations, or nuclear arms control, as might have been the case under the previous Republican Party administrations.

Carter's Human Rights Policy

After assuming office, President Carter faced the challenge of translating the human rights vision that he had articulated in the campaign into an operational policy. This was not easy, as his human rights ideas were deeply rooted in moral convictions but were not integrated into a public philosophy about international affairs. One former aide has noted that because Carter had a moral ideology but no political ideology, his human rights policy reflected "strong moral impulses tethered somewhat loosely to a set of political goals."[33] However, if U.S. foreign policy was to advance the cause of human rights, it was essential to establish realistic policies and priorities that would effectively advance such rights.

The Carter administration sought to promote human rights abroad in a variety of ways. First, it used public diplomacy—pronouncements, policy statements, declarations, and condemnations—to draw attention to the priority of rights and to regimes in which major abuses were occurring. Second, it emphasized human rights initiatives within regional and international organizations, encouraging the further institutionalization of human rights norms. Third, it strengthened the U.S. institutional support for human rights by transforming the Department of State's Office of Human Rights into the Bureau of Human Rights, headed by an assistant secretary of state. A major task of the new bureau was to prepare an annual report on human rights abuses and violations in foreign countries.[34] Finally, the Carter administration used sanctions to promote human rights. For example, during Carter's term, the U.S. government cut its security assistance to at least eight countries and its economic aid to an an even greater number of countries because of major human rights abuses.

As Carter administration officials began to express human rights concerns publicly and privately, profound tensions began to emerge not only between the United States and other governments but within the administration itself. For example, when a reporter asked an administration official in the new administration how the U.S. government viewed continuing Soviet threats against human rights activist Andrei Sakharov, the Department of State issued a statement expressing admiration for Sakharov's role as a champion of human rights within the Soviet Union. "Any attempts by the Soviet authorities to intimidate Mr. Sakharov," the statement went on to say, "will not silence legitimate criticisms in the Soviet Union and will conflict with accepted international standards in the field of human rights."[35] However, Soviet government officials did not appreciate this shift in U.S. foreign policy. In their view, no other state had a right to tell the Soviet government how to treat its citizens. As a result, Soviet Ambassador Anatoly Dobrynin immediately protested to Secretary of State Cyrus Vance, and shortly thereafter Tass, the Soviet news agency, denounced the U.S. statement as an "unsavory ploy." Given the Soviet Union's superpower status and the need to balance human rights concerns with other legitimate interests, such as arms control, nuclear proliferation, and global order, the United States immediately backed off from its public denunciation of Soviet human rights. However, this was not the case with lesser powers, especially Latin American authoritarian regimes with whom the U.S. strategic interests were minimal. As a result, the United States pursued a more vigorous human rights policy toward countries such as Argentina, Brazil, Guatemala, and Uruguay than toward Indonesia, the Philippines, and South Korea, where security interests were at stake.

However, as Carter officials discovered, pursuing human rights often necessitated trade-offs with other core interests. As one observer noted at the time, although self-determination, majority rule, minority rights, and international order are all desirable, most of the time we can enjoy only some of these good things in life, and then only at the expense of others. "Refusing to accept this fact of life is like refusing to grow up because adults lead such sordid lives."[36] To develop a more coherent human rights strategy, Carter signed a presidential directive on human rights (P.D. 30) to clarify goals and establish clear policy priorities. Among other things, the directive established priorities among major types of human rights, emphasized the role of positive sanctions, prohibited aid to regimes guilty of serious rights violations, and encouraged the use of international financial institutions in promoting human rights.[37] Despite these explicit guidelines, the tensions surrounding the administration's human rights initiatives persisted as the administration sought to balance human rights with other important foreign policy goals.

Assessing the Policy

Despite inconsistent policy implementation, some scholars and officials regard Carter's human rights policy as a major foreign policy success. Brzezinski, for example, identifies human rights among the foremost foreign policy achievements of the Carter administration. In his view, the human rights policy was important because it encouraged the identification of the United States with the ideals of justice, equity, majority rule, self-determination, and human dignity.[38] Others credit the reduction of human rights abuses in authoritarian regimes (e.g., Argentina, Indonesia, and Uruguay) to the international human rights campaign.

However, this policy was also strongly criticized by many. Some argued that it was hypocritical because of its selective and inconsistent application. Others, such as Joshua Muravchik, argued that the policy lacked balance because it focused attention on individual human rights abuses while overlooking system-wide violations by totalitarian regimes. As a result, the Carter administration emphasized the less serious human rights abuses of authoritarian regimes while neglecting the more egregious systematic suppression of freedom in totalitarian regimes.[39] In addition, Carter's human rights policy was criticized for its conceptual confusion about rights. Rather than clarifying and prioritizing rights, some critics suggested that Carter added to the conceptual muddle. For example, Jeane Kirkpatrick, who served as U.S. ambassador to the United Nations during the Reagan administration, argued that Carter increased conceptual confusion by the broadening of the definition of rights. As Kirkpatrick noted, "Human rights in the Carter version had no specific content, except a general demand that societies provide all the freedoms associated with constitutional democracy, all the economic security promised by socialism, and all of the self-fulfillment featured in Abraham Maslow's psychology."[40]

In short, the tradition of political idealism contributed decisively to the foreign policies of President Carter. The tradition not only provided a worldview by which international events and developments were assessed but also served as a source of inspiration and guidance in public affairs. As this case study suggests, the development and implementation of Carter's human rights policy were a direct by-product of the president's idealistic worldview.

Moral Reflections

I have suggested that ethical traditions influence the conceptualization of issues and the development and execution of policies.

- In light of this case study, what are some distinctive policy features that are rooted in the tradition of political idealism?
- What policy strengths and weaknesses can be attributed to idealism? If President Carter had relied on political realism rather than idealism in defining and implementing human rights, how might the policy have differed?
- Would a human rights policy rooted in political realism have been more effective, or less effective in promoting international human rights? Why or why not?

Summary

Ethical traditions play an indispensable role in international relations. In a world in which moral values are being increasingly undermined and neglected, traditions provide a structure for identifying and applying relevant moral norms to international relations. By illuminating widely shared moral values, ethical traditions help guide individual and collective political action, thereby contributing to the development of humane foreign policies and just international structures. Ethical traditions also provide the moral architecture necessary to critique and assess the foreign policy behaviors of states and the international structures of global society. Ethical traditions are not self-validating. As a result, the plurality of traditions requires that the competing and conflicting claims of different traditions be examined with care and reconciled when possible.

CHAPTER FOUR

THE ETHICS OF INTERNATIONAL HUMAN RIGHTS

[Human rights] have become a kind of *lingua franca* of ethics talk so that much of the discussion about ethics in international relations takes place making use of the vocabulary of rights.

R. J. Vincent[1]

There are goods more important than order. There are wrongs worth righting even at the cost of injuring order.

Charles Krauthammer[2]

The news media regularly reminds citizens in the developed nations that there is much suffering in many poor, undemocratic states of the Third World. This suffering, manifested by hunger, disease, religious persecution, ethnic discrimination, forced expulsion, torture, and even death, is sometimes the result of natural disasters. More frequently, however, this suffering is a direct by-product of ethnic conflict and civil war among major groups seeking political power. For example, the post-Cold War disintegration of Yugoslavia led to a bitter ethnonationalistic war within Bosnia-Herzegovina among Croats, Muslims, and Serbs that resulted in an estimated 300,000 deaths and more than a million refugees. Similarly, the conflict among Somali clans in the early 1990s led to the total breakdown of public order, resulting in a bitter civil war that left hundreds of thousands of Somalis dead, mostly from starvation. In Rwanda, the animosity between Hutu and Tutsi peoples led to a tribal genocide in 1994 that claimed more than 800,000 lives and left more than two million refugees. Individuals, nonpolitical groups, and societies themselves also perpetuate significant suffering when they carry out actions that threaten the dignity of persons. For example, some societies continue to tolerate and even support practices that are widely condemned, such as slavery, child labor, female genital mutilation, and ethnic cleansing.

This chapter examines the quest for human dignity in global society. Because the international community is a society of societies, each with its own social structures, political and economic institutions, and cultural traditions, defining human rights and identifying policies and structures that are likely to enhance human dignity is an especially challenging task. Although the international community is comprised of many distinct cultures, it is also a society of human beings—a global community of 5.8 billion persons, each entitled to dignity, respect, and equal treatment by government authorities regardless of citizenship or nationality.

Individual rights can be defined and justified in either positive or normative terms. The positive, or empirical, approach describes the individual rights that are already claimed. Positive rights consist of those personal entitlements that are defined by existing domestic statutes or international treaties and conventions. According to the positivist perspective, individuals are entitled to rights because governing bodies have established binding rules and conventions that give effect to such rights. The normative, or moral, perspective defines the rights that ought to be protected. Normative rights include those human rights whose validity depends on the inherent moral legitimacy of the claims. Thus, the normative conception entails rules and principles that are regarded as binding, independent of the statutes and international treaties adopted by states. In sum, whereas positive rights are rooted in fact, normative rights are based on morality.[3]

In defining human rights, it is important to recall that morality can itself be differentiated between positivist and normative conceptions.[4] A normative conception of morality consists of rules and principles that are considered binding regardless of whether they are in fact universally upheld. By contrast, a positivist conception of morality consists of the rules or directives that are in fact upheld as obligatory by what individuals say, believe, or do. However, whether the rules and directives of conventions, such as the Universal Declaration of Human Rights or the International Covenant on Civil and Political Rights, are part of a moral structure will depend on whether persons (as well as groups and states) believe that such rules *ought to be upheld*. As Alan Gewirth has noted, for customs to become morality, there must be a normative component.[5]

The distinction between international morality and international mores is significant because it highlights the important moral role of international treaties and conventions in strengthening the definition and enforcement of human rights in global society. International human rights directives are frequently considered part of international law but not part of international ethics. However, if morality includes rules that people believe should be enforced in global society, such directives are an important part of international morality. Thus, in exploring human rights as a problem of international ethics, this chapter examines the role of international human rights law in the quest for human dignity and global justice.

This chapter has five parts. First, it examines the nature and origins of the human rights doctrine in terms of alternative human rights theories and in light of the problem posed by cultural pluralism. The challenge of competing interpretations of human rights is illustrated with a case study on caning in Singapore. Second, this chapter explores the role of human rights discourse in contemporary international politics, focusing on the international law of human rights. Third, it assesses the limits and possibilities, the problems and prospects, of international protection of human rights. Fourth, it illuminates the difficulties in providing international human rights protection with a case study on the failure of the international community to rescue Rwanda from mass murder. Fifth, it sets forth a number of guidelines that can contribute to the development of a prudent and effective human rights foreign policy.

The Idea of Human Rights

The idea that human beings have individual rights is of comparatively recent origin. Throughout antiquity and the medieval age, Western political thinkers emphasized the development of just political communities by calling attention to the duties and responsibilities of individuals. Human dignity was assumed to be a by-product of participation within and obligations toward a political community. However, with the rise of humanism, the modernization and integration of markets, and the political consolidation of nation-states in the sixteenth and seventeenth centuries, European societies became increasingly urbanized, secularized, and fragmented. In addition, with the consolidation of state power, government authority expanded significantly as it made ever-increasing claims on individuals. At the same time, political thinkers began to emphasize the basic (or natural) rights of persons in political society, the conditional authority of government, and the necessity for limiting the power of rulers to minimize the possibility of tyranny and political oppression. The development of ideas such as these resulted in the theory of political liberalism, a revolutionary doctrine that was to provide the most comprehensive and compelling definition and justification of human rights in the modern world.[6] However, what is important to emphasize at this point is that human rights claims emerged within the context of political liberalism and were expressed fundamentally as claims of individuals against the state.[7]

Although the notion of human rights is a relatively modern political discovery, its development is rooted in a number of major ideas from ancient and medieval political thought. One of the most important of these ideas was the Stoic belief in the universality of moral reason, a concept that reinforced the notion of moral equality of persons and priority of political obligations to all human beings. Because individuals were joined by reason to all persons, their political obligations were not limited to the city-state, as the Greeks had believed, but extended to the universal community.[8] These two Stoic ideas—the universality of moral reason and the priority of the universal community—were significant because they contributed decisively to the rise of natural law, from which the notion of natural rights first emerged in the seventeenth century.

Christianity has also contributed significantly to the human rights idea by emphasizing, among other things, the inherent worth and dignity of every person and the conditionality of temporal obligations.[9] Christianity affirms the dignity of persons not only by claiming that human beings are created in God's image but also by granting the ultimate divine gift— salvation through Jesus' atonement—to all persons. Most significantly, Christianity asserts that God has established a divine, transcendent moral order to which all human beings are subject. In effect, human beings are subject to two authorities: the temporal power of the state and the divine commands of God. According to the Scriptures, citizens should render to Caesar the things that belong to Caesar and to God the things that belong to God. However, when conflict develops between these two realms, citizens should obey God rather than human authorities.

Although some thinkers have argued that human rights are not of Western origin, it is clear that the idea of individual rights is a historical product of European politics and rooted in Western political thought.[10] Some of the most important Western ideas that contributed to the emergence of the human rights idea included the following: (1) a transcendent moral order exists whose norms can be apprehended by reason;[11] (2) human rights are part of the natural order of creation; (3) human beings have inherent worth and need to be treated as ends rather than means; and (4) human beings are fundamentally equal. As originally developed, human rights were rooted in the moral assumptions about human nature. Thus, the notion of human rights was from its inception an ethical idea—a claim based on morality.

Theories of Human Rights

As first articulated, human rights are natural rights rooted in the moral nature of human persons. This perspective can be defined as the *moral theory of human rights,* because the claim that persons are entitled to fundamental entitlements is grounded in morality. According to this classical theory, persons are entitled to particular benefits or goods by virtue of their humanity, that is, their essential moral worth as human beings. Because human rights are rooted in the fundamental dignity of persons, they are timeless and universal, applicable to all individuals regardless of race, gender, age, ethnicity, or nationality. Moreover, because these rights are rooted in the unique moral nature of persons, they exist independently of the communities, societies, and states in which people live. Thus, human rights are extralegal, deriving their legitimacy from their inherent (or moral) validity, not from constitutional or legal provisions or particular actions by states and international organizations.[12]

In the modern world, the idea of human rights has gained increasing influence. As noted by R. J. Vincent, the idea that human beings have rights as humans "is a staple of contemporary world politics."[13] Whereas the moral theory of human rights provided a convincing argument in the seventeenth and eighteeth centuries, in the modern world that theory has been increasingly challenged by alternative conceptions of rights. The earliest major challenges to the classical doctrine of individual rights were developed in the nineteenth century by such political thinkers as Edmund Burke and Jeremy Bentham. Burke, a late eighteenth-century British parliamentarian, argued that human rights are rooted in communal customs and traditions, not in abstract reason and universal morality. As a result, human rights are not individualistic claims justified by reason but rather benefits that persons receive through participation in political society. Bentham, a cofounder of utilitarianism, was even more critical of human rights by disavowing the idea altogether.[14] Because Bentham believed that there was no such thing as transcendent morality or natural law, human rights were entirely fictitious. To speak of individual rights was to speak nonsense. Because human rights were rooted in civil laws, the rights derived from the "imaginary" laws of nature were themselves imaginary.

Although political thinkers have continued to challenge the idea of human rights since Burke, Bentham, and others first called into question the morality of individual rights, discourse on human rights continues to dominate contemporary international relations, and notwithstanding the denial of human rights by postmodern scholarship, intellectuals have continued to develop alternative conceptions and justifications of the human rights idea as they seek to develop a more compelling justification for them. To illustrate some of these different perspectives, several alternative human rights theories are briefly sketched here.

One alternative approach seeks to define and justify human rights in terms of basic physical needs. According to the *human needs theory*, persons are entitled to physical survival and security because without them, human life is impossible. Thus, human rights claims are rooted in the requirements of sustaining life and personal well-being.[15] Although this theory has the advantage of focusing on the tangible needs of human life, it fails to illuminate which physical requirements are essential. Moreover, it assumes that human dignity is necessarily achieved by giving priority to the physical dimensions of life.

Charles Beitz has developed a *social justice theory of human rights* that justifies rights in terms of distributive justice rather than the moral nature of persons.[16] According to this theory, human rights are entitlements, based on social justice norms, that ensure the well-being of persons. Beitz claims that because the classical doctrine of natural rights limits entitlements to personal security and fails to include socioeconomic claims, the social justice model provides a more comprehensive account of human rights. Beitz's model, however, has significant limitations. Because distributive justice necessarily depends on the cultures and capabilities of communities, human rights are conditioned by context. Moreover, by defining rights in terms of the distributive capabilities of a particular community, the social justice theory dissolves the fundamental distinction between government goals, such as providing welfare entitlements, and individual rights.

A third approach is the so-called *constitutive theory of human rights*, which specifies the rudimentary rights that are necessary for the enjoyment of other human goods. According to Henry Shue, a proponent of this theory, human beings are entitled to those rights without which other desirable goods are impossible to attain. Shue argues that there are three such rights: security, subsistence, and liberty. These rights do not represent a complete list of basic rights, nor are they necessarily more desirable than other rights.[17] Rather, they specify the collective requirements that are necessary in fulfilling other desirable human goods. Although Shue argues that basic rights are collectively necessary to secure other goods, it is clear that individuals frequently enjoy basic rights to different degrees, thereby calling into question the mutual interdependence of basic rights.

A fourth approach, the *social-scientific theory of human rights*, seeks to justify human rights on the basis of cross-cultural consensus. Because of the high degree of cultural pluralism in the contemporary world and because of the continually changing role of mores and values in different societies, finding a high level of consensus on human rights is likely to prove elusive. However, even if significant international agreement were to be found, such an approach would still not offer a compelling argument for human rights, because a moral claim cannot be deduced from empirical facts.

In sum, although scholars continue to differ on how best to define and justify human rights, there is widespread political agreement that such rights claims are legitimate and provide a basis for making demands within states and the international community itself. Before examining the widely accepted international legal principles and conventions on human rights, I briefly address the problem posed by the doctrine of universal human rights in a global community characterized by cultural pluralism.

The Problem of Cultural Relativism

As noted previously, the international community is a society of multiple societies, each with its own languages, historical traditions, cultural norms, and religious and moral values. Cultural pluralism is a fact of global society. However, if moral, religious and political values differ from society to society, and if human rights conceptions will necessarily reflect the cultural environment in which they are defined and applied, are all cultures equal? If not, whose culture is normative? When values and human rights conceptions come into conflict, who is to determine which interpretation is authoritative?

Because of the widespread relativity of values found in the world, some thinkers have concluded that there can be no international morality. The only morality that can exist is the morality of each particular society. If global society is simply the addition of shared cultures and morality, no doctrine of human rights is possible. The challenge posed by cultural pluralism is how to reconcile universal human rights claims with the fact of cultural and moral relativity.

There are two important points that need to be made about the claims of cultural relativism, one empirical and the other normative. Empirically, the claim of total moral diversity is simply untenable. As A. J. M. Milne has noted, moral diversity cannot be total because "certain moral principles are necessary for social life as such, irrespective of its particular form."[18] Milne argues that there is a common morality shared by all peoples. This morality involves such moral norms as justice, respect for human life, fellowship, freedom from arbitrary interference, and honorable treatment. However, every community also is based on a "particular" morality that is derived from each community's distinctive institutions, social order, and cultural values. As a result, the actual morality of a community involves both a common and a particular morality. Universal human rights are those rights rooted in a shared, or common, morality.

At a normative level, the claims of the doctrine of cultural relativism are similarly untenable because the fact of cultural relativity is not an ethical argument at all. To state that the world is comprised of different cultures is a descriptive statement. Its validity wholly depends on whether the empirical assertion is true. However, the doctrine of cultural relativism claims more than mere description. Because moral values are assumed to be valid only in their particular cultural contexts, cultural relativists claim not only that the values of one society are inapplicable to other societies but that no moral hierarchy among cultural systems is possible. Cultural relativists thus seek to derive an ethical doctrine from the fact of cultural pluralism. But as Vincent has observed, the doctrine of cultural relativism cannot logically rank cultures or pass judgments about them. All the doctrine can do is assert that values are rooted in the particularities of each culture.[19] Cultural values might deserve equal respect, but whether they are worthy of such respect depends on the impact of such norms on persons' behavior and quality of life. In short, because it is impossible to derive morality from empirical conditions, cultural relativism must remain a descriptive fact, not a normative proposition.

In reconciling cultural relativism with the universality of human rights, it is important to emphasize that universalism and relativism are not mutually exclusive categories but rather different ends of a continuum. The choice is not between the extremes of *radical universalism*, which holds that culture plays no role in defining the morality, and *radical cultural relativism,* which holds that culture is the only source of the morality. Rather, the affirmation of human rights in global society will necessarily be based on an intermediary position that recognizes both the reality of cultural pluralism and the imperative of rights claims rooted in universal morality. This is the view taken by Jack Donnelly, who defines his approach as "weak cultural relativism." According to him, such a position recognizes "a comprehensive set of *prima facie* universal human rights" while still allowing "occasional and strictly limited local variations and exceptions."[20] In defining and promoting international human rights, the challenge is to assert and defend the universality of basic rights while recognizing that the formulation and application of rights claims will depend in part on the social and cultural context in which rights claims are asserted.

A case study on flogging in Singapore illustrates the tension between universalism and cultural pluralism.

CASE NO. 4-1
CANING IN SINGAPORE

Background

In 1994 Michael Fay, an eighteen-year-old American youth, was found guilty of vandalism in Singapore after he and several other adolescents spray painted about fifty automobiles in a high-income area of the city. Fay was sentenced to six lashes with a cane, four months in prison, and a $2,200 fine—a punishment that was consistent with the severe penalties imposed on lawlessness in the quasi-authoritarian city-state of Singapore but that seemed grossly excessive from an American perspective. Because the punishment involved flogging, a practice long considered inhumane in the West, the Singapore court verdict precipitated an intense debate in the United States that focused on the justice of Fay's punishment as well as the relative effectiveness and morality of the Western and Asian approaches to law and order.

Although Singapore is a modern, economically prosperous city-state, it is a tightly regulated society with limited political freedoms and strict social and cultural controls. Economically, Singapore is a relatively free, competitive market system, prospering greatly from global trade; however, politically and socially Singapore is a quasi-authoritarian state, an illiberal society with significant governmental controls over political, social, and cultural life. According to one comparative study of political and civil freedoms, in 1994–95 Singapore ranked toward the bottom of the countries classified as "partly free."[21] For example, Singapore permits the detention of suspects for up to two years. It also requires organized groups of ten or more to register with the government, and permission from the police is required for any meeting of more than five persons. In addition, Singapore's police must approve speakers at all public functions. Socially, the regulations seem even more draconian: Public acts such as chewing gum, spitting, or feeding birds carry a fine of several hundred dollars; there are even severe penalties for failing to flush a public toilet or eating in the subway.

Flogging, as practiced in Singapore, consists of tying a prisoner to a wooden trestle and striking him or her on the buttocks with a damp rattan cane. Although the effects of caning depend on the number and intensity of the strokes, the punishment involves intense physical suffering, frequently resulting in the tearing of skin tissue that leads to permanent scars. It is a generally accepted principle of international law that torture is an unacceptable form of punishment. For example, Article 7 of the International Covenant on Civil and Political Rights, which went into force in 1976, declares, "No one shall be subjected to torture or to cruel, inhuman or degrading treatment or punishment."

The Moral Debate over Caning

When Fay was sentenced to six lashes, an intense public debate emerged in the United States over the appropriateness of such punishment and the relative effectiveness of Singapore's criminal justice system. The debate increased in intensity when President Bill Clinton condemned the punishment as "excessive" and called on Singapore's president, Ong Teng Cheong, to commute the sentence. In response to Clinton's appeal, President Cheong decreased the caning from six lashes to four, with the punishment being served on May 5, 1994. After an additional month in prison, Fay was released and then returned to the United States to live with his father.

The discourse precipitated by the caning of Fay was fundamentally a public debate of alternative theories of political society and human rights—a debate between the "Asian School" and Western liberalism. Had Singapore been a poor, backward, corrupt society and had the United States not experienced significant social and moral decay in recent years, it is unlikely that the Fay verdict would have erupted in widespread public debate. However, Singapore is not a corrupt Third World nation, nor is the United States an example of civic virtue and social development. Indeed, Singapore has become a modern, dynamic economic society, providing ample economic and social benefits to its people in an urban environment of safety, low crime, social order, and economic prosperity. By contrast, the United States, the leading industrial democratic society in the world, has experienced a dramatic loss of social order, involving the breakdown of family life, the disintegration of neighborhoods, and the dramatic rise in crime. The cultural and social decay of the United States is dramatically illustrated by a comparison of Los Angeles and Singapore, cities of roughly the same size: In 1993 Singapore had 58 murders and 80 rapes, whereas Los Angeles had 1,058 murders and 1,781 rapes.[22]

Lee Kwan Yew, the former long-term prime minister of Singapore and the chief architect of the country's political and social system, believes that the social and cultural decline of the West is due to its excessive emphasis on individualism and freedom. The East Asian approach to political society has the advantage, he believes, in more effectively balancing the claims of social and communal goods with the demands of individuals. In his assessment of the social decline of the United States, Kishore Mahbubani, an official of Singapore's foreign ministry, writes, "This social deterioration is so drastic that it cannot possibly be the result of a mere economic downturn or fewer resources for law and order. To Asian eyes, it suggests that something fundamental has gone wrong in the United States."[23] Mahbubani goes on to suggest that the source of social ills in the United States is its ideology of excessive individualism and personal freedom, which has helped to undermine the family and other social institutions. The celebration of individual freedom, in his view, has had an ironic outcome, contributing to social decay and a cultural decline that now threatens the personal security and economic and social well-being of individuals. In particular, Mahbubani suggests that the rights of criminals have been given precedence over the rights of victims: "It is obvious that this enormous reduction of freedom in America is the result of a mindless ideology that maintains that freedom of a small number of individuals (criminals, terrorists, street gang members, drug dealers), who are known to pose a threat to society, should not be constrained . . . even if to do so would enhance the freedom of the majority."[24] For Mahbubani and other East Asian officials, American culture has become flawed because of its excessive emphasis on individual rights that has in turn weakened social institutions and impaired the criminal justice system.

In sum, the moral debate over caning was rooted partly in alternative conceptions of political society and human rights. What was considered cruel treatment in Western societies was regarded as necessary punishment to protect social and political life in Asia.

Moral Reflections

This case raises a number of important issues about the conceptualization and implementation of human rights.

- Is caning torture, as the West asserts, or a harsh punishment, as some Third World countries claim?
- When states hold different conceptions of human rights, as was the case in this dispute, which party is to decide whose political morality is correct?
- Does Western political morality emphasize individual rights and freedoms excessively?
- Is the Western emphasis on individual rights claims morally superior to the Asian approach that emphasizes communal obligations? Why or why not?
- How should the West respond to Asian claims that countries such as Singapore have a more stable and secure social order precisely because they emphasize social and community obligations rather than celebrate individual rights?

The International Law of Human Rights

Despite the divergent theories, competing ethical and philosophical justifications, and contested interpretations of human rights, there is widespread *political* acceptance of the idea of human rights in the contemporary world. This political agreement is evident in the significant body of international law of human rights that has developed through the codification of norms, rules, and directives in binding conventions. Although international human rights law first began to emerge in the nineteenth century with norms such as the prohibition against piracy and slavery, such laws have developed mainly since the end of World War II.

The first major modern international legal agreement to highlight human rights in contemporary global society was the UN Charter. Although the charter is essentially a constitutional document delineating the institutional structures and functions of the UN system, it is also an important human rights document because it specifies the promotion and protection of human rights as one of the major purposes of the United Nations. In its preamble, the charter reaffirms faith in "fundamental human rights" and then calls on member states to promote and encourage "respect for human rights and for fundamental freedoms" (Article 1). Later, the charter delineates some of the international human rights obligations that member states should promote (Article 55), calling on states to take individual and collective actions in support of these norms.

In 1948, the UN General Assembly adopted the Universal Declaration of Human Rights. Because of its inclusive, comprehensive nature, the declaration is generally recognized as the charter of international human rights, providing its most authoritative global definition.[25] The declaration does not distinguish or rank different types of human rights; rather, it affirms a comprehensive listing of basic, civil, political, social, economic, and cultural rights. The inability to develop a listing of foundational rights and to discriminate between rights and worthy socioeconomic goals was due in great measure to the growing ideological conflict between the two major powers—the United States and the Soviet Union. As a result, the declaration is rooted in a plural conception of human rights, with the West championing civil and political rights and the East championing socioeconomic rights. It is important to emphasize also that although the declaration is not formally international law (it was adopted as a resolution, not as a binding treaty), it is nonetheless viewed as part of the international law of human rights, providing direction in the development and codification of human rights norms.[26]

The international law of human rights is expressed in a number of legally binding agreements. The two most important of these are the International Covenant on Civil and Political Rights and the International Covenant on Economic, Social, and Cultural Rights (see table 4-1), which

---

Table 4–1: Selected International Human Rights

According to the *International Covenant on Civil and Political Rights* (1966), states are obligated to respect and promote a wide variety of basic rights. These include

>   the right to life and physical security of the person;
>   freedom of thought, religion, and expression;
>   freedom of association and peaceful assembly;
>   due process of law and a humane penal system;
>   freedom from torture; and
>   the right to legal equality and nondiscrimination.

According to the *International Covenant on Economic, Social and Cultural Rights* (1966), states are obligated to respect and promote such rights as

>   the right to work and to enjoy an adequate standard of living;
>   the right to just working conditions, including fair compensation;
>   safe and healthy working environment and periodic holidays;
>   the right to form trade unions and to strike;
>   the right to education;
>   the right to social security; and
>   the right to participate in cultural life.

Both covenants emphasize that human rights must be available on the basis of equality and nondiscrimination.

---

together essentially legislate what the declaration proclaims.[27] Although the drafters of the declaration had originally intended to follow up their work with a single treaty, Cold War rivalries delayed its development and adoption by more than a decade. Moreover, rather than drafting a single convention, superpower politics resulted in two different agreements, with Western democracies identifying much more with the convention on political and civil rights and the communist states identifying much more with the convention on social and economic rights.

Although the UN has sought to proclaim the interdependence and indivisibility of human rights, political leaders, representing various types of political regimes and diverse cultural traditions, continue to espouse different and at times conflicting conceptions of human rights. International tensions over human rights doctrine are inevitable when statesmen proclaim divergent political ideologies. However, rather than assessing the legitimacy of the different human rights claims and seeking to reconcile the relative merits of conflicting theories, international organizations have simply expanded human rights, incorporating new claims advocated by influential transnational political groups. For example, new rights claims that have been gaining legitimacy in the international community include "the right to development" and "reproductive rights."[28]

The limited consensus on human rights doctrines, coupled with the ever-expanding list of rights, has had a deleterious effect on the moral foundations and priority of international human rights claims. Because of growing pluralism and confusion about human rights, it has become increasingly difficult to differentiate between basic rights claims (e.g., freedom of conscience and freedom from torture) and secondary rights claims (e.g., the right to work and the right to a jury trial).

This contemporary confusion about human rights was amply evident at the 1993 World Conference on Human Rights, the largest international meeting on human rights in twenty-five years. The aim of this UN-sponsored conference was to bring together government and nongovernment representatives to develop a post-Cold War declaration on international human rights. In preparation for this gathering in Vienna, several regional meetings were held to develop distinctive human rights perspectives and concerns within each geographic region. Whereas Western states did not hold a preparatory meeting, African leaders met in Tunis, Latin American and Caribbean leaders in San Jose, and Asian and Pacific delegates in Bangkok. Each of these meetings issued a declaration named after the city in which officials gathered.

Although each of the regional declarations represented alternative perspectives from the political liberalism championed by the West, the Bangkok Declaration represented a blatant challenge to the idea of basic human rights rooted in limited, democratic government. In that declaration, Asian leaders proclaimed the universality of rights but then argued against such universality by noting that rights "must be considered in the context of . . . national and regional particularities and various historical, cultural and religious backgrounds." Moreover, after affirming the sanctity of state sovereignty, the Bangkok Declaration notes that the promotion of human rights is to be carried out mainly through domestic institutions, not in response to foreign political pressure. Indeed, the declaration emphasizes that foreign aid should not be conditional on the observance of human rights. From an international relations perspective, the Bangkok Declaration is important because it presents a radical departure from the traditional Western conceptualization of human rights, capturing the growing antipathy toward Western democratic values and the priority that the West assigns to political and civil rights.

In view of the increasing conceptual pluralism of human rights, the development of a consensus at the Vienna conference among government representatives from 171 countries proved to be a daunting task. However, what enabled the conference to issue a collective declaration was not the development of greater agreement about the nature of human rights but rather a procedural decision that the Vienna proceedings would be carried out through a "consensus" in which the conference decisions would be based on unanimity. This meant that the final declaration had to be approved by all 171 governments or there would be no final action at all. Because there was significant international pressure to adopt a concluding declaration, efforts to resolve competing and conflicting norms would have delayed the proceedings and possibly threatened the conference itself. As a result, the aim of the conference proceedings was to develop a comprehensive statement that partially satisfied each of the regional groups and many of the 2,000 nongovernmental organizations represented at the conference.

The Final Declaration and Action Program of the World Conference on Human Rights, known as the Vienna Declaration, is a long statement divided into a preamble, a declaration of principles, and a plan of action. The statement of principles, the most important section, includes a reaffirmation of widely accepted political, social, and economic rights but noticeably omits such core rights as freedom of religion, freedom of assembly and association, and freedom of speech. Indeed, the document places its greatest emphasis on social and economic rights, giving at best cursory coverage to civil and political rights associated with limited, democratic government. From a liberal perspective, the major shortcoming of the Vienna conference was the failure of the United States and its allies to press the importance of democratic government in promoting human rights. Thus, one critic suggested that the Vienna Declaration was "a hodgepodge collection of high principles, stolen wording and bad compromises" and was likely to be used by authoritarian rulers "to justify old and new human rights violations."[29]

Because respect for human rights depends in great measure on the underlying political and cultural values of the international community, the Vienna conference is significant because it illuminates the contested and increasingly pluralistic political foundation of global society.[30] However, to the extent that human rights are approached from an increasingly pluralistic or multicultural worldview, the international law of human rights is likely to be regarded as less authoritative. The challenge for the international community is to delimit human rights and to emphasize only those rights considered essential to human dignity.

Human Rights and Foreign Policy

When gross human rights violations occur in global society, who is responsible for halting and punishing such evil? Are foreign governments morally responsible, individually or collectively, for minimizing human suffering from poverty, hunger, torture, genocide, and war? Do citizens from one state bear moral responsibilities for the personal security and well-being of persons in other states? As noted earlier, one of the basic ethical norms of global society is that moral obligations are not defined by territorial boundaries. However, if individuals, groups, and states bear moral obligations toward human beings in foreign lands, it is much less evident how such moral obligations should be fulfilled. In this final section, I examine the role of governments in promoting and protecting human rights in foreign countries. My aim is to illuminate some of the constraints and possibilities in developing a foreign policy on human rights.

Although UN membership requires that states promote human rights domestically and internationally, there is no international consensus about the role that human rights norms should play in foreign policy. Not only do regimes differ as to which human rights are most important, but governments also differ in the priority they assign to human rights goals in international affairs. The United States, which as noted earlier has been inspired periodically by moral idealism in its foreign policy, has undoubtedly been the strongest proponent of human rights in world politics. However, its approach has also varied greatly, from the public expressions of humanitarianism by such presidents as Woodrow Wilson and Jimmy Carter to the quiet realpolitik of Richard Nixon and Ronald Reagan. Moreover, northern European countries, such as Norway, Denmark, and the Netherlands, have emphasized socioeconomic rights through their foreign aid and humanitarian assistance programs. Still other major powers, such

as Japan and Germany, have deemphasized human rights altogether, believing that the definition and expression of basic rights must be derived
from the particular political and cultural environment of each nation-state.

There is no simple way by which states can promote international
human rights in other countries. The idea of human rights is, after all, subversive to the idea of an international society of sovereign states.[31] It is
subversive for at least two reasons. First, because human rights are, as
George F. Kennan has observed, inextricably related to the cultural values
and political, economic, and social structures of society, it is impossible
to demand human rights reforms without also demanding corresponding
changes in other aspects of society on which those rights depend.[32] Some
regimes might tolerate human rights violations even though their laws and
prevailing cultural and political norms affirm individual rights. However,
most human rights abuses involve more than a failure to live up to domestic rules. Instead, they are a direct by-product of a deficient (often an antidemocratic) political culture and an inadequate institutionalization of
human rights norms. Thus, when a government demands that another state
fulfill its human rights standards more fully, it typically involves a challenge not only to that society's government rules but also to its prevailing
cultural mores.

Second, the idea of human rights is subversive because, although pre-
tending not to threaten the existing structures of global society, it establishes norms that governments commonly disregard and even deliberately
violate.[33] Notwithstanding the widespread popularity of human rights,
there is a large gap between the international declarations and conventions
on human rights and states' actual behavior. As a result, the idea of human
rights is potentially revolutionary because its effective application would
involve significant behavioral reforms. Moreover, in those regimes in
which individual human rights are systematically threatened by the government itself, it would necessitate the radical transformation of both the
structures of government and the underlying social, cultural, and political
norms and values.

Preventing Mass Murder

The international protection of human rights in the modern world is an
especially difficult task not only because human rights are regarded as part
of the domestic jurisdiction of governments but also because governments
themselves abuse rights. Indeed, the most serious human rights violations
in the twentieth century have been due not to war, intergroup conflict, or
domestic disorder but to deliberate government campaigns of mass murder
and genocide, or what Stanley Hoffmann terms "the institutionalization of
cruelty."[34] In addition, as R. J. Rummel has observed, governments in the

twentieth century have been far more brutal to their own people than to foreigners. Whereas international and civil wars have resulted in the death of 35 million persons, Rummel found that domestic killing by authoritarian and totalitarian regimes has claimed the lives of 169 million persons, nearly four and a half times the rate of wartime deaths.[35] Rummel argues that the genocide and mass killing by governments—a phenomenon he calls *democide*—are a direct result of the development of authoritarian and totalitarian regimes possessing arbitrary, unconstrained power. The two most destructive regimes have been the Soviet Union and communist China, which together are responsible for murdering 97 million persons, or more than half of all the twentieth century's democide.[36]

If the promotion of human rights is a legitimate end of foreign policy, surely the protection of life from genocide and mass murder must be regarded as an essential element of a comprehensive human rights policy. Regrettably, however, states have rarely used their individual and collective power to halt the most serious violations of human rights. For example, major powers did not attempt to halt either the Soviet communist government's deliberate starvation of 5 million Ukrainian peasants in the 1930s or to prevent the mass murder of 6.5 million Soviet peasants (kulaks) who were resisting collectivization. Moreover, the international community did nothing to prevent the Chinese communist government from slaughtering more than 20 million of its citizens in the 1950s and 1960s or to halt the Cambodian Khmer Rouge from mass murdering 2.4 million of its citizens in the 1970s. From time to time governments have tried to prevent genocide when such mass murder threatens regional security. This was the case with Pakistan's mass murder of 1.5 million Bengalis in Bangladesh (formerly East Pakistan) in 1971, when, in response to this genocidal campaign, some 10 million persons fled to India. This influx of refugees precipitated India's military intervention that ultimately led to West Pakistan's political independence. In 1992–95, Western powers failed to halt ethnic cleansing in Bosnia in which Serbs killed or drove out tens of thousands of Muslims from hundreds of villages to create homogeneous ethnic communities. Even more seriously, the West failed to halt the 1994 genocide in Rwanda that resulted in the deaths of more than 800,000 persons. Also, in mid-1998, Serb forces were carrying out a brutal repression of Albanians in the Serb province of Kosovo.

Why have major powers failed to halt the brutality of modern authoritarian and totalitarian regimes? Why have they failed to protect innocent masses from the breakdown of domestic regimes and the spread of civil strife? To a significant degree, states have been reticent to protect human rights in foreign countries because they have been unwilling to challenge the norm of sovereignty and to risk war over interests not considered vital to the nation. Historically, states have used military force to protect core interests, such as territorial security, but have been reluctant to use force to pursue secondary interests, such as the welfare and humanitarian needs of foreign societies. Thus, the pursuit of a humanitarian foreign policy is often reduced to a fundamental choice between political autonomy or human rights, between sovereignty or the alleviation of suffering, and, unless compelling national interests are involved, regimes are likely to give sovereignty precedence over cosmopolitan human rights. Thus, when war broke out in the former Yugoslavia in 1991, nearby European powers refused to use military power to prevent the killing of more than 200,000 persons and the displacement of nearly two million others. When civil war broke out in Rwanda between the two rival groups (Tutsis and Hutus), the major powers, with the exception of France, did little to halt the genocide that resulted in the mass murder of nearly 800,000 persons and the displacement of more than two million refugees.

To illuminate the tensions between sovereignty and suffering, between power and human rights, I next examine the 1994 Rwanda genocide, arguably the most egregious violation of human rights in the post-Cold War era.

CASE NO. 4-2
THE RWANDA GENOCIDE

Background

Rwanda is a small nation of about eight million inhabitants in central Africa that is populated by two different peoples: the Hutus and the Tutsis. Although both groups speak the same language, enjoy the same type of food, share similar religious beliefs, and have lived side by side for centuries, they differ in physical appearance and in the vocations they pursue. The Hutus, a short, Bantu people, have historically lived as peasants cultivating the land; the Tutsis, by contrast, are a taller people from northern Africa who have generally worked in cattle grazing. Moreover, Rwanda's Hutu majority (85 percent of the population) has been historically ruled by the Tutsi minority (15 percent of the population). Even during the colonial rule that began in the late nineteenth century, German and Belgium colonial rulers governed through the Tutsi authorities.

In response to growing demands by the Hutu majority for self-determination, Rwanda gained its independence from Belgium in 1959. After gaining power, the Hutus sought to redress historic political, social, and economic inequalities, resulting in reverse discrimination against the Tutsis. As a result, hundreds of thousands of Tutsis fled Rwanda to neighboring states, especially Uganda and Burundi. In the 1980s, Tutsis established a guerrilla force, the Rwandan Patriotic Front (RPF), which sought to end oppression against Tutsis. To halt the cycle of violence, Hutu President Juvenal Habyarimana and Tutsi military leaders signed a power-sharing peace agreement, the

Arusha Accord, in Arusha, Tanzania, in 1993. The aim of the accord was to bring the ongoing conflict between the ruling Hutus and the RPF to a halt by establishing a cease-fire, a sharing of power among competing groups, internationally supervised democratic elections, the repatriation of refugees, and the integration of RPF with the government's armed forces.[37] To ensure the accord's implementation, the UN Security Council established an observer force of 2,500 troops, known as the UN Assistance Mission to Rwanda (UNAMIR).

The Genocide

On April 6, 1994, as President Habyarimana was returning to Kigali, Rwanda's capital, two missiles hit his jet as it approached the airport. The plane spun out of control and crashed, killing all passengers. Within hours of Habyarimana's death, Hutu militia, led by the Presidential Guard, began a systematic massacre of Tutsis and Hutu moderates, including the government's prime minister and ten Belgian members of UNAMIR assigned to protect her. This action led Belgium to withdraw its 400 other troops, virtually paralyzing the UN force.[38] Encouraged by political and civic extremists, Hutu killing spread quickly throughout the land, resulting in the systematic murder of tens of thousands of civilians. One of the largest massacres occurred in mid-April in the western city of Kibuye, when more than 5,000 Tutsis were rounded up in a stadium and then slaughtered. Although the government forces were well equipped with modern weapons, the genocide was carried out by tens of thousands of Hutus at close quarters with primitive weapons. "If people murdered with machetes," writes David Rieff, "it was because the Hutu leadership had conceived of a genocide that would involve the entire Hutu people."[39]

The genocide did not end until the RPF took control of major Rwandan centers by mid-June. By that time, however, the Hutus had killed at least 800,000 Tutsis and moderate Hutus, making this genocide campaign one of the deadliest and most destructive in modern times.[40] One observer has written that the Rwandan genocide "claimed more lives more quickly than any campaign of mass murder in recorded history."[41] Moreover, the RPF's rapid conquest of Rwanda led to one of the largest and fastest refugee movements ever, with almost two million persons fleeing to neighboring states within the first two weeks of the Hutu exodus.

The Failure of International Humanitarian Protection

In light of the disintegration of Rwandan society, the mass killing, and the displacement of some 2.2 million refugees, what actions should neighboring African states have taken to prevent or, at a minimum, to limit human suffering? What actions should the major powers have carried out when the evidence of mass killing first came to light? Should an international peacekeeping force have been deployed, and, if so, what should have been its short- and long-term missions? Which states should have participated in and paid for such an operation?

When the genocide began, the only foreign troops in Rwanda were some 1,400 troops of the UN observer force. UNAMIR, created solely to assist implementation of the Arusha Accords, was not authorized to use force to keep peace. Thus, when the mass killing began, the UN force was unable to deter mass killing, and after Belgium recalled its troops in mid-April, the remaining UN troops were kept in the barracks. Subsequently, the Security Council, on the recommendation of UN Secretary-General Boutros Boutros-Ghali, reduced the observer force to 270 troops. In the meantime, however, as international leaders became aware of the mass killing, Boutros-Ghali reversed his recommendation by calling for a 5,000-member peacekeeping force. The Security Council, however, refused to support his request. The United States opposed the proposed peacekeeping operation partly because of cost (the U.S. share of peacekeeping operations is 30 percent) but also because of a lack of clarity about the operation's mission and organization. Speaking about the need for a Rwandan peacekeeping operation, President Bill Clinton said that it was important for the United Nations to learn "when to say no."[42]

Only one major power (France) temporarily deployed troops in Rwanda to limit further killing. Because France had been a supporter of the Hutu government, it carried out a temporary humanitarian intervention to prevent Tutsi military forces from retaliating against fleeing Hutus. The French interventionary force established a security zone in the southwestern part of Rwanda, thereby providing foreign protection for a two-month period (June 23 to August 21). It has been estimated the French intervention was responsible for saving the lives of tens of thousands of fleeing Hutus.

However, states did provide significant humanitarian assistance to the large Rwandan refugee camps in Zaire, Tanzania, and Burundi. Major international governmental and nongovernmental organizations played a key role in providing humanitarian supplies and medical aid. The United States, in particular, gave significant financial and humanitarian assistance, and when a cholera epidemic began to spread among the 1.2 million Hutu refugees in Goma, Zaire, the U.S. government authorized the deployment of 4,000 soldiers to assist the relief effort and to establish controls to prevent the spread of cholera. However, the introduction of U.S. forces was solely for humanitarian relief rather than peacekeeping.

The Rwanda genocide and the subsequent displacement of refugees suggest that, despite the claims and rhetoric of international human rights, foreign states are not eager to intervene to prevent mass killing. Despite increasing acceptance of the international law of human rights, the protection of such rights is still regarded as an obligation mainly of states. As one scholar has observed, "Until the great powers in the Security Council are willing to act together, and to absorb comparatively small numbers of casualties to prevent the large-scale slaughter of innocent people, there will continue to be after-the-fact hand-wringing and emergency aid efforts. And once again it will have been too late for everything except the grief."[43]

Moral Reflections

During his trip to Africa in 1998, President Clinton expressed regret that the international community had not acted more decisively in halting the Rwanda genocide.

- In light of his apology, should Western powers have intervened in Rwanda to prevent the mass killing?
- Does the international community, and especially the United Nations, bear a collective responsibility for its failure to protect innocent Rwandan civilians from systematic mass murder?
- When it became evident that society-wide killing was underway in Rwanda, should the United States and other major powers have intervened to halt the genocide?
- Was the unilateral intervention by the French morally justifiable?

Three years after the genocide, more than 100,000 Hutus remained in Rwandan prisons awaiting trial for their alleged participation in the 1994 killing. Because Rwanda's limited judicial system has been able to prosecute only a small portion of the prisoners, the road to domestic justice and ultimately national reconciliation is likely to be long and difficult.

- Given the extraordinary brutality of the genocide and the large number of persons awaiting trials, how should Rwanda attempt to address this past society-wide evil?
- Should some nonjudicial options be considered in seeking to expedite trials?
- Could some form of political forgiveness be considered as an instrument of national reconciliation?

Promoting Human Rights

Because of difficulties and grave risks entailed in curbing governmental genocide and mass murder, states concerned with human rights have tended to emphasize individual human rights abuses and to neglect systemic, society-wide genocidal campaigns. Western democratic countries have typically promoted civil, political, social, and economic rights selectively. For example, as noted in the previous chapter, the Carter administration's human rights policy focused on individual human rights abuses carried out by authoritarian regimes and neglected the more serious oppression of totalitarian regimes. President Ronald Reagan radically transformed this policy by focusing on the systemic abuses of human rights by totalitarian regimes. Because communist governments were considered a major obstacle to human dignity, the Reagan administration sought to advance human rights by allocating significant aid to anticommunist political groups and Third World regimes threatened by revolutionary Marxist movements. Western European countries, in contrast, have emphasized human rights through quiet diplomacy, giving precedence to social and economic rights through humanitarian programs and foreign aid transfers.

How should major powers promote human rights in global society? What norms should guide their actions? In devising an effective human rights policy, the challenge consists of improving rights without unduly threatening the decentralized nature of global society. In light of the human rights foreign policy experience of the United States during the 1970s and 1980s, the following four principles can contribute to the development of a more prudent and effective human rights policy: (1) the priority of actions over declarations, (2) the necessity of developing preconditions for sustaining and protecting basic rights, (3) the superiority of quiet over public diplomacy, and (4) the imperative of humility and modesty. Each is discussed here.

1. Giving priority to actions over rhetoric is important in promoting human rights because the bilateral and multilateral initiatives on human rights have traditionally focused on declarations and conventions. However, the achievement of rights does not depend on pronouncements, constitutions, and international conventions. The emphasis on human rights pronouncements has no doubt contributed to the widespread acceptance of the human rights idea in global political discourse, but it has also had a deleterious effect in fostering the illusion that constitutions, bills of rights, and conventions are sufficient for the implementation of rights. However, declarations and conventions are not self-activating. Robert Goldwin has observed that it is regrettable that so much time and energy has been devoted to creating the illusion that enunciating rights will necessarily lead to their enforcement. He writes that it is either "a conscious fraud, or a naive faith in the magic of words" to assert that recognizing the human right to enough food will resolve the problem of hunger.[44] Thus, some scholars argue that excessive emphasis on the rhetoric of rights can be counterproductive to the advancement of human dignity of persons because it can distract attention from the task of securing basic human rights.

2. Developing socioeconomic and political preconditions is also essential in maintaining a credible and effective human rights policy. As noted earlier, because human rights cannot be separated from the institutions and practices of government or the social and cultural mores of society, it is impossible to promote specific human rights norms in other societies without also changing other dimensions of those societies. Thus, a credible human rights policy must cultivate the essential social, political, and economic preconditions for human rights.

3. Quiet diplomacy is also important in devising a sound human rights

policy. The reason that quiet, confidential diplomacy is important in addressing human rights is that states are reluctant to alter their policies solely in response to foreign pressure. Soviet leader Leonid Brezhnev once remarked that "to teach others how to live cannot be accepted by a sovereign state." Although President Carter's highly public human rights policy elevated human rights to a prominent place in U.S. foreign relations, there is considerable disagreement over the extent to which such open diplomacy contributed to an improved observance of human rights. Some scholars have argued that the use of public pronouncements, condemnations, and sanctions not only failed to encourage human rights but also further isolated nondemocratic regimes.[45] William Gleysteen, Jr., a former U.S. ambassador, has written that condemnatory public statements about human rights are "[O]ne of the most tempting but most counterproductive [foreign policy] instruments."[46] The difficulty of linking human rights to economic interests is also illustrated by the failure of the United States to use most-favored-nation status to foster more humane treatment of dissidents. When President Clinton assumed office, he sought to promote human rights in China by making economic trade conditional on the improvement of human rights. However, as Case No. 7–1 suggests, the policy of granting China most-favored-nation status backfired and forced the president to delink trade from human rights. Given the complexity and sensitivity of human rights, a prudent foreign policy should be formulated with care and implemented with sensitivity, preferably through confidential channels.

4. Finally, a prudent human rights policy should be modest in scope. This is true for at least two reasons: first, to minimize moral ethnocentrism and second, in order to decrease moral self-righteousness and hypocrisy. In calling attention to the dangers of "cultural imperialism," Kennan has written that Americans who profess to know what other people want and what is good for them "would do well to ask themselves whether they are not actually attempting to impose their own values, traditions, and habits of thought on peoples for whom these things have no validity and no usefulness."[47] To be sure, avoiding moral judgments in developing and executing a human rights policy is impossible. However, a state that seeks to foster rights in foreign countries should proceed tentatively, recognizing that international society is comprised of a plurality of cultures and worldviews.

Modesty is especially important in minimizing moral self-righteousness and hypocrisy. Self-righteousness typically arises from excessive confidence in one's own rectitude and the certainty of iniquity in another. However, if a human rights policy is to be credible, the articulation and application of norms must be undertaken dispassionately with the realization that moral indignation itself can impair judgment. Herbert Butterfield wisely noted earlier in the twentieth century that "moral indignation corrupts the agent who possesses it and is not calculated to reform the man who is the object of it."[48] At the same time, human rights also can contribute to hypocrisy when they are not articulated and promoted in a wise, prudent manner. Hypocrisy—the pretentious use of moral slogans for national gain—can arise when a state clothes its national interests in moral (human rights) language, thereby seeking to gain universal approbation. Thus, when human rights are used to justify national interests, the credibility of international morality, and especially of human rights, can be jeopardized.

Summary

Despite the existence of significant pluralism on specific human rights doctrines, there remains widespread international agreement about the utility of human rights claims. This consensus is best affirmed and expressed through the substantial body of contemporary international law on human rights. Because international political society is anarchic, international institutions do not have the authority to ensure compliance with human rights norms. As a result, the international enforcement of human rights ultimately depends on the policies of foreign states, especially major powers, and on the actions of international organizations and policies of states. However, formulating a credible and effective human rights foreign policy is especially difficult because human rights practices are normally a reflection of the social and cultural values of countries. Because states normally interpret the international enforcement of rights as a qualification of national sovereignty, the international pursuit of human rights will necessarily require modesty of purpose and diplomatic sensitivity.

CHAPTER FIVE

THE ETHICS OF FORCE

Saints can be pure, but statesmen, alas, must be responsible.

Arthur Schlesinger[1]

The aggressor is always peace-loving; he would prefer to take over our country unopposed.

Carl von Clausewitz[2]

There is something heroic in the effort to inject morality in the Hobbesian situation par excellence—when states, locked in war, squirm on the floor of survival. It is good to remind statesmen that the ends do not justify all means, that restraints should be observed even in an angry war, that humanity must somehow be preserved.

Stanley Hoffmann[3]

States seek to influence international affairs through various types of power, ranging from positive sanctions to coercive threats, from "soft power" co-optive strategies that induce desired outcomes to "hard power" strategies that compel through military coercion. Although states rely on different policy instruments to influence the behavior of other states, force—the application of coercive power—remains the ultimate instrument for pursuing vital national interests in global society.

Sometimes international relations are categorized in terms of mutually exclusive conditions of war and peace in which force is applied in the former but not the latter. However, such analysis greatly oversimplifies reality because all interstate relations are in part a by-product of the distribution of power among states. As a result, it is preferable to view the relations among states on a continuum between the extremes of peace and war, with most international relations occurring between these two ideal-type conditions. Although only a small portion of international relations are determined by military force, all relations among states are based partly on coercive power, with most of this power held in reserve as political and military capital. Just as financial capital provides the foundation for investment and economic development, such strategic capital provides the basis for the credible implementation of foreign policy.

This chapter explores the political ethics of force by addressing questions such as the following: In pursuing legitimate national interests in global society, is it morally permissible to threaten and, if necessary, to use force? If force is legitimate, what types of threats and what types of force are morally appropriate? Once war begins, what moral principles should govern the use of force? Is the just-war theory an adequate moral framework for assessing modern war? Finally, is the just-war doctrine applicable to domestic insurgencies? In light of international morality, are guerrilla wars morally legitimate?

In examining the ethics of force, this chapter is divided into three parts. In the first part, I briefly sketch the nature and role of force in global politics by focusing on three alternative moral traditions of force: pacifism, amoral realism, and principled realism. In the second part, I examine the ethics of traditional interstate war, focusing on the just-war theory. After describing the major elements of this theory, I illustrate the role of just-war analysis with a case study on the Persian Gulf War. Finally, I examine the nature and ethics of unconventional force, illustrating the moral challenges posed by such policy instruments with a case study on the Reagan Doctrine.

Three Moralities of Force

Historically, three distinct perspectives have dominated the moral analysis of force: pacifism, principled realism, and amoral realism. The first assumes that war and violence are never morally permissible, whereas the last is based on the conviction that military force is politically and strategically necessary to protect vital national interests. Between these two polar positions is an intermediate perspective that assumes that resorting to violence should be a last resort and that, in the event of war, destruction and human suffering should be minimized.

Pacifism

The pacifist approach prohibits the threat and use of force because, in accordance with a rule-based ethic, it assumes that violence can never be a morally legitimate means to provide national security or to secure moral goods such as human rights, international justice, and peace. In its prioritization of values, pacifism holds that peace and nonviolence are the highest norms and can never be compromised to secure other ends, however important they might be. For example, the Dutch Renaissance scholar Erasmus believed that the cost of war was so great that even if a war is won, "you will lose much more than you gain."[4] Thus, for him as well as for other pacifists, force is never a legitimate means by which to protect national interests or to pursue international justice. In sum, the pacifist perspective on global politics offers a simple and categorical rule: Do no violence.

Although pacifism uniformly condemns war and violence, this moral tradition has been expressed in a number of different ways. Four major types of pacifism are pragmatic, humanistic, vocational, and structural. *Pragmatic pacifism* is based on a secular, humanistic worldview, advocating nonviolence in the belief that such a strategy is more effective in promoting long-term global peace. According to this version, modern warfare has become so destructive that it can no longer serve as a vehicle of peacemaking or peacekeeping. Nuclear pacifism, which specifically rejects national security based on nuclear weapons because of their enormous destructive potential, is a particular version of this type of instrumental pacifism.

Humanistic pacifism, another expression of this tradition, assumes that life is sacred and thus that killing is morally impermissible, even in defending other moral values. War is immoral because it destroys that which is sacred. Humanistic pacifism, which is frequently expressed through nonresistance or nonviolent resistance, condemns war and the preparation for war. Like religiously based pacifism, this type of pacifism seeks to protect human life at all costs; however, whereas humanism justifies life through a secular worldview, religious pacifism justifies its commitment to nonviolence and nonresistance through religious convictions.

A third type of pacifism is *vocational pacifism*. According to this perspective, violence and war are morally unacceptable because they are inconsistent with the vocation of Christianity. Some Christians, such as Mennonites and Brethren, believe that the Gospel of Christ calls on Christians to renounce the instruments of power and violence in this world and to model "revolutionary subordination."[5] To follow Christ means to renounce the evil ways of this world, especially its reliance on power and force. Menno Simmons, the founder of the Mennonite sect, once observed, "Our fortress is Christ, our defense is patience, our sword is the Word of God, and our victory is the sincere, firm, unfeigned faith in Jesus Christ. Spears and swords of iron we leave to those who, alas, consider human blood and swine's blood well-nigh of equal value."[6]

James Turner Johnson argues that the roots of vocational pacifism, or what he calls sectarian pacifism, lie in the teaching and witness of the early Christian church, which he suggests called on believers to renounce the world and withdraw from its evil demands.[7] According to Johnson, sectarian pacifists did not seek to resolve the problem of violence in political society; rather, they sought to establish separate communities in which they could live their lives in accord with the demands of their religious convictions. As a result, this tradition expressed itself historically in such sectarian developments as the rise of monastic Christian orders in the medieval era, the spread of Anabaptist sects in sixteenth- and seventeenth-century Europe, and the growth of "peace churches" in contemporary America.

A fourth type of pacifism is *structural pacifism*, or what one scholar calls utopian internationalism.[8] This tradition was first expressed in the Middle Ages in the writings of Dante Alighieri and Marsilius of Padua and subsequently developed by the Renaissance humanist Erasmus and by such modern philosophers as Jean-Jacques Rousseau and Immanuel Kant. In the contemporary age, this perspective has been expressed by the World Federalist Movement, which seeks to create a world federalist state as well as more modest transformational projects, such as the World Order Models Project, guided and elaborated by Richard Falk.[9] According to structural pacifism, because war and the preparation for war are immoral, global institutions need to be transformed so that the risk of war is reduced, if not eliminated. To realize their utopian dream, structural pacifists favor a radical restructuring of international political society, shifting power from sovereign states to a common global authority. Like sectarian pacifism, structural pacifism abhors war and seeks its elimination. However, whereas the former seeks to resolve the problem of violence through withdrawal, the latter attempts to eradicate war by establishing a more inclusive society based on a "superstate" that would prevent war altogether.

Although pacifism is an important moral tradition, it provides little help to the soldier or the statesman in structuring moral reasoning about the defense and protection of vital interests in global society. Because the highest priority is life and peace, it does not allow for the possibility of using force for pursuing other moral objectives. Pacifism's chief end is the abolition of war and violence. As a result, this tradition provides a potent moral critique of the security structures of the Westphalian and post-Westphalian international systems but offers little guidance to decision makers pursuing justice within and among states.

Amoral Realism

This perspective represents the direct opposite position of pacifism. Whereas pacifism prohibits war and violence, amoral realism assumes not only that war is a legitimate instrument of policy but also that morality does not constrain war. Indeed, assuming the legitimacy of war's ends, amoral realism believes that the only norm governing the conduct of war is military victory. Moreover, because morality is absent in the international community, global order is achieved not by the pursuit of "moral" foreign policies but rather as a direct by-product of the balance of power among states.

Although several variants of amoral realism have been developed, two of the most important are the "cynical" perspective and the "jihad," or religious war, perspective. Both are similar in that they believe that morality is silent in wartime, denying that moral limits exist on the conduct of war. Whereas cynics justify force on the basis of self-interest, adherents to the jihad doctrine justify unlimited violence on the basis of religious convictions. The cynical perspective is the most radical because it denies morality altogether, both in the justification and in the prosecution of war. According to this perspective, because moral values are simply subjective preferences, they have no constructive role in determining and judging political action in global society. To the extent that force is justified in international relations, it is based on prudential judgment divorced from moral values. In addition, because the aim of going to war is to prevail, there are no inherent moral limitations in defeating the enemy.

The cynical perspective of force is illustrated by Thucydides' account of the Athenian subjugation of the island of Melos in the Peloponnesian War. The Athenians, believing that their own security and well-being lay in a credible balance of power with Sparta, their arch-rival, sought to extend their imperial control over Melos as they had over most other islands in the Aegean Sea. The Melians, however, refused Athenian entreaties, desiring instead to remain free from foreign control. After being rebuffed, the Athenians determined to compel Melos to surrender and become part of the Athenian Empire. Athenian diplomats were sent in an attempt to persuade Melos to surrender. According to Thucydides, the Athenians cynically told the Melians that justice depended on the distribution of power, in which "the strong do what they have the power to do and the weak accept what they have to accept."[10] When the Melians refused to surrender, the Athenians laid siege to the island, eventually forcing their unconditional surrender.

A *holy war* is one that is waged for a religious cause. Because its purpose is assumed to be in accord with the divine will, it involves unlimited use of force in a holy cause. Historically, the two most important expressions of holy wars have been the Islamic jihad and the Christian-inspired crusade. The jihad, or religious war, is rooted in Islam's conviction that the world is divided into two realms—the House of Islam, where Islamic law prevails, and the House of War, comprising the non-Islamic world.

Between these two realms there is a "morally necessary, legally and religiously obligatory state of war."[11] Because Islam is assumed to be universally applicable, Muslim believers have a duty to convert or at least to subjugate unbelievers. It is important to emphasize that in Islam the struggle between good and evil is both a spiritual contest and a temporal conflict. As Bernard Lewis notes,

> Muhammad, it will be recalled, was not only a prophet and a teacher, like the founders of other religions; he was also the head of a polity and of a community, a ruler and a soldier. Hence his struggle involved a state and its armed forces. If the fighters in the war for Islam, the holy war "in the path of God," are fighting for God, it follows that their opponents are fighting against God. And since God is in principle the sovereign, the supreme head of the Islamic state—and the Prophet and, after the Prophet, the caliphs are his vice-regents—then God as sovereign commands the army. The army is God's army and the enemy is God's enemy. The duty of God's soldiers is to dispatch God's enemies as quickly as possible to the place where God will chastise them—that is to say, the afterlife.[12]

Although Islamic scholars differ on whether and to what degree morality limits violence in jihad, it is clear that there are comparatively few restrictions placed on the conduct of war, especially when compared with the just-war tradition.[13] The aim in the jihad, as in the crusade, is to defeat and destroy the enemies of God. Total war is morally permissible.

The *crusade*, which shares with jihad a divine justification for war, is characterized by a conflict between good and evil in which total force is used to defeat the enemy. Roland Bainton has written that the crusading idea requires that war "be fought under God and with his help, that the crusaders shall be godly and their enemies ungodly, and that the war shall be prosecuted unsparingly."[14] The origins of the crusading idea are found in the biblical accounts of Old Testament religious wars and in particular in the efforts of ancient Israel to gain control of the promised land. According to Deuteronomy 7, the Lord commanded Israel to expel seven nations or peoples from their territory, giving them the following mandate: "[T]hou shall smite them, and utterly destroy them; thou shalt make no covenant with them nor show mercy unto them." Bainton argues that the crusade goes beyond a holy war in that it was fought "not so much with God's help as on God's behalf, not for a human goal which God might bless but for a divine cause which God might command."[15] The sincerity of the warriors, he goes on to suggest, was evidenced by the fact that war booty was consecrated to God.

The first major religious crusades occurred at the end of the eleventh century, when Pope Urban II called on Christians to recapture the Holy Land from the Turks and in particular to free Jerusalem. Throughout the twelfth and thirteeth centuries, western European military forces carried out numerous expeditions to the Middle East, seeking to reclaim Palestine from the Muslims and seeking to establish strategic centers free from the threat of Muslim forces. The crusading idea was subsequently expressed in a number of different domestic and international conflicts, culminating with the Peace of Westphalia. That treaty brought the Thirty Years' War to a close by giving secular rulers sovereign authority within their states, including the right to determine their country's religion.

Throughout the Renaissance and Reformation, the crusading spirit pervaded many European countries as Christians fought among themselves to establish within society the true religion, to purify their churches from heretical beliefs, and to ensure civil compliance with religious norms. For example, during the Spanish Inquisition in the fourteeth and fifteenth centuries the Roman Catholic Church used torture and violence to punish heretics and to ensure conformity with established religious beliefs. During the conquest of America in the early sixteenth century, Spanish conquerors relied on the crusading idea, modified by the just-war theory, to justify the subjugation and Christianization of heathen indigenous peoples. Protestants, too, resorted to military force to ensure compliance with religious beliefs. In sixteenth-century Geneva, Reformation leader John Calvin sought not only to use city government to promote the good and prohibit evil but also to ensure that civil authority reinforced true religion. A century later, Puritan leader Oliver Cromwell sought to institute pietistic Christian norms in one of the most thoroughgoing efforts to legislate morality since the codification of the Mosaic Law.[16] For our purposes, what is significant about Cromwell's Puritan revolution is the extent to which the crusading idea influenced the conduct of military conflict and civil rule. As with other religious wars beforehand, morality was applied to force through a Manichean worldview in which political and military conflict was defined in the religious categories of believer and infidel.

Principled Realism

The third approach, principled realism, represents an intermediary position between the extremes of pacifism and amoral realism. It assumes that all interstate relations, including war, are subject to widely acknowledged moral standards. Because power and force are fundamental realities of the international community, the quest for peace and justice among states can be only imperfectly realized, and then only when power and force are incorporated into the calculus of decision making. Like pacifism, principled realism affirms international moral constraints on war, but whereas pacifism proscribes all war and violence, principled realism assumes that force can be an instrument of justice. Although violence is regarded as evil, it is not necessarily the greatest evil. As a result, some moral values—such as the protection of the innocent, the recovery of something wrongfully taken, the punishment of evil, and the defense against aggression—may justify the use of force. According to this perspective, just as an individual has the right to resist injustice, so too a state has the right to use force, individually or collectively, to repulse aggression and to resist and punish evil.

The doctrine that best expresses the approach of principled realism is the *just-war theory*, an ethic rooted in ancient Greek and Roman philosophy and in the teachings of the early and medieval Christian church.[17] The just-war theory is significant because it provides a moral framework for defining and assessing the use of force. Fundamentally, it seeks to limit the violence of war by seeking to restrain the possibility of war and also the destructiveness of war itself. To constrain the possibility and practice of war, the theory provides norms for judging when war might be morally justified and, in the event that a war is justified, how such a war should be limited. The aim of the theory is not to justify war but to bring international relations under the control of morality so that, if moral norms were followed faithfully and consistently by the disputing parties, it would reduce the risk of war.

It is important to emphasize that the origins and development of the just-war theory were rooted not in the limitation of violence but in the quest for political justice. For early and medieval Christian thinkers, the main challenge was to define not how violence might be limited but rather to define the circumstances that might necessitate force in ensuring justice. For example, Ambrose of Milan, an early Christian bishop, argued that when a Christian is confronted by an armed robber, he may not use force in self-defense, "lest in defending his life he should stain his love for his neighbor." However, if the armed robber attacked a neighbor, the Christian, in fulfilling his duty to love others, had a moral obligation to defend the innocent victim. Failure to defend the neighbor would itself be morally wrong and would make the Christian as culpable for the attack as the robber himself. The principle of charity thus places a major duty to care for others, allowing, as a last resort, limited force to halt injustice.[18]

The Theory of Just War

The just-war theory is comprised of two parts: the *jus ad bellum*, the justice of going to war, and the *jus in bello*, justice in wartime. Because the theory is rooted in natural law, one scholar has defined these two dimensions as "war-decision law" and "war-conduct law."[19] According to this theory, if war is to be considered moral, it must fulfill the norms required for the justification of violence as well as the norms for prosecuting a war. A war might be waged for unjust reasons but still be prosecuted in a just manner. Conversely, even if the reasons for going to war are completely just, the war itself could be prosecuted in an immoral manner, resorting, for example, to indiscriminate attack on civilians. In short, if a war is to be moral, it must satisfy all just-war norms.

Although the just-war theory has been historically interpreted in a variety of different ways, there is a general consensus about its essential elements. The theory's core norms are listed in Table 5–1.

Table 5–1: Elements of Just-War Theory

I. The *jus ad bellum* has traditionally included the following six norms:

1. *Just cause*: The only legitimate justification for war is to deter aggression, to defend against unjust attack, or to right a grievous wrong. Although the theory does not specify what constitutes a just global order, the effort to alter territorial boundaries by force or to extend political and economic control in foreign lands is considered unjust. Aggression is immoral and gives rise to a just cause to resist by force.

2. *Competent authority*: The use of force is morally permissible only when it is legitimate, that is, authorized by government. Violence prosecuted by non-government groups or private individuals is immoral.

3. *Right intention:* A war is just only if it seeks to restore a just peace. The goal of war must be to right the evil that justifies war in the first instance. Because war is, as Clausewitz once remarked, the pursuit of political objectives by other means, the aim of warfare must be only to alter specific conditions or morally unacceptable actions of an enemy state.

4. *Limited objectives*: A war is just only if its goals are limited. An unconditional, unlimited war of attrition is morally unacceptable. Additionally, goals and means must be proportionate. This means that the good to be realized by prosecuting a war must be commensurate with the probable evil resulting from war, or, as Robert Tucker has put it, "[T]he values preserved through force must be proportionate to the values sacrificed through force."[20]

5. *Last resort:* Before a state can legitimately resort to war, it must exhaust all peaceful means. War can be morally legitimate only when a state has made every effort through measures short of war (e.g., diplomacy, multilateral negotiations, and sanctions) to seek to redress the evil. Before violence can be justified, nonviolent measures must have been exhausted. Like proportionality, this is a difficult norm to apply, requiring uncommon prudential judgment.

6. *Reasonable hope of success*: The use of force against an aggressor must have a reasonable chance of success. Good intentions are not sufficient. A war that is unlikely to achieve its limited goals is immoral.

II. The *jus in bello* establishes norms governing the use of force in wartime. It includes the following two principles:

7. *Discrimination*: Military force must be applied only against the political leadership and military forces of the state. Every effort must be made to discriminate between combatants and noncombatants, soldiers and civilians, to minimize civilian casualties. Direct attacks against civilian targets, such as neighborhoods, hospitals, and schools, are morally impermissible. Indiscriminate mass destruction of cities is similarly impermissible.[21]

8. *Proportionality*: The destruction inflicted by military forces in war must be proportional to the goals they are seeking to realize. An indiscriminate war of attrition that seeks to eliminate the enemy society altogether is not morally justified. The goal should be to use the minimum level of violence to achieve the limited aims of a war.

It is important to emphasize that the aims of the *jus ad bellum* are limited in scope. The quest for political justice within states is not a central focus of just-war theory. For example, it does not seek to remedy the injustices resulting from the past arbitrary delineation of state boundaries that might have disregarded cultural, linguistic, and ethnic affinities of people, nor does it attempt to relieve the suffering of citizens living in oppressive regimes. Although the absence of political self-rule or the existence of political oppression is morally unacceptable, such injustices do not justify international war. Rather, they give people a right to demand self-determination and just rule. In effect, extreme domestic injustice may justify revolution but not war. I explore exceptions to this conclusion in chapter 6 in discussing the morality of foreign intervention.

It is also important to note the presumptive conservative character of *jus ad bellum*. Fundamentally, the just-war theory is a status quo doctrine rooted in the existing Westphalian order of sovereign states. Although the theory does not explicitly endorse the anarchic global system, it presumes its moral legitimacy, seeking to advance a just peace within the context of Westphalian norms. For example, the norm of competent authority is typically applied to existing governments, not to potentially legitimate nations seeking to secede from an existing state or to political groups seeking to topple a regime. In addition, the just-cause norm is generally interpreted within the context of territorial international law, which regards aggression—the forceful violation of territorial boundaries—as the most serious justification for war. To be sure, the territorial boundaries of many states have little to do with global justice. In Africa, especially, the boundaries among states were often established arbitrarily by imperial powers without taking into account the distribution of tribal, ethnic, and cultural affinities. Nevertheless, international law accepts the existing order as legitimate, proscribing war as a means to establish more just territorial boundaries.

Because the just-war theory seeks to promote a just peace within the international system of nation-states, there is a significant correspondence between the theory and international law, especially the most fundamental norms that govern the rights and duties of states. According to international law, states are entitled to political independence and territorial integrity but also share a duty to respect the sovereignty of other states by not interfering in their internal affairs. Most important, states are obliged to settle disputes peacefully without resorting to force. However, if a state is the victim of aggression, it has the inherent right to use force in self-defense. International law thus shares with the just-war doctrine a presumption against force. However, whereas the former provides a legal system for defining states' rights and duties, the latter provides the moral architecture for assessing the morality of force in interstate relations.

To illustrate the role of just-war norms in conventional, interstate conflicts, I next examine the ethics of the 1991 Persian Gulf War.

CASE NO. 5–1
THE ETHICS OF THE PERSIAN GULF WAR

Background

On August 2, 1990, Iraq carried out a massive surprise invasion of its tiny neighbor Kuwait. Iraq's much larger and qualitatively superior military forces smashed through Kuwait's defensive positions. Within twenty-four hours, Iraqi forces had taken control of all key Kuwaiti military and government centers and had installed a puppet regime. Within two days, Iraq's initial invasion force had grown to more than 120,000 soldiers and 850 tanks, with a significant portion of those forces stationed along Kuwait's southern border, potentially threatening Saudi Arabia. Within days of the invasion, Saddam Hussein, Iraq's dictator, announced the formal annexation of Kuwait.

Although numerous developments might have contributed to Iraq's decision to attack Kuwait, two factors were especially important. First, Iraq disputed its southern border with Kuwait, claiming that the existing territorial boundary was unjust and historically incorrect. Iraq had periodically pressed Kuwait for a readjustment of the border, seeking in particular to gain sole access to the rich Rumaila oil field along the border and the control of two islands at the end of the Euphrates delta. Kuwait had refused Iraq's demands, arguing that the borders were legitimate, having been established by Britain in 1922 in the aftermath of the Ottoman Empire's collapse.

Second, Iraq faced major financial pressures because of its long and costly war with Iran in the 1980s. Although Kuwait had provided Iraq with some $10 billion during the war, when the war terminated in 1988, Iraq had a foreign debt of over $80 billion, making economic reconstruction difficult. If Iraq was to modernize its economy and replenish its military forces, it needed to reduce its oppressive debt, and the only way to do this was to increase its foreign sales of petroleum, its main export. In its effort to increase oil revenues, Iraq claimed that Kuwait was undertaking actions that impaired Iraq's economic reconstruction. In particular, it charged Kuwait with two acts of "financial aggression"—selling more than its allotted OPEC quota, thereby depressing petroleum prices, and pumping ("stealing") an excessive amount of oil from the jointly owned Rumaila field. As a result, Iraq demanded that Kuwait not only forgive Iraq's debt of $10 billion but that it pay reparations of $13 to $15 billion. Kuwait refused these demands.

Although Saddam Hussein had no doubt expected that Western nations would oppose his actions, he had calculated that, as the most powerful state in the region, his invasion could not be challenged. However, he failed to anticipate the international condemnation of his action and especially the determination of President George Bush to redress the aggression. Immediately after the invasion, the U.S. government froze some $30 billion of Iraq's and Kuwait's assets in its jurisdiction. Moreover, with Syria and Turkey closing their Iraqi pipelines and foreign ships refusing to pick up Iraqi oil, Iraqi oil exports came to an abrupt halt.

In a virtually unprecedented action, the UN Security Council passed more than a dozen resolutions opposing Iraq and seeking the restoration of Kuwait's sovereignty. In its first action, the Security Council condemned the invasion and then declared Iraq's annexation of Kuwait null and void. It then adopted numerous actions, including comprehensive sanctions, to force Iraq to withdraw from Kuwait. However, after these actions failed to change Hussein's policies, the Security Council authorized (in Resolution 678) UN member states to "use all necessary means" to force Iraq's withdrawal from Kuwait if it had not done so by January 15, 1991. It is significant also that the Arab League, the principal alliance of twenty-one Arab states, condemned Iraq's action and called for the liberation of Kuwait.

After Iraq failed to comply with the international community's demands, a massive multilateral force, spearheaded by the United States, carried out a forty-six-day war to liberate Kuwait. The allied war began with a massive bombing campaign that eliminated Iraq's air force, destroyed its nuclear weapons development centers and chemical weapons facilities, eliminated the country's military and civilian communications networks, and severely weakened its ground forces. In addition, the bombing damaged the country's infrastructure, especially the transportation system. After six weeks of aerial bombardment, the allied forces launched a ground campaign involving the largest deployment of armored forces in the history of warfare. Within two days allied forces had liberated Kuwait, and within four days they had routed Iraq's armed forces, killing thousands of its soldiers and decimating its armored forces. The ground campaign ended within 100 hours of its beginning as Iraq agreed to cease-fire terms imposed by the allies.

The Just-War Doctrine and the Persian Gulf War

Was the Gulf War just? Was the allied military campaign justified, and was it prosecuted in a moral manner? Prior to the allied liberation campaign and in the aftermath of the war, scholars and politicians, especially in the United

States, debated these issues, carrying out an unprecedented moral debate about the justice of this war. Although there was significant disagreement about which actions were morally appropriate prior to and during the war, the debate about the morality of force was framed by just-war criteria. Just-war doctrine provided the framework for moral argumentation. Even President Bush took pains to use the moral language of just war to justify his decisions.

The case for resorting to force to liberate Kuwait was morally compelling because each of the six *jus ad bellum* criteria were fulfilled. First, because Iraq's invasion was clearly illegal (contrary to international law) as well as unjust (contrary to international political morality), the resort to force was in accord with the just-cause norm. Regardless of the legitimacy of Iraq's territorial and economic claims against Kuwait, Iraq was duty bound to use peaceful methods to settle its dispute with Kuwait. Iraq's attack was thus an act of war, giving Kuwait the inherent legal and moral right to use individual and collective force to repulse the aggression. Clearly, this conflict provided evidence that the just-cause criterion had been fulfilled. Indeed, Johnson argues that Iraq's aggression provides "as clear and unambiguous a case as one could hope to find in the real world."[22]

Second, the competent-authority norm was also fulfilled because the use of force was authorized by the U.S. Congress as well as the UN Security Council, the most authoritative multilateral peacekeeping and peace-enforcing body in the world.

Third, the right-intention criterion was also fulfilled by the just purpose of liberating Kuwait. The aim was not to conquer Iraq or to topple its dictatorship. The goal was simply to restore Kuwait's sovereignty and to halt the unjust humanitarian and strategic consequences of Iraq's invasion.

Fourth, although it was clear that the allied objectives were consistent with the limited-objectives norm (liberating Kuwait), determining whether the war's ends and means were proportionate presented particular challenges prior to the war. Although in retrospect it is clear that the liberation of Kuwait and the military defeat of Iraq justified the evil of war, at the time of the crisis it was difficult to be certain of the relationship between means and ends. Would the evil from the liberation campaign be commensurate with the evil already inflicted on Kuwait? What if Hussein resorted to weapons of mass destruction? Despite the potential for significant destruction, the evil inflicted by Hussein—an evil involving human rights abuses, the pillaging of Kuwait's treasury, and the violation of core norms of global society—was so extensive that there seemed to be a compelling case for proportionality.[23]

Fifth, the use of force was also in accord with the principle of last resort. This norm is especially difficult to apply because, as Michael Walzer has observed, there is no moral theory to guide its application.[24] As a result, the decision to use force will ultimately be based on political and strategic considerations, areas in which moral philosophers have no special competence. Although critics and advocates of the war were deeply divided on whether this had been fulfilled, it was clear that additional time would not necessarily have resolved the dispute. Throughout the five-month intervening phase between the invasion and the liberation campaign, allies had individually and collectively sought to resolve the conflict through diplomatic negotiation and through the pressure of comprehensive economic sanctions, but Iraq remained belligerent and uncompromising.

Finally, the probable-success norm was also fulfilled because there was complete certainty about the outcome of the allied liberation campaign. The allies had put together a multilateral force of more than a half million combatants, backed by an extraordinary arsenal of air power and armored forces. There was little doubt that the allies, spearheaded by the United States, would prevail militarily. The only questions were how destructive the war would be and how quickly it would be won.

The Moral Debate

The most significant moral opposition to the war came from religious and political elites who believed that additional time was necessary to satisfy the last-resort norm. For them, UN-imposed economic sanctions needed more time to work. However, in their eagerness to avoid war, they failed to appreciate that, from an international legal perspective, the condition of war had already begun when Iraq invaded its neighbor on August 2. More significant, these elites failed to recognize that sanctions were a source of deep moral harm and were themselves inconsistent with the just-war norm of discrimination because the harm fell disproportionately on civilians rather than on the political and military officials of the state. To the extent that comprehensive sanctions would have been given more time to work, they would have imposed an increasingly intolerable burden on the most vulnerable members of society, namely, women, children and the aged. Walzer has noted that opponents of the war who supported a prolonged blockade of Iraq "seem not to have realized that what they were advocating was a radically indiscriminate act of war, with predictably harsh consequences."[25]

Some religious and political leaders also opposed the war out of fear that the war would be disproportionate. Following a much publicized National Council of Churches' (NCC) "peace pilgrimage" to the Middle East in mid-December, leaders of mainline Protestant denominations declared that resorting to force to settle the conflict was "morally indefensible." They claimed that forcibly liberating Kuwait would "unleash weapons of mass destruction" and result in hundreds of thousands of casualties. "It is entirely possible," the NCC leaders noted apocalyptically, "that war in the Middle East will destroy everything."[26] On January 15, the day before the air campaign began, NCC Protestant leaders again urged President Bush not to resort to war because "it is unlikely that this battle can be contained in either scope, intensity, or time." In their view, the risk of war was "out of proportion to any conceivable gain which might be achieved through military action."[27]

The problem with the pacifistic pronouncements of the preachers and the bishops did not lie merely in the inadequacy of their view but also in the failure to morally assess their own position. By failing to seriously consider the use of force to halt oppression and aggression, religious elites were in effect condoning the occupation and annexation of Kuwait. Walzer notes that "it is very bad to make a deal with an aggressor at the expense of his victim," for then we "make ourselves complicitous in the aggression."[28]

Allied military planners also made significant efforts to apply discriminating force in the war. Indeed, some observers of modern war have suggested that the Persian Gulf War was the most discriminate war ever. Despite the significant destruction involved in both Iraq and Kuwait, allied forces limited civilian casualties and achieved an unprecedented level of compliance with the discrimination norm through the use of precision-guided munitions, such as laser-guided "smart" bombs and cruise missiles. At the same time, however, although Iraq's infrastructure was also classified as a legitimate target, the destruction of communications and transportation systems, electric power centers, water pumping stations and purification plants, and government buildings led some war critics to question the morality of such action.[29] Still, it cannot be denied that from a purely military standpoint, the destruction was almost wholly centered on military targets. By contrast, Iraq's missile attacks on Israel and Saudi Arabia were highly indiscriminate, intentionally targeting population centers.

The norm of proportionality, the second element of the *jus in bello*, was also fulfilled in significant measure by the allied liberation campaign, which sought to achieve the stated aims of war with the least destruction possible. The goal was to use overwhelming but discriminating force to achieve the liberation of Kuwait as quickly as possible and with the fewest casualties. However, it needs to be emphasized that estimating the proportionality of evil between means and ends is a highly subjective prudential judgment. The difficulty in ascertaining the morality of the means-ends relationship is due in great part to the difficulty in assigning a value to the goal of restoring sovereignty. How can the value of national liberation be determined? Is the restoration of sovereignty worth 1,000, 5,000, or even 50,000 lives?

Some scholars argue that the allies failed to fulfill the proportionality norm because of the disproportionate losses among combatants (50,000 to 75,000 Iraqi deaths vs. several hundred deaths for the allies). Tucker argues that the war's disproportionality was problematic not so much because it was an unfortunate by-product of military battle but because it was directly intended. The American strategy, influenced by the failure of Vietnam, was designed to use overwhelming force to achieve clear, achievable goals in a short span of time.[30] Jean Bethke Elshtain, for example, attributes the "extraordinary lopsidedness of deaths and casualties" to the use of "excessive firepower," especially in the bombing of "the Highway of Death," on which Iraqis fled Kuwait City with some 15,000 vehicles. In her view, the destruction along that highway was not "a fight by *jus in bello* standards but a massacre."[31] Although Elshtain is correct in emphasizing the just-war tradition's insistence on tempering justice with mercy, the proportionality norm applies not to the relationship of combatant casualties but to the relationship between the means and ends of war. As Francis Winters has observed, there is nothing in the moral logic of self-defense that can support the notion that "great powers may justly fight only when they reduce themselves to functional equality with small powers."[32]

Moral Reflections

From the foregoing review, it is evident that just-war criteria influenced the military liberation of Kuwait. Although some just-war elements were fulfilled more fully than others, there is substantial evidence that the resort to force and the prosecution of the air and land wars was unusually consistent with just-war principles. Still, some theorists have questioned both the timing and the prosecution of the liberation campaign.

- In light of this case study, was the allied resort to force warranted by Iraq's actions?
- Did the six-month interlude between Iraq's invasion and the commencement of the military liberation campaign provide sufficient opportunity to exhaust nonviolent conflict-resolution alternatives?
- Should more time have been allowed for comprehensive sanctions to affect Iraq's society? Was sufficient time allowed to fulfill the just war's last-resort principle?
- In terms of *jus in bello* (war conduct) norms, was the targeting of the economic infrastructure morally legitimate?
- More particularly, was the destruction of Iraq's communications and power centers, transportation networks, and water stations consistent with the discrimination norm?
- Was excessive force used in defeating Iraq? In view of the allied goals (the liberation of Kuwait), were the military means proportional to the political ends of the war?

The Ethics of Unconventional Force

Having examined the ethics of force in conventional interstate wars, I now turn to the role of coercive power in unconventional military conflicts. Although traditional international wars have been the most important types of military conflict since the nation-state system emerged in the mid-seventeenth century, in recent decades the Westphalian model of conflict has become less important as the number and intensity of internal wars have increased. Since the end of World War II, and especially since the end of the Cold War, domestic unconventional wars have become much more prevalent as nonstate actors and political groups have used violence to challenge the nature, boundaries, and governance of existing states.

During the Cold War, these internal wars were frequently influenced by conflicting ideologies and often supported and guided by the superpowers. However, with the collapse of the Soviet empire, intranational wars have been increasingly based on self-determination claims of ethnonationalist groups demanding either complete secession from a state or increased political autonomy. As a result of these political demands, many states have faced increased political turmoil and instability, resulting in weakened domestic authority or even the complete collapse of internal order. The rise in the number of "quasi" or "failed" states is due principally to this phenomenon. According to one study, of the 164 wars during the 1945–95 period, only 38 (23 percent) were conventional interstate wars. Of the other 126 internal wars, about half were based on domestic ideological disputes, whereas the other half were based on self-determination claims.[33]

The expansion of domestic civil strife and internal wars is significant because these domestic military conflicts are generally carried out partly through irregular forces using unconventional strategies. As a result, they differ considerably from the conventional interstate military conflicts discussed earlier. Whereas classical Westphalian wars involve a direct contest between the military forces of two or more states, the internal, ideological wars of the Cold War era and the domestic, ethnonationalistic wars of the post-Cold War era generally involve military force that, although frequently as violent and destructive as conventional warfare, is not easily encompassed by traditional Clausewitzian concepts of war. Moreover, the moral principles used to assess traditional wars are not easily applied to contemporary unconventional wars because classical moral theories, such as the just-war doctrine, are concerned fundamentally with interstate violence, not with domestic civil wars. Indeed, internal wars are morally problematic from a just-war perspective because only "competent authorities" are permitted to prosecute wars. However, as noted previously, most contemporary domestic wars are fought precisely to determine which groups are entitled to exert political authority within the boundaries of a state.

During the Cold War, the ideological conflicts in the Third World typically involved two major types of action—insurgency and counterinsurgency. *Insurgency*, also known as guerrilla war, involves a protracted political and military effort by irregular forces and illegal political organizations seeking to topple an existing regime. The aim of such a war is to force the collapse of the government through unconventional military tactics, including guerrilla warfare and even periodic terrorist attacks. The strategy of insurgency is not to directly engage a regime's regular forces in battle but to exhaust them through hit-and-run tactics, low-level military actions, and popular action programs and propaganda campaigns designed to gain the people's political support. *Counterinsurgency*, by contrast, involves a government's effort to counter guerrilla military actions both by maintaining political support of the masses and by overtly and covertly challenging the coercive operations of the insurgent forces. The military aspect of counterinsurgency is especially difficult because it requires effective intelligence and limited military operations by well-disciplined forces. Typically, however, regular military forces have tended to overreact to insurgents' terror and hit-and-run operations, further alienating the regime from the people.

During the Cold War, both the United States and the Soviet Union were involved, directly and indirectly, overtly and covertly, in these internal wars. The superpowers typically used a variety of coercive instruments short of war to influence the outcome of these conflicts. These unconventional strategies ranged from secret operations (e.g., clandestine raids and covert operations) to overt political, economic, and military support to occasional small-scale military operations. Because many of these Third World conflicts involved insurgency or counterinsurgency, both superpowers participated in these unconventional internal wars. In its involvement in these military disputes, the United States developed a variety of strategies that collectively were defined as *low-intensity conflict (LIC)*, which typically involved four types of unconventional military actions: pro-insurgency (supporting insurgent forces), counterinsurgency (fighting against revolutionary guerrillas), peacetime contingency operations (such as police-type actions), and military "shows of force" that display military capabilities.[34]

LICs pose major ethical challenges in part because they rely on unconventional war strategies and use irregular forces. Insurgencies, as previously discussed, seek to defeat the enemy not through direct military engagements but rather through wars of attrition based on hit-and-run tactics and attacks on society's infrastructure and on key civilian institutions. A major aim of insurgents' military operations is to foster fear, demoralize its people, weaken society, and undermine the economy. To effectively carry out their military operations, insurgent forces rely on secrecy, surprise, and small-scale operations, frequently involving support from civilians. Indeed, insurgencies and counterinsurgencies are morally problematic because, by engaging civilians as supporters and as active participants in the war, they undermine the just-war norm of discrimination that differentiates combatants from noncombatants.

Despite the moral challenges posed by unconventional operations, some scholars have defended the right of fighting oppression with unconventional force. Walzer, for example, argues that notwithstanding the moral problems of guerrilla war, insurgency can be a morally legitimate means of fighting oppression.[35] Whether fighting against a tyrannical regime is moral will depend on both the conditions that justify violence against a regime and the range of legitimate methods available to rebels. Charles Krauthammer similarly provides a qualified defense of guerrilla tactics when the existing oppression is the greater evil.[36] Although political socie-ties presume the legitimacy of the existing political order, Krauthammer correctly observes that order is not the sole collective good. As the U.S. Declaration of Independence suggests, when a regime becomes tyrannical, people have a right to rebel and constitute a new, legitimate government authority. In short, internal, unconventional wars, such as interstate wars, can be morally permissible, provided that their ends and means are just. However, unlike traditional wars, unconventional military operations pres-ent greater challenges in ensuring that the means of violence are morally acceptable.

To explore the morality of force in unconventional conflicts, I next as-sess the ethics of the Reagan Doctrine, a doctrine that supported and justi-fied U.S. participation in Third World unconventional wars.

CASE NO. 5–2
ETHICS AND THE REAGAN DOCTRINE

Background

In the November 1980 presidential election, Republican Party candidate Ronald Reagan defeated Jimmy Carter. During the election campaign, Reagan charged that the Carter administration had been "soft" on Soviet communism and had failed to effectively challenge Soviet expansionism in developing countries. In addition, Reagan charged that Carter had allowed the U.S. military power to deteriorate and had failed to advance America's interest in promoting political and economic freedom in the world. Candi-date Reagan promised that, if elected, he would restore American military strength and challenge Soviet expansionism by supporting regimes threat-ened by revolutionary communism and assisting peoples seeking to over-come tyranny, especially communist oppression.

The Reagan Doctrine

Unlike other presidential doctrines (e.g., those of Truman and Nixon), the Reagan Doctrine did not emerge from a single speech or initiative but from a series of addresses, declarations, directives, and policy actions undertaken in the president's first term of office. Krauthammer, who first coined the term in 1985 and was responsible for the concept's popularization, argued that the Reagan Doctrine involved two core features: the rollback of Soviet expansionism and the protection, promotion, and consolidation of democ-racy.[37] In his view, the doctrine was rooted in the administration's overt sup-port of regimes threatened by Marxist insurgency and in its support of anti-communist liberation movements.

One of the Reagan administration's early initiatives that contributed to the development of this doctrine was U.S. policy toward El Salvador, a coun-try threatened by virulent guerrilla war. Although the U.S. government limited its direct military involvement, it provided substantial economic and military assistance to prevent Marxist revolutionaries from toppling the government. The goal in El Salvador was not only the defeat of the guerrillas but also the strengthening of democracy in that land. Because the U.S. policy toward El Salvador in early 1982 involved both a military strategy of countering insurgency and a political strategy of further institutionalizing democracy, Robert Kagan suggests that the Reagan Doctrine "may have been born in El Salvador in 1982."[38]

One of the most significant expositions of the emerging new doctrine was a speech given in June 1982 before the British Parliament at Westminster. In that speech, regarded as one of the most important addresses during his eight-year presidency, Reagan proclaimed that the United States would launch a "crusade for freedom," supporting democracy wherever it had a chance to succeed. According to Reagan, the aim of U.S. foreign policy was not simply to contain communist expansion but to advance the cause of political freedom everywhere, regardless of the ideology of the regime, noting that it would be "preposterous" to "encourage democratic change in right-wing dictatorships, but not in communist regimes." Above all, the long-term goal of the freedom crusade was to "leave Marxism-Leninism on the ash heap of history." The Westminster speech is historically significant because it represented an emerging shift from the traditional Republican foreign policy of containment to democratic expansion, from realpolitik to an ideological crusade for freedom. As one scholar has noted, Reagan's speech "ventured onto new ideological terrain, leaving traditional Republican foreign policy behind."[39]

Some political leaders and scholars thought that Reagan's pronouncements about the duty to promote democracy and oppose communist regimes were overly simplistic and moralistic. For them, Reagan's foreign policy was unwisely based on a Manichean morality that unnecessarily divided the world into good regimes guided by the "forces of light" and bad regimes guided by the "forces of darkness."[40] Although democracy was regarded as essential in securing human freedom, Reagan's critics argued that foreign policy should be inspired and guided not by a crusading spirit for freedom and democratic institutions but rather by a more dispassionate and pragmatic assessment of America's national and global interests.

Some of the early Reagan administration decisions about the global promotion of democracy focused on Eastern Europe. In May 1982, for example, Reagan signed a secret order, National Security Decision Directive (NSDD) 32, setting forth a comprehensive anticommunist national strategy. This directive authorized U.S. officials to challenge the monolithic power of the Communist Party rule in Eastern Europe by providing help to antigovernment groups and thereby strengthening the preconditions for democratic rule. In Poland, for example, U.S. officials were authorized to assist such intermediary political groups as the Catholic Church and the union-based Solidarity Movement. A year later, Reagan signed another secret directive (NSDD 75) that further reinforced the U.S. government's commitment to an active anticommunist global campaign. This directive called on the United States to "roll back" the Soviet sphere of influence by seeking to "contain and over time reverse Soviet expansionism."[41]

Although the Reagan administration's anticommunist crusade was proclaimed as universally valid, the Reagan Doctrine was applied mainly to the Third World. Such a strategy would permit the United States to challenge by proxy the Soviet Union's Third World influence without directly confronting its military power. The aim was thus to support anticommunist liberation movements without directly challenging the Soviet Union militarily. Not surprisingly, the Reagan administration carried out its anti-Marxist revolutionary campaign in small, developing nations, with the major test cases being Afghanistan, Angola, Cambodia, and Nicaragua.

As it emerged in the mid-1980s, the Reagan Doctrine was characterized by five elements. First, the United States sought to directly challenge and curb Soviet power. Although containment, the dominant U.S. Cold War strategy, tried to limit Soviet expansion, the aim of the Reagan Doctrine was much more expansive, involving the rollback of the Soviet sphere of influence. Second, the United States supported limited, constitutional regimes and helped foster democratic institutions that were conducive to human liberty. Third, the Reagan Doctrine used morality to justify its ideological crusade for liberty. Whereas the Cold War doctrine of containment was justified largely on the basis of national interest, this new doctrine was justified by claims of justice. As one scholar has noted, the doctrine was based on the supposition that "what was necessary had to be coupled with a defense of what was right."[42] According to Reagan, supporting anti-Soviet insurgencies was morally legitimate because human beings were entitled to freedom. Fourth, the Reagan Doctrine was characterized by its "overt and unashamed American support for anticommunist revolution."[43] According to the doctrine, the United States would not directly confront Soviet military power but instead would rely on insurgent forces to carry out anticommunist revolutionary insurgencies. The United States would provide military, economic, and logistical support to guerrillas fighting Marxist regimes. Finally, the Reagan Doctrine encouraged prudent interventionism to weaken politically oppressive regimes, to support and strengthen anticommunist regimes, and to help consolidate democratic political systems. Such interventionism involved a variety of LIC strategies, ranging from shows of force to limited military operations, from overt economic and military assistance to covert intervention.

The Ethics of the Doctrine

As noted previously, the major foreign policy aims of the Reagan administration as formulated in the Reagan Doctrine were to roll back the geopolitical power of the Soviet Union and to promote anticommunist, prodemocratic regimes. In assessing the moral merits of the doctrine's goals, it is clear that Reagan's call for a revolution in liberty—involving increased individual freedom, the spread of democracy, and the reduction of totalitarian control—

was morally unassailable. However, if goals are assessed not only in terms of official statements and presidential declarations (declaratory policy) but also in terms of government decisions (operational policy), it is clear that actions were far more concerned with containing and reducing the power of communist regimes than with promoting and consolidating democracy. As a result, the anticommunist struggles were often invested with more moral content than they deserved.[44] For example, Reagan regularly referred to anticommunist insurgents (in countries such as Afghanistan and Nicaragua) as "freedom fighters," even though such military forces were concerned mainly with political independence and self-determination, not with establishing democratic structures.

Although the Reagan Doctrine's advocates recognized that most of the insurgent forces were not democratic or likely to foster democratic institutions immediately, the destabilization of existing Marxist regimes was considered to be a first step in the process of political liberation. In their view, undermining the power of oppressive regimes through LIC strategies, although morally problematic, was necessary in promoting personal liberty. For example, Krauthammer, a staunch defender of the doctrine, wrote: "[I]f indigenous rebels, claiming their right to freedom, meet the (lesser) requirements to justify revolution and call for American support, it is hard to see what morally proscribes us from responding."[45] Robert Johnson, however, notes that the doctrine's goal of fostering liberty was an illusory, unattainable ideal in the Third World regions where it was being applied because the notion of popular will has "no clear meaning in pre-modern societies with little or no democratic tradition."[46] Moreover, Johnson argues that in the Reagan administration's eagerness to morally defend and support anti-Marxist insurgencies, it tended to conflate "democracy" and "independence," thereby legitimizing revolutionary struggles that were anticommunist but not necessarily prodemocratic.[47]

Although significant consensus existed over the moral legitimacy of the doctrine's goals, strategists, scholars, and public affairs commentators were deeply divided over the merits of the doctrine's means. The moral ambivalence over methodology was rooted not only in concerns about supporting anticommunist fighters but also in the legitimation of unconventional guerrilla warfare tactics. From an ethical perspective, the Reagan Doctrine's methods posed two significant problems. First, by supporting covert intervention, the doctrine tended to undermine the territorial integrity and political independence of some Third World countries. Second, by supporting insurgent forces, the doctrine tended to legitimate guerrilla warfare tactics. The first problem concerned the *jus ad bellum,* the second the *jus in bello.*

Foreign intervention challenges global order. Support for antigovernment insurgencies is contrary to international law because it compromises a state's right to political sovereignty and its obligation to honor nonintervention. However, Krauthammer has noted that international order is not the highest value in global society. In his view, because sovereignty "grants legitimacy and thus protection to whoever has guns and powder enough to be in control of a government," respecting sovereignty is not a moral imperative. "There are wrongs worth righting even at the cost of injuring order," he writes.[48] As I suggest in the next chapter, there are some exceptional circumstances that can morally justify direct and indirect foreign intervention, such as the gross abuse of human rights, but from a legal and moral perspective the presumption is always against foreign intervention.

Ultimately, whether covert or overt foreign intervention is morally defensible will depend partly on the scope of human rights abuses and the prospects for eradicating the tyrannical abuse of power. According to Charles Beitz, if insurgents are worthy of support, they should, at a minimum, be genuinely committed to respecting human rights and should represent "a truly indigenous movement with substantial popular support."[49] Determining whether antigovernment forces have popular support in a tyranny is virtually impossible to ascertain. For example, in his assessment of the Nicaraguan anti-Sandinista insurgents (Contras), Beitz concludes that they did not satisfy the popular-support norm. Similarly, Robert Pastor argues that the application of the Reagan Doctrine in Nicaragua was counterproductive because it was based on policies and tactics that were inconsistent with traditional U.S. foreign policy. "To defeat the Communists," writes Pastor, "Reagan adopted their tactics and jettisoned America's purpose: respect for the rule of law."[50] Still, when citizens were given the opportunity to express their view about the Sandinista regime in presidential elections in 1990, they decisively elected the anti-Sandinista coalition to power.

But even if force is morally justified in challenging communist oppression, is reliance on insurgency a morally legitimate way of advancing justice? For example, were the U.S.-supported insurgencies in Afghanistan and Nicaragua morally legitimate? As noted previously, guerrilla warfare is morally problematic because it subverts the basic just-war distinction between soldiers and civilians, combatants and noncombatants. By their very logic, insurgent forces rely on unconventional warfare using irregular forces and guerrilla tactics that seek to undermine society. Although the discrimination norm is an essential element of the just-war theory, it is not the sole criterion. Indeed, because the just-war doctrine provides numerous norms for judging when to go to war and how to fight, judging the moral legitimacy of a particular action—such as giving military and financial support to the Afghan guerrillas (mujahedeen) seeking to topple the Soviet-installed regime in Kabul—must be undertaken by applying all the doctrine's norms. In particular, the justice of war must also be judged in accordance with the legitimacy of the war's goals and the proportionality of the violence inflicted in wartime. Krauthammer, aware of the moral difficulties involved in supporting unconventional warfare, justifies the Reagan Doctrine's support for anticommunist insurgencies as "the lesser of two evils," believing that the evils of guerrilla war are justified by the aim of overthrowing tyrannical regimes.[51]

Did the Reagan Doctrine contribute to the rollback of Soviet influence in the international community? Did it undermine Marxist regimes? Did it contribute to the expansion of democracy, especially in the Third World?

The most important test case for the Reagan Doctrine was the U.S. support for the insurgency in Afghanistan, regarded by James Scott as the "cornerstone" of the Reagan Doctrine.[52] In supporting this anti-Soviet insurgency throughout the 1980s, the U.S. government provided nearly $3 billion of covert military assistance, including the transfer of highly sophisticated antiaircraft Stinger missiles. The success of the mujahedeen insurgency, which resulted in major Soviet military losses, eventually forced the Soviet Union to withdraw from Afghanistan as well as to reappraise its foreign policy. Although the insurgency helped defeat the Soviet Union, it contributed little to the development of a more pluralistic society. Indeed, in the post-Cold War era, Afghanistan has been ruled by Islamic fundamentalists who have imposed an even more totalitarian government than was the case under the Soviet-installed puppet regime in the 1980s.

Despite the uneven application of the Reagan Doctrine to Nicaragua, some scholars claim that the Reagan administration's initiatives toward that country might have contributed to its transition from a radical Marxist regime in the early 1980s to a democratic system in 1990. Unlike Afghanistan, in which the Soviet forces were forced to withdraw, the Soviet-supported Sandinista regime was not defeated militarily, in part because of the comparatively modest, sporadic support from the United States.[53] Nevertheless, the Reagan administration's policies contributed to Sandinista reforms, without which the return of democracy in 1990 would have been unlikely. "Guns alone could force the Sandinistas from power," writes Kagan, "and guns alone, therefore, provided sufficient pressure to force them to make changes to preserve power."[54] However, if the Contras' military threat was essential to Nicaragua's shift toward democratic rule, Kagan also argues that it was not sufficient to achieve democracy. In his view, the continuation of Reagan administration policies would probably not have resulted in the February 1990 elections but would have "meant many years of inconclusive struggle."[55] U.S. military support for the Contras was thus a necessary but not a sufficient condition for democratization. Other factors that ultimately contributed to the elections included the Central American Peace Plan initiated by Costa Rican President Oscar Arias, ongoing congressional initiatives and debates, the dramatic decline of Soviet power in the late 1980s, and the renewed commitment of the Bush administration to a peaceful resolution of the regional conflict.

Assessing the international impact of the Reagan Doctrine is especially difficult because practitioners and scholars differ as to how and when the doctrine was implemented. Nevertheless, there can be little doubt that during the 1980s the relative international influence of the Soviet Union declined precipitously. As former Secretary of State George Shultz noted in his memoirs, by the end of the 1980s "[t]he Brezhnev Doctrine was dead, with the execution due in some considerable part to its opposite number, the Reagan Doctrine."[56] Some scholars have claimed that the decline of Soviet influence was due mainly to internal economic and political conditions; others, however, have credited the decline of the Soviet Union and the ending of the

Cold War to Reagan's vigorous anticommunist campaign.[57] Although scholars and public officials are similarly divided over the impact of the Reagan Doctrine, there can be little doubt that U.S. foreign policy contributed partly to the decline of communist influence and the expansion of democratic regimes in the 1980s.

Moral Reflections

The Reagan Doctrine raises numerous critical issues about the role of moral values and unconventional force. Although there is little doubt that the Reagan Doctrine's aims of democratization and increased individual liberty were morally worthy, it is much less clear that the moral and strategic crusade against communism was similarly justified.

- Were the goals of the Reagan Doctrine morally legitimate?
- Because communist regimes were regarded as the principal obstacle to the promotion of human rights, did this belief justify the anticommunist liberation campaign?
- In light of the just-war theory, did the Reagan Doctrine's anticommunist strategy justify the use of indirect and covert force?
- Was the strategic, military, and political support for anticommunist forces consistent with international law and international ethics?
- In view of the morally problematic nature of guerrilla warfare, was support for insurgent forces morally warranted?
- Would direct U.S. military confrontation with the Soviet Union have been morally preferable to proxy wars?

Summary

Although war is evil, it can be morally justified in exceptional circumstances. Normally, such circumstances will require that other alternatives be exhausted and that the goals and methods be consistent with international morality. The just-war doctrine provides a framework by which to judge both the morality of going to war and the morality of combat. Although the just-war doctrine is applied mainly to international war, it provides an ethical framework for assessing the morality of other military strategies short of war as well. The use of unconventional force, such as guerrilla warfare, is especially problematic because civilians are encouraged to support and directly participate in these operations. In the end, the moral legitimacy of coercive threats, covert operations, and limited military operations, including guerrilla warfare, depends on both the goals and means justifying such strategies.

CHAPTER SIX

THE ETHICS OF INTERVENTION

Probably more lives have been lost to ethnic, religious, or ideological crusades than to simple [national] greed.

Lea Brilmayer[1]

Respect for sovereignty in itself is not a moral imperative. It cannot be. The sanctity of sovereignty enshrines a radical moral asymmetry. It grants legitimacy and thus protection to whoever has guns and powder enough to be in control of a government.

Charles Krauthammer[2]

[H]umanitarian intervention [is] obligatory where the survival of populations and entire ethnic groups is seriously compromised. This is a duty for nations and the international community.

Pope John Paul II[3]

Foreign intervention involves the direct or indirect use of power to influence the affairs of other states. Intervention can be undertaken openly or covertly, individually or collectively, and involve relatively noncoercive actions, such as propaganda and official condemnation, to coercive measures, ranging from economic sanctions to direct military intervention. Moreover, intervention can be undertaken for a variety of purposes, including economic imperialism, countering prior intervention, promoting political objectives, protecting human rights, and fostering national security.

In this chapter, I examine the nature, legality, and morality of military intervention—the most extreme type of foreign intervention. Such intervention involves the individual or collective use or threat of use of force against another state to influence its domestic affairs. This chapter has three parts. First, it examines the legality of nonintervention and briefly assesses the extent to which it has been practiced by states in contemporary international relations. Second, it analyzes some of the arguments used to morally justify state sovereignty and its corollary, nonintervention. Third, it examines two different types of intervention: strategic and humanitarian. The first, commonly used by the superpowers during the Cold War, involves foreign military penetration for security, political, or ideological purposes. By contrast, humanitarian intervention involves military intervention to uphold human rights in the face of genocide, famine, and war. Because of the great human suffering that has resulted from the disintegration of states, the international community has responded to many major gross human rights violations by authorizing multilateral interventions in such countries as Iraq, Somalia, Rwanda, Haiti, and Bosnia.

International Law and Intervention

The most fundamental pillar of international society is state sovereignty. This legal right ensures states juridical equality, political independence, and territorial integrity. Because states have the right to determine their domestic affairs, no foreign state may unilaterally violate the territorial boundaries of another state or interfere in its internal affairs. Moreover, states have a duty to respect the political independence and territorial integrity of other states. Thus, the norm of nonintervention is a corollary of state sovereignty, for without the former the latter is impossible.

The norm of nonintervention has been defined and proclaimed in numerous sources. The most important legal prohibitions against intervention are contained in the UN Charter, which states (Article 2.4) that UN members are obligated to "refrain in their international relations from the use of force against the territorial integrity or political independence of any other state." In 1965, the General Assembly passed Resolution 2131, which states in part,

> No State has the right to intervene, directly or indirectly, for any reason whatever, in the internal or external affairs of any other State. Consequently, armed intervention and all other forms of interference or attempted threats against the personality of the State or against its political, economic, or cultural elements are condemned.[4]

Five years later, the General Assembly passed Resolution 2625, titled the Declaration on Principles of International Law Concerning Friendly Relations and Co-operation Among States, which reiterated the nonintervention norm.

Regional international organizations have also affirmed the priority of the nonintervention norm. For example, the Organization of American States (OAS), the regional organ of Latin American states, defines the principle in a highly absolutist, restrictive manner. According to its charter, direct and indirect intervention in the internal affairs of other states is totally prohibited (Article 15). Such prohibition applies not only to armed force but also to other forms of interference or attempted threat against "the personality of the State or against its political, economic and cultural elements" (Article 18).

The norm of nonintervention is so foundational to the contemporary international system that even the United Nations is prohibited by the charter (Article 2.7) from intervening in the domestic affairs of its member states. The United Nations can take actions under Chapter VII of the charter that might involve military operations against the wishes of a state.[5] However, such actions are exceptional and are taken only in response to a serious threat to international peace. In general, international law as expressed in numerous charters and conventions is unambiguous about nonintervention: States and other actors have a duty to respect countries' political independence.

Although nonintervention is the most basic constitutive norm of international society, states have historically intervened in the affairs of other states. Indeed, intervention has been so common in modern international relations, according to Michael Mandelbaum, that the history of global politics is "in no small part the history of intervention."[6] Mandelbaum attributes the prevalence of intervention to the oligarchic distribution of power, which allows strong states to intervene in the domestic affairs of the weak.

Historically, foreign intervention has been undertaken for a variety of reasons, including economic expansion, strategic interests, territorial security, and humanitarianism. For example, during the nineteenth century, major European powers intervened in Asia and Africa to establish colonies that could, among other things, provide a source of raw materials, cheap labor, and a market for goods. In the early part of the twentieth century, the United States intervened in a number of Central American countries (e.g., Cuba, the Dominican Republic, Haiti, Nicaragua, and Panama) to foster domestic political order and reduce economic corruption. Although such interventions were designed to prevent European powers from interfering in the Western Hemisphere, they also served to reinforce the dominant political role of the United States in the region.

During the Cold War, when the two superpowers dominated global politics, the most important motive for intervention was strategic security. Although both the United States and the Soviet Union were more powerful militarily than any other hegemonic powers in history, they nonetheless feared each other and sought to increase their power and influence through bilateral ties and multilateral alliances. Moreover, they intervened militarily in other states to protect and promote vital national interests or to advance ideological goals. Thus, for example, when the Soviet Union intervened in Czechoslovakia in 1968 and in Afghanistan in 1979, it did so to strengthen communism in those states; when the United States intervened in the Dominican Republic in 1965 and in Grenada in 1983, it did so to challenge antidemocratic forces. According to Mandelbaum, during the Cold War, American interventionism was driven almost exclusively by the great rivalry with the Soviet Union:

> Korea and Vietnam, where the United States fought the most protracted wars of the Cold War era, were spaces on the board of global geopolitics; the United States was attempting to defend those spaces for fear that, if the Soviet Union and its clients occupied them, the Soviets would be emboldened to challenge Western positions elsewhere.[7]

Territorial security has also been an important motive for military intervention, especially among lesser powers. When a state perceives that its territorial boundaries and economic well-being are threatened by the deliberate actions, political instability, or government oppression in neighboring countries, the threatened state might seek to protect its interests through foreign intervention. For example, when India intervened in East Pakistan (Bangladesh) in 1971 after the Pakistani government began a war against the Bengali people, it did so because India perceived the war and the mass human rights violations as a threat to its own security. Similarly, when Tanzania intervened in Uganda in 1978, it did so, according to its officials, not because the dictatorial regime of Idi Amin was violating human rights but because the record of gross human rights violations was a source of major regional instability, threatening the territorial security of Tanzania. In other words, while gross immorality was being carried out, the rationale that justified foreign intervention was national security rather than the violation of human rights.

However, the gross violation of human rights has served as a justification for some foreign interventions. When the United States intervened in Cuba in 1898 and declared war on Spain, it did so in part to overthrow an oppressive dictatorial regime that was committing gross human rights violations. Moreover, when the United States intervened in Somalia in 1992, it did so mainly to reestablish political order to resume humanitarian relief to millions of people threatened with starvation.

In short, although the international system proscribes foreign intervention, states have, from time to time, violated the sovereignty of other states when they have perceived that their national interests or the global common good would be advanced by such action.[8]

The Ethics of Nonintervention

I suggested previously that international law explicitly affirms state sovereignty and its corollary obligation of nonintervention. However, if the norms of sovereignty and nonintervention have legal validity, do they also possess moral authority? Is state sovereignty a key moral principle of global society? Is nonintervention a foundational norm of global order? What ethical priority do these norms have in international society?

The claim that nonintervention is a morally valid norm in global society is based on several core assumptions and values: (1) the existing anarchic international system is morally legitimate, (2) peoples have a moral right to political self-determination, (3) states have a juridical right to sovereignty and territorial integrity, (4) states have an obligation to resolve conflicts peacefully, and (5) force is an illegitimate instrument for altering the existing territorial boundaries. In exploring the moral basis of nonintervention, I first examine the nature of political legitimacy in the international system, focusing on how domestic and international legitimacy is used to justify nonintervention. I then examine two types of intervention—strategic and humanitarian—and seek to show how moral arguments have been used for each.

Political Justifications

Political thinkers have offered two types of justifications for sovereignty and nonintervention. One argument is based on the legitimacy of states in the international system; the other is based on the legitimacy of a regime in terms of its people. *International legitimacy* assumes that existing states, as sovereign members of the decentralized, state-centric international community, are entitled to recognition and respect and to the right of political autonomy and its corollary, the right against nonintervention. International legitimacy is not rooted in the character of regimes but in the existing Westphalian order, whose viability depends on the political autonomy of states. If a state is functioning as a politically independent community, it is entitled, according to this perspective, to the rights and obligations of the international society of states.

Domestic legitimacy, by contrast, assumes that states are entitled to respect and support when they fulfill their core obligations as states. According to this perspective, state autonomy is conditional on the fulfillment of basic duties. Fundamentally, this means that states have a responsibility to honor people's collective claim to self-determination and to protect the basic rights of individuals, including freedom of conscience, freedom from torture and arbitrary arrest, and freedom to own property. Given the wide disparity in human rights conceptions, domestic legitimacy is generally defined in terms of the extent to which communal self-determination is practiced. Thus, from a domestic perspective, whether a state is entitled to the right of nonintervention will depend mainly on subjects' approval of the regime itself and to a lesser extent on a regime's protection of basic human rights.

The notion of international legitimacy is generally rooted in the claim that states, like people, have a right to be free and to govern themselves. This argument, based on the application of social contract theory to international relations, assumes that the relationship of persons to domestic society is analogous to the relationship of states to global society.[9] According to this argument, just as individuals have inherent rights such as life and liberty, so too political communities have basic rights, including the freedom and the political independence to define, preserve, and pursue communal interests.

Whereas international legitimacy emphasizes the rights and duties of states, domestic legitimacy emphasizes the rights of persons within communities. Although the comparison of individuals and states can be useful in illuminating and defining ethical rights and obligations within international society, states and persons are not morally equivalent because the former are merely artifacts designed to protect and promote the rights of people they represent. According to this perspective, states are not inherently moral actors but rather conceptual entities whose legitimacy is wholly derived from their ability to sustain and foster the communal well-being of persons. In particular, states derive their domestic legitimacy, that is, their right to rule and to be obeyed, from their capacity to protect and advance people's individual and communal rights.

It is one thing to assert that states, which are entitled to the right of nonintervention, must be legitimate internationally and domestically. It is quite another to define what these notions mean and how they should be applied to contemporary international relations. Are all states and quasi-states entitled to sovereignty and nonintervention? If not, how, and by whom, is the legitimacy of states to be determined? What role should foreign actors play in determining state legitimacy, and what should be the role of the people? In times of domestic conflict and civil wars, which political communities are entitled to recognition and thus to political autonomy?

Michael Walzer has provided a useful criterion for judging state legitimacy. For him, states are entitled to political autonomy when they fulfill two conditions—viability and communal support. According to Walzer, a legitimate community is one that can pass the "self-help" test; that is, it must be capable of existing without external aid. He claims, "A legitimate government is one that can fight its own internal wars."[10] Walzer, following John Stuart Mill, argues that the only legitimate self-determination is that which is earned through struggle because only through the long and arduous quest for self-rule will people develop the habits and virtues necessary to sustain political autonomy. One political community cannot give another self-determination; the requirements for authentic self-rule must be indigenous and can be acquired only when individuals and groups struggle to affirm the right of self-determination. Walzer writes, "As with individuals, so with sovereign states: there are things that we cannot do to them, even for their own ostensible good."[11] Although self-help is no doubt important in developing indigenous self-determination, the self-help argument is morally problematic because it runs the risk of equating political success with justice and might with right.

For Walzer, communal legitimacy is based on a community's capacity for self-determination. Such capacity, he suggests, depends on the "fit" between a political community and the government, that is, whether a regime represents "the political life of its people."[12] Walzer writes, "The moral standing of any particular state depends upon the reality of the common life it protects and the extent to which the sacrifices required by that protection are willingly accepted and thought worthwhile."[13] Communal legitimacy is not achieved through periodic elections but rather through the protection and promotion of a people's shared cultural, religious, social, and economic life. For Walzer, communal consent involves representation of a "special sort," rooted in the shared values, experiences, and hopes of a people bonded together through time. Just as individuals have a right to defend their homes, citizens also, he suggests, have a right to protect their homeland and the values and institutions that sustain it politically and economically. However, if this communal life is to enjoy international legitimacy, it must be authentic, which means that solidarity must exist between government and subjects. Thus, a state's right to political autonomy is rooted in the right of individuals to protect their collective life from foreign domination.

Jefferson McMahan has similarly argued that the legitimacy of the state rests on the degree to which a regime protects and promotes "communal self-determination."[14] For McMahan, communal self-determination involves the right of human communities to govern themselves freely and independently. Although democratic practices and institutions would no doubt be conducive to communal self-determination, McMahan argues that democratic government is not a prerequisite. In his view, self-determination does not require self-government. Rather, a political community must be able to control its own destiny and to govern its own affairs independently of external influences while maintaining some level of domestic legitimacy.

For McMahan, two criteria are important in ensuring domestic legitimacy. First, a state must be representative of the political community or communities within its territorial boundaries. Second, it must enjoy the support and approval of the mass of citizens.[15] According to McMahan, a state that is representative and enjoys the approval of its citizens is domestically legitimate and thus entitled to the right of nonintervention. A state that is not representative and not supported by the people is thus not a legitimate, self-determining community.

In sum, the moral validity of states depends on two types of legitimacy: international and domestic. Internationally, states are presumptively legitimate by virtue of their ability to exist as independent, viable political communities; domestically, states are legitimate to the extent that they affirm communal self-determination—a norm manifested by a regime's representative character and the extent to which citizens approve and support its government. It is important to emphasize that the right of nonintervention does not depend on a regime's democratic self-rule; rather, it depends on two conditions: international viability and the representative character of a regime. Because the domestic legitimacy of states is more restrictive, it is possible for a state to be internationally legitimate, that is, regarded as legitimate by other member states, while still being considered domestically illegitimate by a significant portion of its own citizens.

Moral Justifications

Political thinkers have offered moral and legal arguments for the ethical legitimacy of sovereignty and nonintervention. The most powerful of these is the utilitarian argument that sovereignty and nonintervention must be honored if order is to be maintained in global society. According to this thesis, intervention is wrong (illegal and immoral) because it fosters international chaos and instability by encouraging counterintervention, military conflict, and even large-scale war. This ends-based morality suggests that if global order is to be maintained, it will occur only by honoring the existing cartography. International order cannot be maintained when states fail to respect the territorial integrity and political autonomy of member states. Stanley Hoffmann has argued that whether or not one finds particular states morally acceptable, it is important to uphold the legal rights of states lest international society collapse "into a state of war or universal tyranny."[16]

In her illuminating study on global order titled *Code of Peace*, Dorothy Jones argues that the international community has an ethical framework—a "code of peace," as she calls it—that states have accepted as normative and legally binding in their international relations.[17] These norms are not derived from states' international behavior but rather are rooted in the shared political doctrines and legal and moral principles embodied in widely accepted treaties, conventions, declarations, and other international agreements. According to Jones, the code of peace involves the following nine tenets:

1. Sovereign equality of states
2. Territorial integrity and political independence of states
3. Equal rights and self-determination of peoples
4. Nonintervention in the internal affairs of states
5. Peaceful settlement of disputes between states
6. Abstention from the threat or use of force
7. Fulfillment in good faith of international obligations
8. Cooperation with other states
9. Respect for human rights and fundamental freedoms.[18]

Because this code specifies the acceptable behavioral mores of the international community, it provides not only a regulatory structure but, more significant here, an ethical system. The code is an ethical system because it establishes binding moral obligations on states that, if fulfilled, have the potential of contributing to peace and stability in the international system.

Walzer similarly builds an ethical theory of peace on the basis of sovereignty and other widely accepted states' rights. These foundational norms collectively form a "legalist paradigm," which provides the moral and legal structure for maintaining international peace. The paradigm includes six key principles:

1. An international society of independent states exists;
2. The states comprising the international society have rights, including the rights of territorial integrity and political sovereignty;
3. The use of force or threat of force by one state against another constitutes aggression and is a criminal act;
4. Aggression justifies two types of action: a war of self-defense by the victim and a war of law enforcement by the victim and any other members of the international society;
5. Nothing but aggression justifies war;
6. After the aggressor state has been militarily repulsed, it can also be punished.[19]

Because aggression is contrary to the legalist paradigm, the use of force against a state constitutes an international criminal act, giving rise to the legitimate use of defensive force. Although this legal framework provides the foundational structure for pursuing and maintaining international peace, Walzer recognizes that global order will not necessarily ensure domestic peace and justice. The paradigm might foster international tranquillity and deter aggression, but it will not necessarily ensure justice for individual people. Regimes that are internationally legitimate might be unjust domestically. As a result, Walzer provides for some exceptions to his legalist paradigm.[20] For example, states may carry out an anticipatory military attack if they have conclusive evidence of imminent attack and may intervene militarily in other states to assist viable secessionist movements or rescue peoples threatened with massacre.

For communitarians, models such as Walzer's legalist paradigm and Jones's code of peace are important in global politics because they provide a framework for sustaining international order and promoting international justice. Although some thinkers might consider structural models such as these in purely legal and political terms, Walzer's and Jones's models need to be viewed as ethical systems because they provide norms that, if fulfilled, can contribute to international justice.

Mandelbaum has observed that international boundaries must be based on some principle and that support for the status quo is the simplest one available. If this norm is discarded, all borders become suspect and the potential for international conflict and disorder are considerable. From an ethical perspective, the problem with this status quo argument is that it assumes that the existing cartography is morally legitimate. However, the existing international order has not been fashioned by norms of justice and human dignity but by arbitrary decisions by military and political leaders. As Mandelbaum notes, "Historically, the prize of independence has gone to those powerful or clever or fortunate or merely numerous enough to achieve it."[21] During the Cold War, the sovereignty norm was widely accepted and enforced by the major powers, but in the aftermath of the disintegration of the Soviet Union, the norm of self-determination has become increasingly powerful, challenging the sanctity of existing boundaries. As a result, the post-Cold War era has increasingly witnessed conflict and chaos as ethnic, religious, and political groups demand increasing political autonomy within existing territorial states. The conflict is rooted in the tension between two foundational norms of the post-Westphalian order: sovereignty and self-determination.

As noted earlier, ethics is concerned with the application of multiple and sometimes conflicting moral norms to individual and collective human conduct. Stanley Hoffmann, for example, has suggested that the contemporary international system is based on four norms: sovereignty, self-determination, self-government, and human rights.[22] Although Hoffmann does not prioritize these norms, it is possible to classify them, as shown in

Figure 6–1: Classification of Global Norms

| | | PRIORITY OF NORMS | |
		Primary	*Secondary*
UNIT	*Individual*	Human Rights	Self-Government
OF			
ANALYSIS	*Community*	Sovereignty	Self-Determination

Source: Developed by the author.

figure 6–1, in terms of unit of analysis (the individual and the community) and level of significance (primary and secondary). Because no ethical formula exists by which potential conflict among these norms can be resolved a priori, tensions must be resolved through arguments based on consistency, impartiality, and potential outcomes.

Although foreign intervention is undertaken for a variety of reasons, two major types of intervention are strategic and humanitarian. The former is carried out to advance the political interests of the intervening power, whereas the second seeks to protect and promote human rights. I next examine the ethics of each of these types of military intervention.

Strategic Intervention

Strategic intervention is foreign intervention that seeks to advance the national interests of an intervening state. Some of the major goals pursued through such intervention include territorial security, regional stability, political interests, economic prosperity, and ideological interests. Examples of strategic intervention include the following: the U.S. intervention in the Dominican Republic in 1965 and in Grenada in 1983, both of which were undertaken to prevent the spread of radical revolutionary regimes, and Vietnam's 1979 intervention in Kampuchea (Cambodia) and Tanzania's 1979 intervention in Uganda, both of which were undertaken to challenge repressive regimes that threatened territorial security and regional stability.

Krauthammer has argued that any foreign intervention should not only meet the test of morality—that is, be judged right in its goals and methods, but also be politically viable domestically, that is, be in the interests of the intervening state. Because intervention uses scarce economic and military resources, states must define those international interests that are important and those that are not. According to Krauthammer, interventions should be undertaken only when key national interests are at stake. He writes, "To intervene solely for reasons of democratic morality is to confuse foreign policy with philanthropy. And a philanthropist gives out his own money. A statesman is a trustee."[23] Thus, for Krauthammer, national goals are not only a legitimate justification for intervention but also a central precondition for any intervention.

Although strategic intervention can be viewed as an undesirable but nonetheless necessary, last-resort action to protect and advance vital state interests within the anarchic international system, such interventions are morally problematic because they violate sovereignty, a cherished norm of the international system. However, because sovereignty is not the sole or even most important norm of global society, the violation of the nonintervention rule might be morally legitimate in exceptional circumstances. Such circumstances might involve protecting a state's vital security interests from destabilizing domestic developments in neighboring states (e.g., civil war, genocide, radical reforms, or revolutionary politics), maintaining a favorable balance of power in a region, or countering strategic initiatives that threaten a state's vital interests. Because the international community recognizes the right of individual and collective defense, strategic interventions carried out to ensure territorial security would thus merit moral legitimacy. However, strategic interventions might also be morally legitimate because the values and interests being pursued by the intervening state are consistent with widely accepted norms of international morality. The national interests of the intervening state need not be inimical to the interests of the intervened state. Indeed, with the exception of the sovereignty norm, both the intervened and the intervening states might share a strong commitment to norms such as global order, human rights, regional security, self-determination, and economic prosperity. In short, interventions guided and justified in terms of national interests are not necessarily unethical.

As with all types of intervention, strategic intervention poses fundamental moral problems. Because the contemporary international community is regulated by a number of important norms, the dilemma of strategic intervention is basically this: Should the nonintervention norm be violated to advance other legitimate goals? Even where compelling evidence exists for overriding the sovereignty norm, scholars have identified norms that should be fulfilled prior to resorting to military action. Some of the most important of these norms have been developed from the just-war doctrine and include the following: (1) *last resort*—no military intervention should be attempted until all nonviolent alternatives have been exhausted; (2) *proportionality*—the evil done by the military action should be proportional to the good achieved by such action; and (3) *prospect of success*—there

must be a high probability of achieving the goals justifying the intervention.[24]

To illustrate the nature, role, and problematic moral character of strategic intervention, I next examine the U.S. intervention in Grenada in 1983.

CASE NO. 6–1
U.S. INTERVENTION IN GRENADA

Background

Grenada, a microstate about twice the size of the District of Columbia, is an
island in the southeastern Caribbean Sea with a population of about 110,000
persons. After receiving political independence from Britain in 1974, Grenada established a parliamentary government, headed by Eric Gairy, an ec-
centric, populist leader. Gairy then sought to consolidate his power by creating paramilitary squads designed to intimidate opposition groups. However,
the shift toward more repression backfired and led to even greater opposition
from left-wing groups, especially a radical nationalist group known as the
New Jewel Movement (NJM). Headed by Maurice Bishop, the NJM emphasized nationalism, mass participation, a Marxist ideology, and closer ties
with Cuba.

In March 1979, while Gairy was out of the country, Bishop led a blood-
less coup, overthrowing Grenada's weak but increasingly corrupt government and establishing his own People's Revolutionary Government (PRG).
Bishop immediately began espousing Marxist ideas and aligned his country
with Cuba and other communist regimes. As a result of Grenada's ideological shift, the Carter administration distanced itself from the PRG and even
considered blockading the island. After Ronald Reagan became president in
1981, the United States became even more aggressive in its opposition of
Grenada's PRG, bringing to a halt virtually all multilateral economic assistance to the island. When Grenada began building a 9,000-foot runway with
Cuban assistance, Reagan administration officials regarded this development
as part of a strategy to radicalize the Caribbean basin and to directly challenge U.S. efforts to extend democratic capitalism in the region.

Moreover, as a result of growing ideological tensions within the PRG,
Bishop was forced to share political power with a hard-line faction headed
by Bernard Coard, the deputy prime minister. When tensions between radical Marxists and hard-line Leninists proved insurmountable, Coard, with the
support of Army Commander General Hudson Austin, carried out a coup
against Bishop, placing him under house arrest. The arrest precipitated public demonstrations, riots, and a breakdown in public authority. A mass dem-
onstration in St. George's, Grenada's capital, resulted in the freeing of
Bishop, but in the ensuing power struggle Austin's revolutionary guards re-
captured and executed Bishop and killed several government and union officials. The guards then turned their guns on the demonstrators, killing up to
100 of them. In the immediate aftermath of Bishop's execution, the new mil-

itary and political leaders, headed by Coard and Austin, announced the creation of a new government headed by a revolutionary military council.

After the massacre, Sir Paul Scoon, the island's governor-general, concluded that foreign assistance was needed to restore order. At the same time, the elected leaders of five neighboring states (Barbados, Dominica, Jamaica, St. Kitts-Nevis, and St. Lucia), comprising the Organization of Eastern Caribbean States (OECS), concluded that the revolutionary conditions in Grenada were a threat to the region's stability. As a result, two days after the October 19 massacre, the OECS, along with Scoon, requested help from the United States to restore order in Grenada.

The U.S. Intervention

On October 25, four days after receiving the request for assistance, U.S. military forces invaded Grenada. The military intervention began with the night landing of Navy commandos near St. George's (to protect the island's governor-general). At daybreak, Marines attacked and captured Grenada's sole functioning airport on the eastern side of the island and then proceeded to take control of the southern, more populated area. Some 5,000 U.S. Army Rangers parachuted into Point Salines on the southern tip of the island, where the new airport was being constructed. Although U.S. forces encountered heavy resistance at first, especially from some several hundred armed Cubans, they rapidly consolidated control over the southern region, capturing the island's rebel leaders and securing all key military objectives within three days. Because the U.S. forces had destroyed all military opposition and consolidated power throughout the island by early November, the U.S. government began withdrawing troops so that by early December only token noncombatant forces remained to assist Grenada in transitioning to democratic rule.

U.S. government officials offered three justifications for taking military action against Grenada.[25] First, U.S. citizens in Grenada had to be protected. In a nationally televised address two days after the intervention had begun, President Reagan stated that the "overriding" reason for authorizing military action was to protect the lives of U.S. citizens seeking to leave the island. Second, the U.S. government was responding to a joint request of eastern Caribbean nations for collective defense, a request that U.S. government officials deemed consistent with Article 52 of the UN Charter, Articles 22 and 28 of the OAS Charter, and Article 8 of the OECS Treaty.[26] Although some international lawyers regarded U.S. action as legally appropriate,[27] others considered the intervention contrary to international law.[28] Third, Grenada's governor-general had requested assistance.[29]

Although government officials publicly defended the intervention of Grenada using these three arguments, the Reagan administration's underlying rationale for the military action, as viewed from a realist perspective, was to halt the spread of Marxism in the Caribbean basin. In particular, the United States intervened to confront the challenge posed by Grenada's radicalization and the threat posed by Soviet-Cuban geopolitical developments within the region.[30] During his first two years in office, President Reagan had repeatedly called attention to Grenada's increasingly radical politics and the threat that its Marxist alignment posed to the region. He believed that Grenada's radicalization threatened not only the Caribbean region but, by extension, the U.S. regional interests as well. As he noted in a speech in March 1983, "It isn't nutmeg that's at stake in the Caribbean and Central America, it's the United States' national security."[31] Thus, after U.S. forces found a large cache of weapons, sufficient to equip a 10,000-person army, and discovered an extensive network of secret bilateral agreements with Soviet-bloc states, Reagan administration officials felt vindicated in their judgment that Grenada's Soviet alignment and increasing militarization had threatened the region's security and the consolidation of democracy in the Caribbean basin.[32]

The Ethics of the Intervention

Was the intervention legal? Was it moral? From a strictly juridical perspective, the invasion was contrary to international law, notwithstanding the Reagan administration's claim to the contrary. It was illegal because it involved the violation of a country's sovereignty without the authorization of a legitimate international organization. This was the widespread view of most states of the international community, which expressed their overwhelming opposition (108 votes for, 9 against, and 27 abstentions) in a General Assembly resolution deploring the intervention as "a flagrant violation of international law." Even most close U.S. allies failed to support its action by abstaining on this UN action.

The OECS did request U.S. assistance, but it is doubtful that the organization's charter allows for collective security intervention against one of its members. Clearly, the preferable approach to intervention would have been to secure authorization by the United Nations and, failing that, by the OAS. According to Chapter VII of the UN Charter, the Security Council is the main institution responsible for determining when threats to international security exist and what actions are to be taken in response to those threats. When the United States intervened in Somalia in December 1991 to halt starvation and in Haiti in October 1994 to restore to power the elected president, Jean-Bertrand Aristide, it did so with the approval of the Security Council.

Although the OAS and UN charters prohibit foreign military intervention, they do not prohibit the use of force for self-defense. When the destabilizing events were unfolding in Grenada following Bishop's execution, the governor-general, along with OECS leaders, perceived security threats as immediate. Thus, they sought help from the major regional power, the United States. Although intervention critics are correct to point out that legally the OECS lacked a clear mandate to address collective defense, they also failed to appreciate the potential dangers from the unfolding events. As Michael Doyle has noted, critics seemed to have had more confidence in the views of distant states in Asia and Africa than in the views of Grenada's close neighbors, who called for the intervention. "Those are neighbors," writes Doyle, "whose democratic practices reflected Grenadian hopes, whose security was proximately involved, whose economies were closely linked to that of Grenada, whose Afro-Caribbean citizens have friends and relatives in Grenada."[33]

However legally ambiguous the intervention might have been, it is significant that the citizens in Grenada were staunchly in support of the U.S. action. In one poll taken soon after the invasion, 91 percent supported the intervention and the toppling of the Coard-Austin revolutionary regime. In a later, more sophisticated poll, 86 percent of the respondents indicated their approval of the intervention.[34] Although the United States undertook the intervention to support its strategic objectives of containing the spread of Marxist revolutionary regimes, it was also evident to Grenadians that the U.S. action was not designed to control the political destiny of the small island. Rather, the U.S. intervention was carried out solely to depose a revolutionary regime that had not only betrayed the people's trust but also was threatening the order and stability of the Caribbean basin. Thus, the aim of the intervention was to establish domestic order and quickly reestablish the preconditions under which Grenadians could resume their task of self-government.

From a strictly ethical perspective, the Grenada intervention was morally ambiguous. This was so because the ends and the means of the invasion—the conditions giving rise to U.S. action as well as the military force used to implement the policy goals—involved both beneficial and harmful effects. Because the main motives for U.S. action were strategic as well as humanitarian, the basic motives of the liberation operation were not solely moral. Although halting the spread of Marxist regimes, promoting stability in the Caribbean basin, and protecting the lives of U.S. citizens from civil unrest were all legitimate justifications for government concern, they did not give rise to an unambiguous call for foreign military action. Moreover, although Bishop and a number of his supporters had been killed, there had been no genocide, no systematic abuse of basic rights, and no gross violations of international human rights. What Grenadians, along with visiting foreigners, had to face were instability, loss of personal freedoms, growing oppression, and rising fear—conditions that one scholar has categorized as "ordinary oppression."[35] Thus, despite the growing dangers within Grenada, there was no unambiguous justification for humanitarian intervention.

However, legitimate authorities had requested help. Concerned about Grenada's growing ties with Cuba and other Marxist regimes, the massacre, and the demonstrations, the island's governor-general requested help. His call for assistance was a request for a rescue operation to help restore civic order. Moreover, the call for foreign help was supported by Grenada's neighbors, who viewed with growing apprehension the increasing instability and rising threat to human rights. Thus, although no widespread suffering had occurred to justify a humanitarian rescue operation, the Grenadians, through their governor-general, called for foreign assistance to restore legitimate self-rule.

Thus, it can be argued that, from an ends-based moral perspective, the intervention was undertaken for the benefit of most Grenadians. It sought to restore the ability of Grenadians to govern themselves, recognizing that the beneficence of such action also involved detrimental actions, such as the temporary violation of their nation's political sovereignty. As noted previously, public opinion polls strongly supporting U.S. military action suggest that notwithstanding its moral ambiguities, the Grenadians viewed the intervention as politically desirable and morally justifiable. The military action might have been a necessary evil but, according to Grenadians, its good outcomes far outweighed its costs.

Finally, in judging the morality of the American intervention, it is useful to briefly apply the just-war norms of last resort, proportionality, and prospect of success. Because little time was allowed to consider policy alternatives, the last-resort norm was probably not fulfilled. A week after Bishop was placed under house arrest, he was executed, and a week after NJM leaders and supporters were massacred, U.S. forces landed on Grenada. Although the United States had been opposed to Grenada's increasingly radical geopolitical alignment, the precipitating events arose suddenly and unexpectedly, allowing limited time to consider policy alternatives. Although other nonviolent policies could have been pursued, it is doubtful that other strategies would have achieved the desired objectives with less violence and lower political and economic costs. Second, in terms of the norm of proportionality, policy makers and military strategists tended to agree that the suffering and destruction from the anticipated intervention would be far less than the current and future humanitarian suffering and political oppression from a revolutionary regime. For most Grenadians, the estimated costs and destruction from military intervention were clearly justified by the anticipated good to be achieved through the restoration of civic order. Finally, given the extraordinary military power of the United States, there was complete certainty that the military operation would succeed, that is, that the just-war doctrine's "probability of success" norm would be fulfilled.

Moral Reflections

This case study raises a number of important ethical issues about the nature and role of military intervention.

- Was the U.S. strategy to contain the spread of Marxism in the Caribbean a morally legitimate foreign policy goal? Can the pursuit of strategic geopolitical goals, such as the containment of Marxism, be morally justified?
- Did the growing instability and repression in Grenada justify U.S. military action? Moreover, because political communities demonstrate communal viability through their capacity for self-government, did the foreign intervention impede or advance indigenous political self-determination?
- Because U.S. action was taken in response to requests for help from

the island's governor-general and the leaders of the OECS, were these requests sufficient to justify U.S. action legally and morally?

- Because it is unlikely that the just-war doctrine's last-resort norm was fulfilled prior to the invasion, should the United States have exhausted other peaceful alternatives, allowing the Coard-Austin junta to consolidate power? Or did extenuating circumstances justify an immediate military response?

- Because Grenada established a peaceful, democratic political system in the aftermath of the invasion, did this outcome justify the morally ambiguous intervention in 1983?

Humanitarian Intervention

According to Jack Donnelly, humanitarian intervention is foreign intervention that seeks "to remedy mass and flagrant violations of the basic human rights of foreign nationals by their government."[36] Although the most flagrant violations of basic rights have historically occurred in oppressive, dictatorial regimes, the most serious human rights abuses since the end of the Cold War have been due to civil war and the breakdown of government authority. Thus, although Donnelley's conceptualization might have been adequate during the Cold War, it is increasingly incomplete in addressing the gross human rights violations of the post-Cold War era. As a result, I define humanitarian intervention as foreign intervention (whether unilateral or multilateral) carried out to limit human suffering and death because of government oppression or because of a country's political disintegration.

In the contemporary era, the major threat to human rights in global society has come from "quasi" or "failed" states, that is, political communities in which government authority is weak or absent. Failed states generally result from two developments: first, the decline in the government's perceived legitimacy because of its unwillingness or inability to respond to popular demands and, second, the growing demands by ethnic, religious, and political minorities for increasing political autonomy. These two developments have led to growing civil strife and the breakdown of government authority in numerous countries, including Liberia, Rwanda, Sierra Leone, Somalia, Sudan, the former Yugoslavia, and former Soviet republics such as Azerbaijan, Georgia, Russia, and Tajikistan. Each of these territories has suffered from human rights abuses involving lawlessness, starvation, genocide, and mass migration. For example, the disintegration of Somalia's political system following the overthrow of the dictatorial rule of Siad Barre resulted in bitter conflict among Somali clan leaders (known as warlords). This conflict destroyed much of Somalia's infrastructure and impeded humanitarian distribution of food, resulting in widespread famine. The tribal conflict between the Hutus and the Tutsis in Rwanda similarly resulted in enormous human violence and suffering, including the death of more than a half million persons and the forced migration of more than two million Hutus. Finally, the disintegration of Yugoslavia in the aftermath of the Cold War resulted in a bitter war among Serbs, Croats, and Muslims, with the most intense fighting taking place over the political future of Bosnia-Herzegovina. This conflict is estimated to have caused some 200,000 deaths and displaced more than one million refugees.

Humanitarian intervention—foreign intervention designed to prevent and minimize gross human rights violations—poses legal and moral problems. Legally, humanitarian intervention challenges the established norm of state sovereignty; morally, it challenges the right of communal self-determination. As noted previously, because nonintervention and self-determination are not the only or even the most important norms in the international system, statesmen must devise prudential policies that take into account competing principles, including the demand for order and justice, stability and human rights. Thus, when gross human rights violations occur in a foreign country, statesmen must determine whether, when, and how their governments should respond.

As with strategic intervention, humanitarian intervention is generally justified if it passes two tests: a political test and an ethical test. First, humanitarian intervention must be in the interests of the intervening state or states. This condition is satisfied when the intervening state perceives human rights abuses in a foreign country as either a *general* threat to the order, legitimacy, and morality of global society or, as is most often the case, a *particular* threat to its own economic prosperity, political influence, and territorial integrity. The intervening state might also regard the breakdown in civic order and the growing human rights abuses as a legal obligation in fulfillment of bilateral and multilateral treaty obligations. For example, the United States viewed the breakdown in civic order in Haiti in the early 1990s as its major foreign policy responsibility because of Haiti's geographical proximity to the United States. Similarly, European states were considered to have primary responsibility for containing and resolving the war in the former Yugoslavia. Their geopolitical responsibility was perceived to be rooted in geographical proximity, historical ties, and close ethnic and religious bonds between European and Serbo-Croatian peoples.

Second, humanitarian intervention must be in the interests of the people and communities of the intervened state; that is, the evil of military intervention must be justified by the good accomplished in the penetrated state. Because the aim is to relieve the famine, genocide, and human suffering, this condition is satisfied when existing human rights violations are reduced or eliminated and preconditions are established that prevent their immediate recurrence. It is important to emphasize that right intentions are not a sufficient condition to justify humanitarian intervention. As noted in chapter 2, because an ethical policy must be judged in terms of its goals, means, and likely outcomes, a morally legitimate intervention must be just in its goals as well as its methods and results. Noble intentions are not enough. A policy designed to relieve human suffering through military intervention must, if it is to be considered moral, have a high probability of successfully achieving its goals in both the short and the medium term.

Even when these two conditions are satisfied, the decision to intervene is never easy because it normally will involve trade-offs among relevant norms. In particular, humanitarian intervention will involve a choice between nonintervention and human rights, sovereignty and suffering. Nonintervention is an important norm in the international community, but it is not the only, or even most important, moral principle applicable to the foreign relations of states. The challenge for the statesman is to weigh the relative merits of nonintervention, human rights, and other relevant norms to promote both peace and justice.

To illustrate the nature and role of moral values in humanitarian intervention, I next examine the nature, role, and effects of the U.S. intervention in Somalia in 1992.

CASE NO. 6–2
THE SOMALIA INTERVENTION

Background

The U.S. military intervention in Somalia in December 1992 was precipitated by a massive famine that had led to the death of more than 300,000 persons and threatened the lives of another one to two million. The famine was a direct result of bloody civil war among rival clans that had developed from the ouster of the military dictatorship of General Mohammed Siad Barre, who had ruled Somalia from 1969 until January 1991. Following the overthrow of the Siad Barre regime, civil authority had broken down, and much of the country, especially the Somalian capital of Mogadishu, was in virtual anarchy. When lawlessness intensified in late 1991, the United Nations halted humanitarian relief efforts until a cease-fire could be arranged. In April 1992, the UN Security Council authorized a 500-member peacekeeping force—known as UN Operation in Somalia (UNOSOM I)—to protect the relief convoys. When this force proved inadequate, 3,000 more peacekeepers were added. However, even this larger UN force proved incapable of maintaining rudimentary order and could not even ensure the distribution of food in the face of massive starvation.

In light of a deteriorating political situation, President George Bush authorized the intervention of U.S. forces into Somalia to permit the resumption of humanitarian relief.[37] The U.S. intervention was unique in the annals of international relations because it was the first time that the United Nations had authorized a largely single-state military intervention without an invitation or consent of the government. Such consent was impossible because no functioning government existed in Somalia. Indeed, the gross human rights violations were a direct by-product of a civil war among warlords, each vying for the right to rule Somalia. Thus, on December 3, the Security Council adopted Resolution 794, which endorsed the U.S. offer to lead a multinational peacemaking force. Unlike other UN peacekeeping operations, the goal of this interventionary force, justified under Chapter VII of the UN Charter, was not to keep contestants apart but to impose order through military force. The aim, however, was not political but humanitarian because the goal of establishing order was to allow the resumption of humanitarian relief to prevent further starvation.

Operation Restore Hope began in mid-December with the landing of 3,000 U.S. Marines. The U.S. forces quickly increased to nearly 28,000 soldiers and in time was supplemented by some 10,000 troops from other countries. Although the Unified Task Force (UNITAF) was formally a multinational operation, in actuality it was a unilateral military operation authorized by the Security Council. The planning, organization, and execution of the interventionary force was carried out solely by one foreign state—the United States. Organizationally, the intervention was similar to Desert Storm, the U.S.-led military operation that liberated Kuwait from Iraq in early 1992.

After U.S. Marines landed unopposed, they quickly consolidated control over Mogadishu and its port and airport and then extended control over the urban centers and villages in central Somalia, where the famine was most severe. Within a month, U.S. military forces had established secure transportation links to key urban centers, thereby ensuring the effective distribution of humanitarian relief. After achieving its basic mission of establishing basic political order and ensuring the distribution of famine relief, U.S. forces were gradually reduced, so that by May 1993 only about 5,000 American soldiers remained from the original deployment.

On May 4, the United States ended its peacemaking task and formally transferred authority to a new, large (20,000 soldiers and 8,000 support staff) UN peacekeeping mission—UNOSOM II. Unlike the earlier mission, UNOSOM II had a greatly expanded mandate, authorized not only to maintain order but also to help create the conditions and institutions considered necessary for peaceful self-rule. Whereas the first peacekeeping mission was limited to ensuring famine relief, UNOSOM II, as authorized by Security Council Resolution 814, called for the "consolidation, expansion, and maintenance of a secure environment throughout Somalia" and "the rehabilitation of the political institutions and economy of Somalia." In effect, the original peacekeeping mission was extended from keeping order and facilitating humanitarian relief to nation building. In addition, the new peacekeeping operation is important because it was justified, for the first time in UN history, under Chapter VII of the UN Charter. Finally, UNOSOM II is important because, unlike the first mission, the United States pledged to support this operation with 4,000 soldiers, including a 1,300-member Quick Reaction Force.

In view of UNOSOM II's broader peacekeeping mandate, conflict was inevitable between UN forces and the dominant Somali warlord, General Mohammad Farrah Aideed, and his Somali National Alliance (SNA) forces. After SNA troops ambushed UN peacekeepers, killing 24 Pakistani soldiers, the Security Council authorized UN forces to "take all necessary measures" against those responsible for this attack. Over the next four months, conflict between Aideed's SNA and UN peacekeepers intensified, culminating in one of the deadliest battles in UN peacekeeping history. The October 3 firefight, which was precipitated by a surprise raid by U.S. Army Rangers on an SNA center, killed 18 U.S. soldiers and injured 78 and killed or injured between 500 and 1,000 Somalis. Shortly thereafter, President Bill Clinton, under heavy congressional pressure, announced that he was modifying the U.S. role in Somalia from what two U.S. diplomats described as "its admittedly overambitious vision of assertive multilateralism and rebuilding failed states."[38] According to Clinton, U.S. forces would no longer seek to forcefully disarm Somali clans and would withdraw all forces no later than March 31, 1994, even though additional forces were temporarily authorized to increase the security of existing troops deployed in Somalia. Subsequently, UN Secretary-General Boutros Boutros-Ghali and the Security Council set March 31, 1995, as the final date for the withdrawal of all UN peacekeeping forces.

The Ethics of the Somalia Intervention

From a legal perspective, there is little doubt that the original Somalia intervention was legitimate. Because all civil authority had broken down in Somalia as a result of war, the Security Council-sanctioned UNITAF provided the necessary legitimacy for the U.S.-led operation to restore order and thereby resume humanitarian relief. However, it is important to emphasize that this UN-sanctioned force was legally unprecedented: It was the first time that the Security Council had authorized intervention in a state without its consent.[39]

From a political perspective, scholars and public officials disagreed over the merits of UNITAF. According to Alberto Coll, these political differences were fundamentally between "interest-driven realists" and "values-driven globalists."[40] For the former, humanitarian intervention was unwise because there were no clearly defined U.S. interests in Somalia. For example, John Bolton, the assistant secretary of state for international organization affairs at the time of the U.S. operation and an opponent of the action, has suggested that the fundamental failure of U.S. decision makers was the attempt "to adapt the world and U.S. policy to idealized and untested models, rather than to define U.S. interests and then pursue them."[41] For globalists, however, humanitarian intervention was important to prevent the spread of war and suffering in the African continent, because "[i]nternational society, morality, and basic decency form one whole fabric."[42] Despite the high cost of the U.S. intervention ($2 billion for the military operations alone), globalists, such as Chester Crocker, have argued that U.S. action was well justified in protecting life and in temporarily restoring political order to Somalia. For Crocker, U.S. general interests were served by Operation Restore Hope because the United States, as the leading state in the international system, has an interest in the overall stability and well-being of the global society. Crocker writes, "As the end of the century nears, it is surely wise that we and others broaden our understanding of national interest to include consideration of interests related to global order (sanctity of borders, extension of the Nuclear Nonproliferation Treaty) and global standards (avoiding genocide, mass humanitarian catastrophe)."[43]

From an ethical perspective, there is also little doubt that Operation Restore Hope, the first phase of the military intervention, was morally legitimate. Following the tridimensional framework developed in chapter 2, it is clear that the operation's goals (the restoration of order for humanitarian reasons), means (the use of limited, UN-sanctioned force, undertaken as a last resort), and ends (the restoration of order to resume humanitarian relief) were consistent with moral values commonly accepted in global society. However, if the humanitarian intervention under UNITAF was morally compelling, this was not necessarily the case for the expanded mission of the United Nations under UNOSOM II. Because political viability and self-help are important criteria in determining authentic self-determination, the expansion of peacemaking to include nation building, although legally justified by the United Nations, was politically and morally problematic. Politically, it was problematic because it sought to settle an indigenous war among clans by seeking to demilitarize the warring factions while remaining impartial to their claims. However, if wars are to result in a political settlement, the parties themselves must be involved in the settlement. This normally occurs after the warring parties tire of fighting and make a compromise or when the victorious party imposes a settlement on the loser. However, seeking to build a political order without a prior fundamental settlement among the parties is unlikely to foster a long-term peace. Moreover, because nation building requires significant military forces to encourage and if necessary to impose a settlement on the recalcitrant factions, it is a demanding task that is not well suited to lightly armed multilateral peacekeeping forces. In short, because communal solidarity and legitimacy must be earned by the people themselves, the expansion of UNOSOM's mandate was morally problematic because it impaired authentic political development.

Moral Reflections

This case study raises a number of critical issues about the ethics of humanitarian intervention.

- Was U.S. intervention morally warranted? Given the many other needs in the world, did the Somalian famine present a compelling case for U.S. action?
- In carrying out its foreign policy, should the United States be guided by narrowly defined national interests, or should it seek to carry out initiatives that are consistent with global values?
- This case raises important issues about trade-offs between short-term and long-term goals. Is short-term humanitarian relief morally warranted without also the effort to remedy the underlying conditions giving rise to such needs? Is short-term response to human suffering an adequate moral strategy, or must humanitarian relief also address the fundamental causes of human suffering? More specifically, should U.S. forces have sought to demilitarize the warring factions after successfully establishing the resumption of humanitarian relief?
- Although the U.S. military operation (UNITAF) is generally regarded as morally unassailable and politically legitimate, this is not the case for UNOSOM II. What should have been the mission of this peacekeeping operation? Was the extension of the UN mission to include some nation-building tasks a morally and politically prudent action or should the UN operation have simply sought to prevent the resumption of fighting?
- This case raises issues of moral consistency, especially when compared with the U.S. inaction in the Rwanda genocide (see chapter 4). Although the human needs in Rwanda might have been more pressing than those in Somalia, by what moral calculus could the United States have intervened in Somalia but not in Rwanda?

Summary

The nonintervention norm is an important legal and moral rule in the contemporary international system. In light of the decentralized nation-state system, honoring the sovereignty and territorial integrity of states helps maintain international peace. However, nonintervention is not the only or even the most important norm in global society. Conditions might arise that justify the forceful intervention against another state. Whether military intervention is carried out for strategic or humanitarian purposes, it should be undertaken only when the goals are morally legitimate, where intended goals are likely to be realized, and after peaceful alternatives have been exhausted. Military intervention, especially humanitarian intervention, might be morally warranted to prevent widespread human rights atrocities. As a result, the U.S. intervention in Somalia to prevent starvation was morally legitimate because it prevented the deaths of hundreds of thousands of persons. Similarly, although the major powers (with the exception of France) chose not to carry out military action in Rwanda in 1994, military intervention to halt the genocide in that land (Case No. 4–2) would have also been justified. Still, whether acting unilaterally or multi-laterally, states should regard the violation of the nonintervention norm as an exceptional action that is contrary to the long-term interests of the international community.

CHAPTER SEVEN

THE ETHICS OF ECONOMIC SANCTIONS

A nation boycotted is a nation that is in sight of surrender.
Apply this economic, peaceful, silent, deadly remedy and
there will be no need for force. It is a terrible remedy. It does
not cost a life outside the nation boycotted, but it brings pressure upon that nation that, in my judgment, no modern nation
could resist.

Woodrow Wilson[1]

Wreaking economic havoc on an impoverished developing
country that is already unable to meet the basic needs of its
people hardly commends itself as appropriate action, even if
the foreign or domestic policy of the country concerned merits an international response.

Margaret Doxey[2]

I do not understand how your Christian conscience allows
you [Bishop Tutu] to advocate disinvestment. I do not understand how you can put a man out of work for a high moral
principle. You put a man out of a job and make his family go
hungry so that some high moral principle could be upheld. I
think your morality is confused just as was the morality of
the church in the Inquisition, or the morality of Dr. Verwoerd
in his utopian dreams. You come near to saying that the end
justifies the means, which is a thing no Christian can do.

Alan Paton[3]

States use a variety of foreign policy instruments to influence the behavior
of foreign countries. These include, in order of increasing coerciveness,

145

secret diplomacy, speeches, public condemnation, mild sanctions, comprehensive sanctions, limited military action, military intervention, and war. From an ethical perspective, the most desirable method of pursuing foreign policy goals and of resolving interstate conflicts is through peaceful negotiation. However, when states are unable to resolve disputes through reason and persuasion, they frequently resort to coercive measures, including the use of economic pressures and military force. In the previous two chapters, I examined the ethics of force; here, I analyze the nature, role, and morality of economic sanctions.

The first part of this chapter examines the major goals of economic sanctions and their effectiveness in achieving policy goals. In assessing the relative effectiveness of sanctions, I differentiate between the success in imposing economic hardship and the success in achieving behavioral reform. A case study on trade sanctions and the promotion of human rights illuminates the problem of using economic penalties to encourage policy changes in the target country. The second part of the chapter examines the ethical legitimacy of economic sanctions by applying moral norms derived from the just-war doctrine. Although economic sanctions are normally viewed as an alternative to war, just-war norms provide a useful moral structure by which to judge the ethics of sanctions. A case study on South African economic sanctions illustrates the morally ambiguous role of economic statecraft.

The Aims and Effects of Economic Sanctions

Economic sanctions are a particular type of statecraft used to advance foreign policy goals. According to David Baldwin, sanctions are "influence attempts" in which states seek to exert power over other international actors, that is, to get them to do what they otherwise would not do.[4] The major difference between economic statecraft and military statecraft does not lie in the level of coercion or destructiveness involved but in the nature of the tools used: Military statecraft relies on force to influence other states (through rewards or punishment), whereas economic statecraft relies on economic instruments.

Strictly speaking, economic sanctions can involve positive incentives ("carrots") designed to induce or reward desirable behaviors or negative actions ("sticks") designed to punish actors for illegal or undesirable behaviors, to deter unwanted behavior, and to compel desired political change. According to the logic of positive sanctions, an effective way to influence the behavior of other states is to provide economic rewards, such as an increase in foreign aid, the expansion of foreign loans at concessionary rates, or the granting of preferential trade treatment. By contrast, the logic of negative sanctions assumes that the most effective way to deter unwanted actions or to compel behavioral change is through the imposition of economic penalties. These sanctions might range from modest actions, such as selected quotas, limited tariff increases, or the reduction of foreign aid, to more extreme measures, such as a freeze of foreign assets, a halt to foreign investment, a ban on technology transfers, or a total economic blockade, the most extreme economic measure. Although some scholars have suggested that positive sanctions are much more likely to induce behavioral change than threats or punishment, negative sanctions have been used more commonly in contemporary international relations than positive inducements.[5] Because most economic sanctions are negative in character, the discussion here is limited to this type of statecraft.

The Goals of Sanctions

Historically, states have used economic sanctions for a variety of reasons. James Lindsay, for example, has identified five reasons that states have imposed trade sanctions: (1) *compliance*—forcing a state to alter its behavior in conformity with the sanctioning state's preferences; (2) *subversion*—seeking to remove particular political leaders from office or attempting to overthrow a regime; (3) *deterrence*—dissuading a target state from carrying out unacceptable behavior; (4) *international symbolism*—sending a message to other governments; and (5) *domestic symbolism*—increasing domestic political support by undertaking a popular public policy initiative.[6] In addition, sanctions are imposed as punishment for actions perceived as objectionable. As Kim Nossal has noted, states use economic punishment as retribution for prior harmful or evil acts in the hope that such penalties will rectify past injustices and deter future objectionable behaviors.[7]

Although most major powers have historically used economic sanctions as an instrument of foreign policy, the United States, more than any other country, has relied on economic statecraft in recent decades to seek to influence the behavior of foreign states. For example, one study of U.S. economic sanctions in the post-Cold War era found that during the 1993–96 period, the government imposed sanctions or passed legislation to do so sixty times against thirty-five countries. The major reasons for imposing unilateral sanctions were to promote human rights and democratization (twenty-two times), to punish and deter terrorism (fourteen), to curb and deter nuclear proliferation (nine), to curb drug trafficking (eight), to foster political stability (eight), and to promote workers' rights and condemn prison labor (six). The principal countries targeted with sanctions were Iran (eleven times), Cuba (nine), Sudan (seven), and China (six).[8]

The Impact of Sanctions

One of the most widely accepted ideas about international statecraft is that economic sanctions are an ineffective instrument of foreign policy. Economist Charles Kindleberger asserts that "most sanctions are not effective,"[9] whereas Margaret Doxey concludes her analysis of sanctions by noting that "in none of the cases analyzed . . . have economic sanctions succeeded in producing the desired political result."[10] In light of the perceived ineffectiveness of sanctions, David Baldwin observes that "[i]t would be difficult to find any proposition in international relations literature more widely accepted than those belittling the utility of economic techniques of statecraft."[11] Moreover, after reviewing seven decades of public statements and scholarly literature, M. S. Daoudi and J. S. Dajani conclude that the idea that sanctions do not work is so widespread that this notion has become nearly axiomatic.[12]

In assessing the effectiveness of sanctions, it is important to distinguish between their economic success and political success, between the economic hardship imposed on the target state through sanctions and the degree of political compliance realized through such penalties.[13] Because a major assumption of economic statecraft is that changes in economic welfare in a target state will induce desired policy changes, economic success is generally regarded as a precondition for political effectiveness.

Economic success: What factors influence the economic success of sanctions? According to one major study of 115 sanctions episodes from 1914 to 1990, economic sanctions have achieved their greatest economic harm when the following conditions were met:

- The target state was economically weaker and politically less stable than the sender; in effect, the relationship was asymmetrical. In successful sanctions episodes, the average sender's economy was 187 times larger than that of the average target state.
- The target and sender had a high level of economic interdependence. In successful sanctions cases, the target state depended on the sender for an average of 28 percent of its total trade.
- Sanctions were imposed quickly and decisively, thereby enhancing the political credibility of the sanctions and increasing the potential for economic harm by preventing the target state from effectively adjusting to the imposed hardship.
- The cost of the sanctions to the target state was significant, generally exceeding 2 percent of its gross national product (GNP).[14]

Another factor that can influence the economic effectiveness of sanctions is the level of multilateral participation. Because most economic goods and services are highly fungible (i.e., can be replaced or substituted), broad participation, especially from the major powers, is normally a prerequisite for imposing the desired hardship on the target state. The importance of collective action was illustrated in 1990–91 during the Persian Gulf crisis, when the United Nations imposed comprehensive economic sanctions against Iraq. Because nearly every country honored the embargo, Iraq's GNP declined by nearly 50 percent. By contrast, the U.S.-led economic embargo against Cuba has been relatively ineffective because few major states have supported this thirty-five-year old policy.

Finally, significant participation by nongovernment actors can also increase the economic success of sanctions. Given the increasing independent power of multinational corporations and other private actors, their support for sanctions can greatly reinforce and intensify sanctions. For example, in response to growing U.S. domestic opposition to South African apartheid, private actors encouraged private divestment and directly pressured American banks and corporations to institute disinvestment programs.[15] These private initiatives not only reinforced the policies of Western governments but also greatly intensified them. Indeed, private disinvestment by American financial institutions and corporations brought far greater harm to the South African economy in the 1980s than did government-imposed sanctions.

Political success: Political success refers to the probability that economic sanctions will lead to desired behavioral changes in the target state. The fundamental assumption of economic sanctions is that negative penalties will discourage existing policies and foster behavioral reform. Although economic "sticks" can no doubt affect the behavior of foreign actors, it is doubtful that economic coercion alone will determine the political decisions of foreign states. For one thing, foreign policy decision making is a multidimensional process that is subject to numerous domestic and international influences. Moreover, as noted previously, some scholars have questioned the belief that economic adversity encourages behavioral reform, arguing that positive inducements are far more likely to achieve desirable policy objectives than economic penalties.

What is the historical record on economic sanctions? According to one comprehensive study, economic sanctions during the 1914–90 period were successful in bringing about desired reforms in about one-third of the cases.[16] However, another scholar, using the same data, has argued that the success rate is less than 5 percent![17] Regardless of whether one accepts the optimistic or pessimistic measures of political success, it is clear that the application of economic hardship has not often resulted in desired political outcomes. Although it is clear that major economic sanctions can result in significant hardship to the target state, such adversity does not automatically translate into desired policy reforms. However, to the extent that sanctions foster desired outcomes, their political effectiveness is likely to depend on three factors: the openness of the target society; the scope and significance of the demands placed on the target state; and the level of multilateral participation.

First, economic sanctions are likely to have far more impact on democratic systems than on autocratic regimes. Because military governments and dictatorial regimes depend less on public opinion, international economic pressures are generally ineffective in influencing regime decision making. For example, the economic sanctions imposed by the United States against Cuba, Iran, Iraq, and Libya have failed either to achieve desired policy goals or to undermine these regimes, in great part because they are undemocratic and largely unresponsive to public pressures.

Second, because economic sanctions are a "marginal" tool of statecraft,[18] they are most effective when applied to nonvital issues. When the aim is to topple an existing regime or to compel major changes in international behavior they are likely to be strongly resisted by the target state. For example, the economic sanctions imposed on Rhodesia in the 1970s to foster democratic rule, on Nicaragua in the 1980s to promote political pluralism, and on Iraq in the mid-1990s to comply with UN-imposed weapons disarmament were largely ineffective because the target governments considered such statecraft a direct affront to national sovereignty.[19] The case study on the U.S. policy debate over granting most-favored-nation (MFN) trading status to China illustrates the limitations of sanctions in fomenting major domestic reforms.

Finally, political success requires international support, especially from the major powers and from neighboring states. Global support is important because it increases the political credibility of sanctions. A lack of international cooperation will not only impair the economic effectiveness of the sanctions but also compromise the perception of resolve. As noted previously, the thirty-five-year economic embargo by the United States against Cuba has been a failure in great part because other industrial powers have been unwilling to support U.S. policy.

CASE NO. 7–1
CHINA, HUMAN RIGHTS, AND MFN STATUS

Background

As a result of its normalization of bilateral relations in 1978, the United States began granting China MFN trade status.[20] The granting of MFN, coupled with China's domestic economic liberalization, contributed to China's significant economic expansion and led to a dramatic increase in trade between the two states. By the early 1980s, the Chinese economy was growing at nearly 10 percent per year, the highest rate in the world and one that persisted for another decade. By 1994, the value of annual trade between China and the United States had grown to more than $40 billion, with China's exports to the United States accounting for more than 40 percent of its total trade.

According to the amended Trade Law of 1974, the renewal of MFN depends on a state's honoring the human right of emigration.[21] Because China, unlike the Soviet Union, had not sought to restrict emigration, the United States regularly renewed its MFN status. However, when Chinese authorities massacred an untold number of demonstrators in Beijing's Tiananmen Square in 1989 and instituted their crackdown on dissidents pressing for democratic reforms, the United States imposed modest sanctions but did not withdraw MFN.

The underlying assumption of the Bush administration was that increased U.S. engagement and continued economic expansion through market reforms would help create the social and economic preconditions conducive to greater democratization and increased respect for human rights. Isolating China through economic sanctions would only impede potential reforms. As James Lilley, a former U.S. ambassador to China, observed, the United States could best foster democratic forces and enhance human rights by broadening American involvement in China's economy. "Rapid economic growth and joint ventures," he writes, "have done more to improve the human rights situation in South China than innumerable threats, demarches, and unilaterally imposed conditions."[22]

Human Rights and Trade

During the 1992 presidential campaign, Bill Clinton repeatedly charged that President George Bush was neglecting human rights and coddling China's tyrants. Clinton promised that, if elected, he would confront China about its disregard for international human rights. Thus, when he was elected president, he was confronted with how to reconcile his campaign pledges on human rights with the continuation and expansion of U.S.-China economic relations. Officials within his own administration were deeply divided, with the Department of State being most strongly committed to the enforcement of human rights and the Departments of Treasury and Commerce being far more sympathetic to the demands for strong bilateral economic ties. As the May 1993 MFN deadline approached, both human rights activists and corporate organizations intensified their government lobbying. To reinforce corporate influence, the Chinese government went on a U.S. buying spree, placing orders for more than $1.1 billion in goods: $800 million for Boeing aircraft, $160 million for automobiles, and $200 million for oil drilling equipment.

Rather than giving precedence to either trade or human rights, President Clinton decided in May 1993 to partially satisfy both human rights goals and business interests. He did so by renewing MFN but also by imposing stricter human rights conditions on future MFN renewals. Thus, when the president announced the continuation of MFN, he issued an executive order declaring that future MFN renewals would depend on "significant progress" in se-

lected human rights areas.[23] Because China's trade balance with the United
States exceeded $23 billion at the time, U.S. government officials were hope-
ful that China's large trade surplus would foster greater compliance with
human rights norms.

As anticipated by some, Clinton's confrontational policy did not lead to
improved human rights conditions in China. Indeed, the human rights initiatives were accompanied not only by increasingly repressive treatment of political dissidents and religious minorities but also by strained U.S.-China relations. One scholar estimates that more political arrests and trials occurred
in 1994 than in any year since the Tiananmen Square crackdown began in
1989.[24] The policy of threatening the withdrawal of MFN status if human
rights abuses were not reduced was clearly not working. As a result, President Clinton announced in June 1994 the "delinking" of MFN renewal from
China's human rights record. Although the United States would continue to
promote human rights, it would not make the continuation of MFN status
conditional on China's human rights record. Thus, despite Clinton's condemnation of the "engagement" strategy of previous administrations, his administration has pursued such a policy since 1994.

The Sanctions Debate

The continued human rights abuses by the government of China presents a
classic dilemma between two approaches to economic statecraft: isolation
and engagement, or what one scholar has termed strategies of "asphyxiation" and "oxygen."[25] The first strategy assumes that the United States
should hold China accountable for human rights violations and abuses. Because China has failed to improve its human rights record since the 1989
Tiananmen Square massacre, the United States should impose economic
penalties, withdrawing MFN status at a minimum. The second strategy assumes that notwithstanding human rights violations, the United States
should maintain and increase economic contact, using international economic relations to foster economic development and encourage political liberalization.

Although the continuation of MFN status might not lead to human rights
improvements, the previous analysis casts doubt on the effectiveness of economic sanctions in fostering behavioral change. Sanctions critics argue that
an isolation strategy is likely to be ineffective in fostering Chinese human
rights reforms for three reasons. First, if the United States were to seek to
isolate China, it would stand largely alone. European countries, as well as
China's East Asian neighbors, strongly support a strategy of engagement
and are unlikely to support an alternative policy. Second, although withdrawal of MFN might result in China's loss of $15 billion in U.S. trade reve-
nue, this total would represent a small fraction of China's economy (less than
one-half of 1 percent of China's $3 trillion GNP). Third, and most important,
because a nation's ideology, structure of government, and conceptualization
of human rights are deeply rooted in its core values, the attempt by a foreign

state to influence human rights practices is likely to be interpreted as an affront to national sovereignty and would thus be resisted.

Moral Reflections

This case raises a number of important questions about the appropriateness of economic sanctions as a policy instrument.

- If the aim of the United States is to foster democratic reforms and to help consolidate democratic capitalism in China, what is the most effective strategy to advance these goals: isolation or engagement, punishment or positive incentives? When is isolation and economic coercion preferable to engagement and positive incentives?
- During the mid-1980s, this issue was widely debated with regard to U.S. policy toward South Africa. The Reagan administration's policy of constructive engagement was based on the assumption that the most effective way to weaken the apartheid regime and foster democracy was to maintain a high level of interaction with South Africa. Administration critics, by contrast, argued that the Afrikaner regime needed to be punished, weakened, and isolated by the imposition of comprehensive economic sanctions. The aims of such sanctions were to limit trade, reduce foreign direct investment, and isolate the country from the international community of states. Was the imposition of sanctions against South Africa warranted? Should a similar strategy be pursued against China? Why or why not?
- The China-MFN debate also suggests the difficulty of imposing sanctions when the target and the sending states have a high level of economic interaction. Since the 1980s, U.S. foreign direct investment and volume of merchandise trade have grown significantly. In the mid-1990s, the volume of annual trade between the two countries exceeded $50 billion while foreign direct investment continued to rise. As a result, investors, traders, and consumers have had a significant and growing stake in the policy debates over China. In view of the high level of economic interdependence with China, should domestic economic interests dictate U.S. foreign policy? Should the promotion of human rights be qualified by commercial or business interests?
- This case raises questions concerning the effectiveness of unilateral sanctions, especially when the target state is a strong economic power and unilateral sanctions are likely to lead to trade diversion and thereby result in limited economic harm. In view of alternative sources for imports and exports, is the imposition of unilateral sanctions a prudent policy? Should economic sanctions, especially against a major economic power, be based on multilateral participation?

The Effectiveness of Sanctions

The previously noted general skepticism about the overall effectiveness of sanctions does not derive from the inability to impose economic hardship on the target state but from the dubious assumption that punishment encourages behavioral reform. Although adversity can encourage capitulation, it can also increase resolve and determination, especially if the target state considers the issues of vital national interest. In addition, sanctions can be politically ineffective because economic harm frequently falls disproportionately on the average citizen while only marginally affecting a regime's political and military leadership. For example, when the United States imposed comprehensive sanctions against Panama in 1988 to topple the government of General Manuel Noriega, the sanctions brought severe hardship to Panamanian civilians but had limited impact on government and military officials.[26]

Perhaps one of the reasons that sanctions have generally been considered ineffective tools is that they have been judged successful only when the desired political goals are achieved. As noted earlier, one major study of economic sanctions found that during the 1946–89 period, sanctions achieved behavioral changes in only 34 percent of the cases. Moreover, the study found that during the first half of this period, sanctions were far more effective politically than in the second half, with the success rate declining from a pre-1973 average of 44 percent to an average of only 25 percent in the 1973–89 period.[27]

However, if the success of sanctions is determined not solely by the political and government changes achieved but also as part of a state's overall repertoire for exercising influence and communicating intentions in global affairs, sanctions can be considered far more effective. Indeed, Baldwin argues that the received wisdom that sanctions are ineffective is wrong because sanctions can serve as effective communications symbols in interstate bargaining.[28] Lisa Martin similarly suggests that the role of economic sanctions has been underestimated and argues that sanctions can be especially effective in demonstrating resolve and in sending signals.[29] In her view, such signaling is most effective when carried out multilaterally and when senders demonstrate resolve by their willingness to suffer economic loss. In addition, it is important to note that the effectiveness of sanctions as instruments of communication need not be based on the direct economic harm inflicted by sanctions. As William Kaempfer and Anton Lowenberg have noted, the impact of signals and threats communicated through sanctions is "unrelated to their market or income effects" because private actors can carry out actions that hasten the desired political reforms.[30]

The important role of sanctions as symbols and instruments of communication has been illustrated in many recent sanctions episodes. For example, when the United States imposed economic sanctions on South Africa in 1985 and 1986, it did so to communicate its opposition to apartheid, not for the instrumental purpose of fostering domestic reforms in the apartheid regime. Additionally, when the United States, supported by the Organization of American States and the United Nations, imposed increasingly stringent sanctions against the military regime in Haiti for failing to restore elected president Jean-Bertrand Aristide to power, it did so mainly to signal its commitment to democratic government.

Sanctions imposed as punishment are also generally perceived as successful because all that is required for them to be effective is to cause significant economic hardship on a target state. When the international community imposed major economic sanctions against Haiti in 1991, the hardship was perceived as a legitimate price for the toppling of the elected government. When the United Nations imposed comprehensive sanctions against Serbia in 1992 in response to its continued military aggression against Bosnia and Croatia, the sanctions were considered effective because of the hardship they imposed on Serb society, even though they did not lead to behavioral changes by Serb authorities.

Finally, sanctions are regarded as successful when they inhibit or delay the use of force. Because war is generally far more destructive than economic sanctions, the latter are generally considered a morally preferable tool of statecraft to military force. As a result, economic sanctions can be viewed as successful when they allow the sending state to impose harm on the target state without resorting to military force.[31] However, under this minimalist standard, virtually all sanctions episodes are likely to be viewed as successful, whether or not the target state modifies its policies.

In short, economic sanctions remain a popular tool of statecraft not because they are effective tools of deterrence and compliance but because they are cheap and powerful symbols of communication. Although the instruments of economic coercion might not lead directly to behavioral reform, they can galvanize domestic and international public opinion, thereby weakening the government's authority in the target state. To the extent that economic sanctions weaken and isolate a regime, as was the case with government and nongovernment sanctions toward South Africa in the 1980s (see Case No. 7–2), they can encourage the target state to alter its unacceptable structures and policies. Ironically, economic sanctions are likely to be most effective against small, moderately developed democratic states in which the citizenry is informed and involved in the affairs of state but least effective in authoritarian regimes based on limited political participation.

The Morality of Economic Sanctions

Unlike international relations issues, such as human rights, intervention, and war, scholars have undertaken comparatively little moral analysis of economic statecraft. The limited moral scrutiny given to economic sanctions is no doubt due to the belief that sanctions are preferable to force. However, economic sanctions are not morally neutral foreign policy instruments but rather indiscriminate tools that impose harm on the target state to foster desired political changes. As a result, the conditions and manner justifying the imposition of sanctions involve a variety of ethical issues, ranging from the moral appropriateness of such instruments to the manner in which such instruments are applied. Because sanctions are morally ambiguous policy instruments, it is important, as Baldwin and others have emphasized,[32] that economic statecraft be judged not solely in terms of political and economic criteria but also in terms of international political morality.

One potentially useful approach in assessing the morality of sanctions is to apply principles of the just-war doctrine. Although application of just-war norms to economic statecraft is based on an analogy of two different decision-making environments, just-war theory can nonetheless offer an invaluable ethical structure by which to morally assess economic sanctions. In particular, just-war principles can provide moral standards for judging economic sanctions policies and for assessing issues such as the following: When is economic coercion justified? Are economic sanctions always morally preferable to military force? Does morality require that economic sanctions be targeted directly on a regime's decision makers? How much collateral harm (i.e., harm to civilians) is morally permissible? Must the anticipated harm from sanctions be proportional to the political good they are expected to achieve?

The principles of the just-war doctrine provide a framework for morally assessing economic sanctions. In applying just-war norms to sanctions, it is important to emphasize that the environments giving rise to war and economic statecraft are radically different. The just-war doctrine is mainly a defensive theory of force applicable to states victimized by aggression, whereas economic sanctions are instituted as an alternative to force to punish third parties for objectionable behaviors. Because the environments of war and peace present radically different decision-making contexts, some scholars have suggested that the just-war doctrine is "an ultimately inadequate paradigm for moral analysis of comprehensive sanctions."[33] Others, by contrast, argue that just-war morality can strengthen the ethical assessment of the role of economic sanctions.[34] The following analysis is based on the latter conviction.

The Just-Sanctions Doctrine

The just-war tradition, as noted in chapter 5, involves two dimensions: the justice of going to war (*jus ad bellum*) and justice in wartime (*jus in bello*).

Although these norms were developed to inhibit war and, in the event of war, to inhibit human suffering, they nonetheless provide a useful framework for judging the morality of economic sanctions. All eight principles (see table 5–1), with the exception of the competent-authority norm, can be applied to economic statecraft. Because private actors can contribute significantly to a sanctions regime, the requirement that governments impose sanctions is unnecessary.[35]

Based on the just-war theory, a *just-sanctions doctrine* can be developed involving two dimensions: the justice of whether to use sanctions and the justice of how to apply them. Of the seven principles of the just-sanctions doctrine, the first five provide a moral framework for determining when economic coercion is morally permissible; the last two specify how sanctions should be applied. The following norms comprise the just-sanctions doctrine:

1. *Just cause*: The aim of economic sanctions must be just. This can involve promoting peace among states, but it can also involve promoting human dignity within states when regimes systematically abuse basic rights.
2. *Right intention*: Sanctions are legitimate only if they are imposed to promote just structures and policies. Sanctions are not justified to increase national power or extend economic influence.
3. *Limited objectives*: Sanctions must have limited goals, involving behavioral reform of only those behaviors and institutions that are unjust and evil. In addition, the objectives of sanctions must be proportional to the good that they are seeking to achieve.
4. *Last resort*: The imposition of sanctions must be preceded by other, less coercive instruments. Only when peaceful negotiations have failed is a resort to comprehensive economic sanctions morally warranted.
5. *Probability of success*: The resort of economic sanctions must have a reasonable chance of success. That is, there must be a reasonable hope that the economic hardship inflicted on the target state will result in greater justice.
6. *Discrimination*: Economic hardship must be targeted on the government and the elites that support it. Economic hardship should not be imposed directly on innocent civilians. Following the principle of double effect, economic harm on the masses can be justified only as a by-product of the unintended effects of legitimately targeted sanctions.[36]
7. *Proportionality*: The good intended from sanctions must be proportional to the harm inflicted on the target state.

The application of the just-sanctions doctrine will depend greatly on the particular circumstances in which economic sanctions are employed as well as the specific purposes that they are designed to serve. Earlier, I noted that sanctions are applied for a variety of reasons. If the aim of sanctions is to bring about political reforms or policy changes in the target state, the just-sanctions doctrine can provide an invaluable moral structure for judging policies. However, if the aim of sanctions is simply to punish or to signal resolve, the doctrine's usefulness in moral analysis of sanctions will be limited. As a result, the analysis here focuses solely on sanctions as a tool of behavioral reform.

The Role of Just-Sanctions Norms

In chapter 2, I suggested that an ethical foreign policy must be judged in terms of its intentions, means, and outcomes. The just-sanctions doctrine provides norms by which to judge sanctions at each of these three levels. The first two norms—just cause and right intention—provide the principles for judging the moral legitimacy of sanctions goals. According to these two norms, the imposition of major economic suffering is morally legitimate only if its aims are morally right. The doctrine also provides principles for judging the policy instruments themselves. Specifically, the doctrine provides three norms by which to judge the moral legitimacy of sanctions—proportionality, last resort, and discrimination. Sanctions are just when (1) the harm they impose is proportional to the good they are likely to achieve; (2) other, less destructive alternatives have been exhausted; and (3) economic penalties are discriminatory, targeting harm on political and government officials responsible for a state's decisions and actions. If sanctions are imposed to influence the political behavior of the target state, it follows that the pain and suffering of economic statecraft should be borne mainly by those responsible for government decision making. Finally, the sanctions doctrine addresses the level of outcomes by specifying that sanctions should be applied only if there is a strong likelihood that the political goals will be realized.

Undoubtedly, the most important yet most morally challenging principle of the sanctions doctrine is discrimination. Indeed, one scholar argues that the major moral problem posed by sanctions is their inability to fulfill the discrimination norm.[37] This principle, which demands protection of innocent persons from the harm being imposed by ruling elites, is significant because it establishes limits on the means that can be utilized in pursuing a moral end. However, reconciling economic sanctions with discrimination is difficult because sanctions are blunt policy instruments. Although sanctions remain a popular tool of statecraft because they provide an alternative to force, sanctions are also a morally problematic instrument because they cannot discriminate between civilians and public officials.

Who are the innocents and who are the culpable? As noted previously, the just-war tradition holds that innocent persons are those who have not participated in societal evils giving rise to war or have not been involved in ordering, prosecuting, and supporting war. Because such persons do not bear direct responsibility for instigating and conducting war, the just-war tradition holds that such persons are "innocent" and should not be subject to intentional attack. Thus, the distinction between combatants and non-combatants is rooted in the notion that harm should be inflicted only on those who bear responsibility for the public actions of government. As Michael Walzer has observed, innocent people are those who "have done nothing, and are doing nothing, that entails the loss of their rights."[38] Thus, they are entitled to be free from direct attack.

If we apply these wartime distinctions to sanctions episodes, who are the innocent civilians and responsible decision makers, the sanctions "noncombatants" and "combatants"? From a simplistic perspective, the latter are those who have ordered, implemented, and supported actions deemed illegal and morally reprehensible by the sending state. Innocent civilians are those who have not supported or participated in such actions. Thus, as Lori Fisler Damrosch has noted, the discrimination norm calls on policy makers to "target the perpetrators of violence or other wrongdoing and minimize severe adverse consequences on civilians who are not in a position to bring about cessation of wrongful conduct."[39]

There can be little doubt of the importance of the discrimination norm in developing a morally just sanctions policy. However, applying such a norm is especially challenging because economic sanctions, as noted earlier, are fundamentally nondiscriminatory instruments of statecraft. Indeed, the hardship imposed by sanctions frequently falls disproportionately on low-income sectors of society. "The principal moral dilemma posed by sanctions," write Drew Christiansen and Gerard Powers, "is that the more effective they are, the more likely that they will harm those least responsible for the wrongdoing and least able to bring about change: civilians."[40] In addition, even when efforts are made to target a regime's leadership, political, economic, and government elites are frequently able to divert resources to minimize the hardships brought about by sanctions.

Despite their indiscriminate nature, economic sanctions remain a popular instrument of foreign policy. To a significant degree, the Western elites' preference for sanctions over force is rooted in the belief that the former is almost always morally preferable. For example, during the Persian Gulf crisis, religious elites opposed force, arguing repeatedly that more time was needed for sanctions to work. In making this argument, however, such elites failed to realize, as Walzer has noted, that "what they were advocat-

ing was a radically indiscriminate act of war, with predictably harsh consequences."[41] Because of the morally ambiguous nature of sanctions, some
scholars have suggested that economic sanctions should be imposed only
when humanitarian measures are undertaken to protect innocent civilians.
Such measures might include the exemption of essential goods, such as
food and medicines, and the distribution of aid to vulnerable groups.[42]

The next case study, on sanctions and South African apartheid, illustrates the morally ambiguous nature of economic sanctions. Although such
statecraft no doubt contributed to the abolition of apartheid, economic
sanctions also inflicted significant harm on the black workers.

CASE NO. 7–2
SANCTIONS AND SOUTH AFRICAN APARTHEID

Background

After the Afrikaner National Party gained control of the South African government in 1948, it began to further institutionalize racial separation (apartheid). Racial segregation was well entrenched in South Africa's social, political, and economic structures when the National Party assumed power, but
the effort to establish a comprehensive legal system of racial separation was
unprecedented, leading to significant international condemnation.

International opposition to South Africa's apartheid policies began in the
early 1960s. For example, in 1962, the UN General Assembly passed a nonbinding resolution condemning apartheid, calling on states to break diplomatic relations with South Africa and to stop trading with it. Subsequently,
the Security Council authorized a ban on arms shipments to South Africa
and in 1977 imposed a total arms embargo. Another important action taken
against South Africa in the early 1970s was the imposition of an oil embargo
by OPEC, forcing South Africa to pay much higher costs for petroleum.
None of these actions, however, had much impact on South Africa's government decision making. Indeed, the oil embargo led South Africa to pioneer
in the development of oil extraction from coal, whereas the arms embargo
encouraged the development of a major military arms industry, providing a
significant source of foreign exchange.

In response to growing American public opposition to apartheid, some
municipalities and universities began demanding divestment of stock in
companies involved in South Africa. The aim of the divestment campaign
was not only to force institutions to sell their stock but also to ultimately
force companies to withdraw from South Africa through disinvestment (i.e.,
selling or closing their operations). By 1982, several state legislatures and
city councils had approved measures mandating divestment, and by 1984
more than forty-five colleges and universities had adopted divestment programs. The divestment campaign accelerated in the mid-1980s, culminating
with California's adoption of a $12 billion divestment program, calling for
the sale of South African holdings in state pension funds and in the endow-

ment of the state's university system.[43] It has been estimated that by 1991, more than twenty-eight states, twenty-four counties, and ninety-two cities had adopted divestment measures, resulting in the sale of some $20 billion of stock.[44]

In response to growing public opposition to apartheid, congressional support for economic sanctions began to increase in the mid-1980s. To forestall more severe sanctions being considered by the Congress, President Reagan instituted modest sanctions in September 1985. The following year, however, Congress, overriding a presidential veto, passed legislation instituting more drastic economic sanctions. The 1986 Comprehensive Anti-Apartheid Act, among other things, banned new investment in South Africa, prohibited new U.S. commercial loans and the export of petroleum and computers, banned selected South African imports, and terminated landing rights for South Africa's airlines. The European Community and the British Commonwealth also instituted similar, although more modest, sanctions at this time.

Although government-imposed economic sanctions were symbolically significant, the most influential economic measures were the actions of the international business community, especially the disinvestment by major corporations and the ban on new bank loans. One scholar writes, "The real actors who overturned constructive engagement [the official U.S. foreign policy toward South Africa] were not public, but private—namely, U.S. commercial banks and foreign investors responding to economic and political risks and nongovernmental anti-apartheid organizations that magnified corporate responses to those risks."[45] It has been estimated that of the almost 400 U.S. companies doing business in South Africa in 1984, only 124 remained in 1989. Moreover, the decision by international banks to call in their loans and close their operations had an especially devastating impact. When the Chase Manhattan Bank announced in 1985 that it would no longer make new loans to South Africa, other foreign banks quickly followed suit, leading to an immediate tightening of domestic credit markets. As a result of the cutoff of loans and direct foreign investment, South Africa experienced massive capital outflows and a sharp weakening of its currency. It has been estimated that from 1985 to 1989 net capital outflows were $11 billion, leading to a significant contraction of the South African economy and a loss of at least $4 billion in export earnings.[46]

The Moral Ambiguity of Sanctions

The principal justification offered by public officials and interest group leaders for the imposition of economic sanctions against South Africa was the belief that apartheid was evil and needed to be abolished. Sanctions advocates argued that economic penalties should be imposed on South Africa to punish the regime and compel the government to alter its social and political structures. Some, such as Archbishop Trevor Huddleston and Archbishop Desmond Tutu, argued that sanctions were necessary to convey a moral message, that is, to express outrage at the inhumane and discriminatory system of apartheid. Others advocated sanctions for strategic reasons, basing their argument on consequentialist logic: Economic hardship and international isolation, they believed, would compel structural reforms.

Most sanctions opponents, including British Prime Minister Margaret Thatcher and President Reagan, also shared the conviction that apartheid was discriminatory, undemocratic, and unjust but believed that the application of comprehensive economic sanctions was an unacceptable policy. Sanctions were opposed for two major reasons: first, because they were considered ineffective in fostering domestic reforms and, second, because they imposed unnecessary economic harm on the black labor class.

Some leaders believed that externally imposed hardship was unlikely to encourage domestic structural changes. Indeed, some sanctions critics argued that economic harm and isolation would only encourage Afrikaner resistance. A far better approach, in their view, was to foster increased participation in the global political economy. Chester Crocker, the assistant secretary of state for African affairs who was responsible for developing President Reagan's African policy of constructive engagement, believed that U.S. influence toward South Africa would be realized only by maintaining strong political and economic ties. Similarly, Helen Suzman, a long-term member of the South African Parliament and a leading apartheid critic, repeatedly claimed that only a strategy of economic expansion could foster humane social change. Indeed, she argued that the major improvements in the living and working conditions for South Africa's blacks had been achieved through economic growth. According to Suzman, economic expansion was responsible for increased skilled jobs for blacks, improvements in education and training, recognition of black trade unions, acceptance of black urbanization, and the abolition of "pass laws" regulating the movement of people among different racial communities.[47] If Western states wanted to help South Africa establish the preconditions for liberal democratic society, they needed to facilitate economic expansion, without which no improvement in the black majority's living standards could be achieved. Moreover, only through a strategy of engagement could foreign states help foster capitalistic and democratic norms in preparation for establishing a more just post-apartheid regime.

A second major reason for opposing sanctions was the belief that they were harmful to the economic and social well-being of the nonwhite working class. Alan Paton, author of the influential book *Cry, The Beloved Country* and one of the first major critics of apartheid, repeatedly condemned sanctions, especially disinvestment, for causing unjust harm to black workers. He explained his moral opposition to disinvestment as follows:

> It is my belief that those who will pay most grievously for disinvestment will be Black workers of South Africa. I take very seriously the teachings of the Gospels, in particular the parables about giving drink to the thirsty and food to the hungry. It seems to me that Jesus attached supreme—indeed sacred—significance to such actions. Therefore, I will not help to cause any such suffering to any Black persons.[48]

From the perspective of the just-sanctions doctrine, two major shortcomings of South African economic sanctions were the failure to target economic harm on decision makers and the failure to protect the black majority from unnecessary hardship. In seeking to weaken and isolate the apartheid regime, economic sanctions led to a major contraction of the South African economy that, resulting in mass unemployment and underemployment among blacks. Even targeted sanctions, such as those imposed on the mineral and fruit industries, imposed especially harsh costs on black laborers, as the retrenchment in these labor-intensive industries significantly increased unemployment. Scholars differ significantly over the negative impact of sanctions on the South African labor market. One study predicted that from 1986 to 1990, comprehensive sanctions would lead to more than 1.1 million lost jobs;[49] another scholar estimates the number of lost jobs at 100,000.[50]

Sanctions, especially divestment (the liquidation of foreign assets), also had perverse, unanticipated effects. Rather than strengthening the economic power of the black majority, the sale of foreign subsidiaries, for example, resulted in increased white ownership of major foreign corporations. For example, when Barclays Bank (London) decided to pull out of South Africa in 1987, a large South African conglomerate (the Anglo-American Corporation) acquired the bank, paying substantially less than it was worth.[51] In 1986 alone, the Johannesburg stock market increased in value by nearly $9 billion, in great part because of the purchase of foreign assets at "fire-sale" prices. Moreover, divestment resulted in increasing concentration of South African wealth. According to Merle Lipton, in 1983 four major South African conglomerates (Anglo-American, Sanlam, South African Mutual, and Rembrandt) controlled 70 percent of the Johannesburg stock exchange; four years later, in response to divestment, these groups accounted for 83 percent of all South African stock.[52] In addition, the contraction of the South African economy led to an increase in the economic power of the state. For example, the UN-imposed petroleum and arms embargoes resulted in the expansion of major industries in synthetic fuel (from coal) and armaments. It has been estimated that from 1977, when the UN arms embargo became mandatory, until 1989, the South African arms industry (Armscor) increased employment by more than 100,000 jobs.[53] Moreover, during the 1980s, while the South African economy was experiencing a major slowdown, South Africa's government employment actually increased by 18 percent![54]

In 1990, President F. W. de Klerk freed Nelson Mandela and other political prisoners, unbanned the African National Congress and other black opposition parties, and set in motion a process of radical change that culminated with the election of Mandela as president in 1994. In response to these developments, Western countries gradually eliminated all official sanctions. However, as of 1997, many multinational corporations that had terminated their South African operations in the 1980s either had not returned or had failed to reestablish successful enterprises.

Although many observers now believe that economic sanctions contributed (symbolically, if not substantively) to political change in South Africa, scholars continue to disagree about the role of sanctions in bringing about an end to apartheid and the moral legitimacy of such a policy. As noted previously, there is little doubt that economic sanctions—especially those nongovernment initiatives such as divestment and disinvestment that led to massive capital outflows—were harmful to the South African economy. However, the key issue is not whether sanctions were costly to South Africa but whether they were responsible for ending apartheid. Some anti-apartheid leaders, such as Tutu and Mandela, believe that economic sanctions were essential in ending white-minority rule. Others, especially National Party officials, have suggested that sanctions played a minimal role in bringing about political reform. De Klerk, for example, has observed that although sanctions disrupted the South African economy, "it was not sanctions that brought about change."[55]

Moral Reflections

The South African case study on sanctions raises a number of important ethical issues.

- Can a morally dubious policy be justified to bring about a morally just goal? Because sanctions are indiscriminate, generally imposing disproportionate hardship on civilians, they are morally problematic policy instruments. Thus, can immoral means (comprehensive economic sanctions) be used to achieve justice (the ending of apartheid)?
- From an ends-based approach (consequentialism), the use of economic sanctions is a morally legitimate policy alternative, provided that the intended goals are just and that the likelihood of achieving the desired goals is high. From this perspective, the goal of ending a racially unjust regime is morally just. Moreover, economic sanctions are superior to military force because they involve much less destruction. From a rule-based approach, however, economic sanctions are morally problematic because they fail to protect innocent persons from economic hardship. Thus, because sanctions impose hardship on civilians, should policy makers get their hands "dirty" by using sanctions to foster a more just world, or should they attempt to keep their hands "clean" by refusing to use immoral means to pursue political justice?
- Was the economic hardship brought about by sanctions proportional to the good achieved by the collapse of the apartheid regime? Because the transfer of power from an Afrikaner government to a democratic, multiracial regime was achieved in a relatively rapid and peaceful means, there can be little doubt that the hardship of sanctions was proportional to the outcomes. However, were its means, the society-wide economic hardship, morally justified? Regardless of the desired goals, was the imposition of government and nongovernment economic sanctions morally legitimate?

Summary

Because force is considered the most extreme and least desirable foreign policy instrument, economic sanctions offer a useful instrument short of war. However, as the previous analysis suggests, the use of sanctions as an alternative to force is morally problematic, in part because the effectiveness of such tools is uncertain but, more important, because the impact of such economic hardship can itself lead to unjust results. In sum, although economic sanctions are a potentially useful instrument of statecraft, their role and impact are often morally ambiguous, frequently involving legitimate ends but dubious means.

CHAPTER EIGHT

THE ETHICS OF GLOBAL SOCIETY

We should not view national boundaries as having fundamental moral significance. Since boundaries are not coextensive with the scope of social cooperation, they do not mark the limits of social obligation.

Charles R. Beitz[1]

There is no single operational international code of behavior. There are competing codes, rival philosophical traditions, clashing conceptions of morality. . . . It is true, as some point out, that all statesmen use the same moral language. . . . Unfortunately, from the point of view of moral harmony, this is meaningless. A community of vocabulary is not the same thing as a community of values.

Stanley Hoffmann[2]

The extent of a country's respect for personal self-determination says something very basic about how it is governed. It is an index of a state's responsiveness to its citizens and, by extension, a measure of overall social health.

Alan Dowty[3]

The emphasis in the previous chapters has been on the nature and role of moral norms in the development and execution of foreign policy. In this final chapter, I examine and attempt to offer a preliminary assessment of the moral legitimacy of the international system itself, especially in light of some of the major problems of our contemporary world. A cursory glance at global society suggests that there is great suffering in the modern world, stemming from factors such as war, forced displacement, ethnic and religious discrimination, starvation, poverty, disease, and ecological degradation. Although such evil is caused by many factors, the international system itself is a major source of human suffering. Because global structures permit war, tolerate egregious international economic inequalities, neglect human rights, and abuse the global environment, some scholars and political leaders have concluded that the contemporary system is seriously flawed and morally unjust.

The structures of global society pose major ethical questions. For example, how should the world system be conceived—as a single community or as a group of national societies? Does the moral legitimacy of states depend on their willingness and ability to protect human rights? Who is responsible for the well-being of migrants and refugees? Are the structures, rules, and procedures of global society fundamentally just? Finally, who is responsible for protecting the global commons, that is, the atmosphere, oceans, and land shared by all member states of global society?

Although such questions might seem esoteric and far removed from the realities of global political life, it is clear that the international order has been increasingly challenged because of perceived wrongs and injustices. Some of the international community's major limitations and problems include the arms race, global inequalities, environmental pollution, and human rights abuses. According to some critics of the existing neo-Westphalian order, the international community's structures are morally bankrupt because they have been incapable of regulating military competition. Because there is no common authority, global society encourages states to give excessive emphasis to military security, encouraging arms races among states. This tendency was vividly illustrated during the Cold War, when the superpowers greatly expanded the size and power of their conventional and nuclear forces, diverting scarce economic resources toward military competition and threatening the world with mass destruction.

A more specific challenge to the international system emerged in the 1970s and 1980s, when Third World leaders began to challenge the moral legitimacy of the global economic order. They argued that its structures and procedures were morally flawed, if not fundamentally unjust, because of the large income inequalities perpetuated between the industrial states in North America and Western Europe and the developing nations in Asia, Africa, and Latin America. As a result, Third World leaders advocated a transformation of the global economic system, proposing a set of reforms, known as the New International Economic Order (NIEO), that would shift economic power and resources from the rich, developed North to the underdeveloped South.

Another significant challenge to the global order emerged in the mid-1980s, when environmentalists began calling attention to the decay of the "global commons." According to such critics, because there is no common authority in the international system, there is no effective environmental protection. Although numerous multilateral efforts have been undertaken to protect endangered animal and plant species and to minimize land, water, and air pollution, international system critics have argued that greater political centralization of authority is essential to ensure "sustainable development," that is, environmentally safe economic growth. Although some treaties and conventions have been adopted on global environmental protection, critics still claim that much more needs to be done—and that this can be realized only by a radical transformation of the system itself.

Finally, the moral legitimacy of the existing world order has been challenged because of its failure to protect human rights. Because states bear the primary responsibility for the welfare of persons, the neglect of human rights is directly attributable to them. At the same time, the international community itself is also responsible for the well-being of persons. This is especially the case for 25 million refugees and other displaced persons who have been forced to flee their homelands since the end of the Cold War because of political oppression, civil war, or ethnic and religious persecution.

This chapter has three parts. In the first part, I examine the ethics of protecting the global commons and illustrate this concern with a case study on global warming. In the second part, I examine the nature of international justice, noting some alternative conceptions of and approaches to this moral ideal. I then describe and assess two major perspectives of global society—communitarianism and cosmopolitanism—and illustrate these alternative conceptions with a case study on foreign aid. In the third part, I examine the role of the individual in global society, focusing on the role of persons who migrate from one state to another and on the moral status of refugees.

Protecting the Global Commons

Because no central authority exists in global society to make and enforce rules that manage and preserve the earth's shared resources, protecting the atmosphere, oceans, and soil beyond the jurisdiction of individual states is ultimately a cooperative enterprise among state and nonstate actors. As expected, states maintain widely varied policies and practices on domestic environmental protection. Some modern industrial states have developed a significant body of rules to reduce pollution, regulate waste disposal, and protect biodiversity. By contrast, other states, mostly poor, developing nations, have neglected pollution control, focusing instead on promoting economic growth. The extent to which states implement sustainable development strategies domestically is vitally important because domestic practices will profoundly affect transboundary air and water pollution and thus impact the quality of the earth's atmosphere and oceans.

Global Environmental Protection

In the early nineteenth century, English political economist William Foster Lloyd developed the "tragedy of the commons" metaphor to explain the dangers of parochial, short-term practices.[4] According to the metaphor, villagers raise livestock on private lands as well as on a common pasture. Whereas each farmer carefully regulates grazing on private land, communal land is used freely by all community participants. As a result, the pasture on private plots is well maintained, whereas the village green suffers from overgrazing.

The commons metaphor is helpful in assessing collective-agency issues because it illuminates the dilemma of protecting resources owned or used in common. Because the village commons can sustain only a limited number of animals (this is defined as the commons' "carrying capacity"), the challenge for village farmers is to maximize their individual well-being without destroying the shared land. If each villager defines his interests in terms of the common good, he will allow only limited grazing by his animals. However, if farmers pursue their immediate self-interest and disregard the interests of others, the communal property will deteriorate and eventually be destroyed through overuse.

If the earth is viewed as a global commons, where the soil, atmosphere and water are collective goods, developing long-term, cooperative strategies might help prevent the misuse or overuse of the earth's shared resources.[5] As with the village green, the challenge for states is to manage the earth's bountiful resources by wisely protecting global resources and devising rules and cooperative strategies that foster "sustainable" economic development, that is, growth that is environmentally safe and capable of being maintained indefinitely.

One way that states have sought to protect their own territories from transboundary pollution is through regional treaties and conventions. For example, countries bordering the Mediterranean Sea have established conventions to protect fish stocks and the quality of water. Similarly, countries sharing the Rhine River (France, Germany, the Netherlands, and Switzerland) have established strict rules governing the discharge of pollution into the river. Countries have also developed international conventions to protect global resources, such as the Convention on Fishing and Conservation of Living Resources of the High Seas (1958); the Convention on the International Trade in Endangered Species of Wild Flora and Fauna—CITES (1973); the London Convention on the Prevention of Marine Pollution

(1972); the Montreal Protocol on Substances that Deplete the Ozone Layer (1987); and the Basel Convention on the Control of Transboundary Movements of Hazardous Wastes and Their Disposal (1989).

Perhaps the most significant international initiative to promote global environmental protection was the 1992 UN Conference on Environment and Development in Rio de Janeiro. Billed as the "last chance to save the planet," the conference, generally referred to as the Earth Summit, was the largest international conference ever held, bringing together more than 25,000 participants. In addition to 172 official government delegations, the summit also involved some 15,000 representatives from over 2,000 environmentally related nongovernmental organizations (NGOs). It is important to emphasize that, although government officials played a decisive role in negotiating various declarations and conventions, most of the preparatory work on global environmental protection was carried out by NGOs. By developing awareness and concern about global environmental protection, these organizations fostered international collective action on the earth's resources, biodiversity, and environment. Two major treaties were signed at the Earth Summit: the UN Framework Convention on Climate Change (also known as the Climate Treaty) and the Convention on Biological Diversity (also known as the Biodiversity Treaty). In addition, officials adopted three nonbinding agreements: a declaration of principles for establishing national environmental conservation programs, a statement of how to sustain forests, and a blueprint for promoting environmentally sustainable economic development.

The Ethics of Global Environmental Protection

Protecting the earth's biodiversity, environment, and resources presents political, technical, and moral challenges. Politically, environmental protection requires a mature collective will. Because protecting species, reducing pollution, and conserving resources involves long-term, elusive payoffs, the development and implementation of transnational environmental strategies is difficult, especially when the political decision-making process is focused on short-term goals. However, if the protection of global resources is important, all members of the international community must implement environmentally safe policies. Economic development strategies must be sustainable. As with the protection of the village green, countries must avoid the overuse or misuse of shared resources.

Technically, sustainable development requires the development of new technologies that reduce pollution, conserve energy, and foster the development of alternative energy sources. Most western European and North American governments have greatly reduced the quantity of pollution and industrial wastes to a significant degree through the application of new technologies and more efficient production techniques. Although industrial production in these countries has been made more environmentally safe, much more remains to be done to strengthen the environmental protection and conservation regime. Developed countries need to continue to devise new technologies and encourage more efficient use of energy. Third World nations, for their part, need to become more aware of the effects of industrialization on the environment and to apply energy conservation policies and environmentally safe technologies as a means of encouraging sustainable economic development.

Finally, environmental protection presents a moral challenge by requiring national (state and nonstate) actors to consider the effect of their behaviors on the current well-being of national and foreign peoples as well as on the quality of life for future generations. A moral approach to economic development and the environment will require, at a minimum, an impartial, long-term assessment of the effects of current actions. If development is to be sustainable, that is, available to future generations, economic growth must involve careful use of renewable and nonrenewable resources, ensuring that present demands are balanced against the potential needs and wants of future generations. In addition, a moral approach to environmental protection must ensure that access to the global commons is fair and that the distribution of the commons' resources is similarly perceived as just. This is a most difficult challenge because, as I note in the following, scholars and public officials frequently hold different conceptions of international justice. However, whether justice is defined in terms of the substantive distribution of benefits or the fairness of the procedural rules, egregious inequalities in the use or misuse of global resources is ethically problematic.

To illustrate some of the ethical challenges in promoting environmental protection in the contemporary international system, I next examine and assess the politics and ethics of global warming.

CASE NO. 8–1
THE ETHICS OF GLOBAL WARMING: NORTH–SOUTH PERSPECTIVES

Background

The earth's climate is determined principally by the balance between energy received from the sun, largely as visible light, and the energy radiated back to space as invisible infrared light. However, water vapors and human-made gases (mainly carbon dioxide) can trap solar radiation and thus impair the reflection of infrared light back into space because they trap solar radiation, much like the glass of a plant-breeder's greenhouse. The "greenhouse effect" thus occurs because vapors and gases allow more of the sun's heat to be absorbed by the earth than is released back into space. Although human-made gas emissions are responsible for only a small part (estimated at less than 5 percent) of the greenhouse effect, they nonetheless play a critical role in influencing the earth's climate because carbon dioxide and other gases linger for long periods of time in the atmosphere before dissipating.

At the 1992 Earth Summit, some 166 countries signed the Climate Treaty, establishing a framework for reducing the growth of greenhouse gas emissions. This action was taken in the belief that stabilization of atmospheric pollution was essential in reducing the potential of further global warming. At the time that this agreement was signed, there was some scientific uncertainty about the role of human-made gases and climate change. Subsequently, however, the UN Intergovernmental Panel on Climate Change (IPCC), a group of about 2,500 distinguished scientists, issued a report on climate change that, although tentative and cautious in its conclusions, left little doubt about the role of greenhouse gases in climate change. According to the IPCC report, in the absence of unchanged patterns of fossil fuel (i.e., coal and petroleum) consumption, greenhouse gas emissions will continue to rise, resulting in an increase of the earth's temperature from 1.8 to 6.3 degrees Fahrenheit over the next century. Although global warming could cause some beneficial developments (e.g., increasing agricultural production in northern territories, such as Russia and Canada), environmentalists have warned that climate change could also bring about significant harm, including a rise in the sea level due to thermal expansion, leading to the flooding of coastal lowlands and the destruction of numerous tropical islands.

Although the 1992 Climate Treaty called attention to the need to reduce greenhouse gas emissions from the burning of fossil fuels, it did not establish binding targets for states. As a result, signatory states implemented few if any structural reforms to reduce greenhouse gas emissions. By 1995 it was clear that the 1992 convention was having little impact on global carbon emissions. In view of a growing international awareness that climate change could result in highly destructive developments, a global consensus began to emerge in the mid-1990s that a stricter, more demanding treaty was needed. Thus, after holding eight major preparatory meetings, some 5,000 delegates gathered in Kyoto, Japan, in December 1997 to develop a more authoritative global warming regime.

The principal result of the Kyoto conference was that industrial states established specific pollution targets to help stabilize total world greenhouse gas emissions. The Kyoto Protocol—essentially an addendum to the 1992 Climate Treaty—requires that countries reduce their greenhouse emissions by about 5 percent below their 1990 level no later than the year 2012. To achieve this goal, the protocol establishes specific targets. The European Union must cut its emissions by 8 percent, the United States by 7 percent, and Japan by 6 percent. Significantly, no binding targets were established for developing nations, although they are encouraged to set voluntary reduction goals. Because the accord's overall goal represents a cut of roughly 30 percent in what carbon emissions would be without the protocol, achieving the Kyoto targets will involve significant cuts in the national use of fossil fuels.

The Ethics of Stabilizing Greenhouse Gas Emissions

The Kyoto Protocol raises a number of major ethical issues. I briefly examine three of them: first, the moral justification for differential treatment of the developed (North) and developing (South) countries; second, the ethics of selling and buying pollution rights; and third, the feasibility and desirability of relying on nuclear power as an alternative energy source as a means to reduce carbon gas emissions.

As noted previously, the Kyoto Protocol establishes carbon emission targets for only the industrial countries. The developing nations, led by China and India, vigorously opposed any emissions targets, arguing that, because the developed countries were producing more than 60 percent of the world's greenhouse gas emissions, they should bear the economic and technological cost of curbing fossil fuel use. Moreover, because most of the accumulated greenhouse gas emissions in the atmosphere were caused by the North's industrialization and economic development, Third World officials argued that it was now their turn to bring about rapid industrialization. Because economic growth necessitates increased energy consumption, a rise in the standard of living in developing nations can be realized only through greater fossil fuel consumption, resulting in higher carbon emissions. Thus, even with the implementation of modern technologies, the political demands for economic expansion in the South will inevitably lead to increased energy consumption.

Although the developing nations are now responsible for about one-fifth of the world's total carbon emissions, whether the Third World accepts emissions targets is not an insignificant issue. It has been estimated that, in the absence of any restrictions on coal burning or petroleum use, greenhouse emissions will more than double in the South in response to increased industrialization. According to one estimate, the Third World's share of global gas emissions is expected to rise from about 20 percent in the mid-1990s to more than 50 percent by the year 2025.[6] Developing nations do not assert that they bear no responsibility for global warming, but rather, that existing greenhouse emissions are the responsibility of the North. Third World officials assert that before undertaking significant commitments to reduce greenhouse gas emissions, their countries need to carry out significant economic development. Thus, for the present, the South contends that global warming remains a responsibility of the North. Moreover, if stabilizing atmospheric concentrations of greenhouse gases is a priority for the industrial states, they can pay poor countries to reduce their emissions. However, if they were to do so, some scholars suggest that the cost to the North would greatly exceed any previous international wealth transfers that have taken place in modern history.[7]

The European Union has strongly supported the Kyoto accord and has suggested that its reduction target (8 percent below the 1990 level by 2010) is feasible. The U.S. government, by contrast, has been much less enthusiastic about the agreement. Indeed, the U.S. Senate overwhelmingly passed a resolution (95 to 0) that requires the South's acceptance of binding emission targets before treaty ratification can be considered. For its part, the Clinton administration has indicated that it will not request Senate ratification of the protocol until the South is committed to binding emission targets.

A second important ethical issue involved in the Kyoto Protocol is the provision of "emissions rights." According to the Kyoto accord, states may buy or sell the right to pollute the atmosphere to reduce carbon emissions efficiently. Industrial countries that have high levels of gas emissions may buy emission rights from developing nations that have comparatively low levels of fossil fuel consumption. Thus, the United States, a country with a high level of carbon emissions, could pay Russia for its pollution rights, as its emissions have dropped 30 percent since 1990 because of a decline in industrial production.

Although the introduction of market forces could possibly contribute to the reduction of total world greenhouse emissions, the commercialization of pollution is itself a morally questionable development. For one thing, it removes the stigma that is normally associated with pollution.[8] When an industry violates pollution regulations, a government agency fines the industry. Such a fine is not simply a financial cost to business but also represents a community's moral judgment that the industry's action (excessive pollution) was wrong. However, when pollution is commercialized, it destroys the moral stigma associated with unacceptable behaviors. Moreover, the trading of emission rights is morally problematic because it weakens communal solidarity required in the collective management of global resources. When some countries can fulfill their communal responsibilities toward the global warming regime by buying the right to pollute, global solidarity is weakened, ultimately making the fulfillment of other global commitments more difficult. There are some things that money cannot buy. If the international community is to remain a community, state actors must all participate in fulfilling shared responsibilities.

Finally, the effort to curb fossil fuel use raises ethical issues about relying on alternative energy sources, especially nuclear power. Although the Kyoto Protocol does not address the ethics of nuclear energy, the issue is significant because a number of countries—notably France, Spain, South Korea, Sweden, and Switzerland—have increased reliance on nuclear power to reduce carbon emissions. During the 1980s, France carried out a massive national effort to reduce the burning of fossil fuels by converting to nuclear power, thereby reducing carbon dioxide emissions by 40 percent. By 1994, 78 percent of France's electricity was being generated by nuclear power. Although the United States has been much more hesitant in turning to nuclear power, by 1993 it had 109 nuclear-powered electricity generating plants that collectively were responsible for lowering carbon dioxide emissions by 30 percent. It has been estimated that in the absence of some 450 nuclear power plants throughout the world, global greenhouse emissions would be about 10 percent higher.[9] The moral problem posed by increased reliance on nuclear energy is that nuclear power itself involves significant, albeit rare, environmental dangers and risks. The question of whether shifting from fossil fuels to nuclear power, as France has done, is a wise and morally correct strategy is still open to debate.

Moral Reflections

The Kyoto Protocol raises a number of important ethical issues.

- Because the North is responsible for most of the existing greenhouse gas emissions, should developed countries bear the principal burden in curbing fossil fuel use? Is the protocol's imposition of different standards on the North and the South morally justified?
- Because the developed countries have established high standards of living while implementing various types of policies and strategies that encourage environmental protection, should they transfer these technologies to the poor countries? Should developed countries pay Third World nations to reduce their emissions?
- Is it moral to buy or sell pollution rights? Why or why not?
- Given the risks and dangers associated with nuclear power, is the shift from carbon-burning plants to nuclear power plants morally warranted?

The Nature of International Justice

To assess international society in light of political morality, it is necessary to have a normative standard by which to judge the rightness or justness of the structures and policies of that society. In effect, what is needed is a conception of international justice. However, defining the nature of international justice and its essential principles is a daunting task. Several factors contribute to this difficulty.

The Elusive Nature of International Justice

First, global political justice is difficult to ascertain because of the lack of agreement about such a norm. This is due partly to the absence of an authoritative conception of political justice. Although justice is one of the most frequently examined themes in Western political philosophy, the different normative theories and conceptualizations of political justice have not yet yielded an authoritative definition of the term. Rather, Western political scholarship has provided a multitude of theories and perspectives about different dimensions of the quest for political justice. For example, some theories emphasize the rights and obligations of individuals in developing a just political society, whereas others emphasize the character and responsibilities of government and other public institutions. Still other thinkers approach justice by seeking to identify foundational principles of political society, whereas others focus on the policy outcomes of government. It is significant that throughout most of Western civilization the quest for political justice was viewed as a by-product of the fulfillment of moral obligations. As a result, most classical political theory emphasized the role of duties and obligation in cultivating political justice. Contemporary thinkers, by contrast, have placed priority on rights. In sum, normative political thought provides insights, perspectives, and theories about the nature of political justice but no authoritative framework for determining justice.

A second reason for the elusive nature of international justice is that global society is comprised of a plurality of cultures and moralities. Whereas domestic societies typically are characterized by comparatively coherent and authoritative decision-making structures, the international community has no comparable legal or political institutions. Moreover, domestic societies are typically based on a more coherent political morality. As Stanley Hoffmann has observed, although there is generally a consensus within national communities about what constitutes justice, in the international community there is "a cacophony of standards." Because of the moral pluralism of global society, justice becomes either "a matter of sheer force—carried at the point of a sword—or, when force does not prevail, a matter of fleeting bargains and tests of fear or strength."[10] It is also important to recognize that the quest for international justice is difficult because such a quest might involve conflict with other normative goals. More specifically, as I note in the following, the quest for international order might not be consistent with the quest for justice either within or among states.

Finally, determining international justice is difficult because the notion of political justice can be interpreted in two very different ways. One approach associates political justice with the rightness and fairness of the rules, procedures and institutions of political communities and the consistent and impartial application of such norms. This perspective is sometimes called *procedural justice* because it defines justice in terms of processes rather than outcomes. According to this approach, political justice involves the impartial and nondiscriminatory application of rules and procedures, not the determination of particular desirable goals or moral outcomes. In effect, justice is realized not by pursuing particular ends but by ensuring the fairness of the system. Such an approach is illustrated by the American judicial system, which pursues justice through impartial courts. To ensure impartiality, a judge maintains strict neutrality as he or she enforces strict compliance with norms governing the presentation of evidence and arguments by the prosecution and defense before an impartial jury.

The second approach defines political justice in terms of the rightness and fairness of outcomes. Justice is that which promotes good or right ends. Because this perspective associates morality with particular distributions or results, it is frequently referred to as *substantive,* or *distributive, justice.*[11] Although this approach has become increasingly influential in contemporary political ethics, it is significant that traditional international morality was defined mainly in terms of procedural norms and in particular "the laws of nations." As Terry Nardin has observed, the association of international justice with particular outcomes is a relatively recent development, dating to the current century when the notion of distributive justice began to be applied to international relations.[12]

A sound, comprehensive approach to international ethics should be rooted in both procedural and substantive norms. Procedural norms are important because they emphasize the impartial application of authoritative rules and principles of global society; substantive norms, however, are also important because the perception of justice is partly rooted in the perception of just outcomes. To be sure, the application of distributive justice among member states presents significant challenges. However, the increased moral sensitivity to egregious inequalities within and among nations has fostered a more robust moral assessment of international relations.

Liberalism and Political Justice

From a normative perspective, the dominant ethical paradigm utilized in assessing twentieth-century international relations has been political liberalism. As noted in chapter 3, this tradition emerged in the seventeenth and eighteenth centuries with the political writings of theorists such as John Locke, Jean-Jacques Rousseau, James Mill, Jeremy Bentham, and John Stuart Mill. Fundamentally, liberalism espouses two basic principles. First, because human beings possess rights, the primary task of government is to secure and protect those rights. Second, the most effective way of inhibiting tyranny and promoting the common good is through limited government based on consent.

Because liberalism first developed as a domestic political theory, its application to international society was, as Hoffmann has noted, "little more than the projection of domestic liberalism on a world scale."[13] Indeed, liberals have argued on the basis of the "domestic analogy" that states possess rights and duties comparable to those of individuals in political society.[14] The application of liberalism to global society has resulted in the development of *liberal internationalism*—a doctrine that emphasizes the peacefulness of democratic regimes, a belief in the fundamental harmony of interests among different peoples, and the universality of human rights. In addition, this doctrine, following the claims of early twentieth-century

American liberals such as Woodrow Wilson, asserts that peoples (nationalities) have an inherent right of political self-determination and that this political right is not only consistent with but also conducive to global order.

Liberal internationalism has contributed to the development of two meta-ethical perspectives on international justice: communitarianism and cosmopolitanism. *Communitarianism* accepts the existing community of states as normative, believing that the quest for human dignity is best secured within and through each of the distinct political societies of the international system.[15] Although the state can be an impediment to justice, it also serves as the primary political agency for ensuring human rights domestically and peace and tranquillity internationally. However, the communitarian approach recognizes that establishing legitimate order domestically is not sufficient to ensure human dignity; what is also required is that conditions in the global society of states be conducive to peace and justice among states and, derivatively, to the well-being of persons. Thus, a central concern of the communitarian perspective is to define the obligations that foster and maintain a just order among member states.

Cosmopolitanism, by contrast, seeks to promote human dignity by giving priority to global or cosmopolitan bonds.[16] Its major focus is on the pursuit of just political relations within all relevant communities, including global society itself. Although this perspective views the state as an important structure in fostering human rights, it also recognizes that states can and do abuse rights. Indeed, because states have been a major source of tyranny and human suffering, cosmopolitanists believe that the moral legitimacy of states is conditional on their protection of human rights. In effect, they assume that international morality requires the subordination of state boundaries to human dignity. Thus, whereas communitarianism accepts the legitimacy of the existing international order, the cosmopolitan approach denies the moral significance of the structures of the existing neo-Westphalian order. Because of its idealistic orientation, cosmopolitanism is sometimes referred to as global utopianism.

In comparing communitarianism and cosmopolitanism, it is significant that both perspectives assert the primacy of human dignity but differ in how best to secure and protect human rights.[17] Whereas the former assigns primary responsibility to the state in securing and protecting individual rights, the latter assigns primary obligation to global society itself. In addition, it is significant that both approaches assume the primacy of morality. Indeed, both traditions are rooted in the tradition of "common morality," which regards ethical norms as rationally accessible and universally binding. Despite cultural pluralism in global society, common morality assumes that the quest for peace and human dignity must be based on moral norms that are transculturally authoritative.

International Justice versus Cosmopolitan Justice

Communitarianism and cosmopolitanism give rise to two distinct emphases on political justice. For the communitarian, states are the primary
actors in global society and thus are presumptively legitimate and entitled
to sovereignty, that is, political independence and self-rule. Because communitarianism is concerned mainly with the promotion of a just peace
among states, global political ethics is approached as a quest for *international justice,* involving equity and peace among member states. Because
states vary considerably in their size, power, and economic resources, the
quest for interstate justice is a daunting task. Moreover, because there is
no common power within international society to resolve conflicts, the establishment and maintenance of order is similarly a difficult task. Thus,
when a state commits aggression, communitarians believe that force can
and should be used to defend the legitimate rights of states.

Communitarians recognize that the quest for interstate justice will not
ensure justice within states. Some governments might be unwilling to protect the rights and liberties of persons. Indeed, some regimes might deliberately pursue policies that inflict great harm on their people. However,
when gross injustices occur, the communitarians and cosmopolitanists differ in their readiness to use external force to correct the alleged injustices.
Because communitarians believe that the protection of existing rules of
global society is foundational to domestic and international order, they are
reluctant to override the sovereignty norm in the name of human rights,
believing that in the long run global order is essential to human rights. As
a result, communitarians are willing to intervene only as a last resort. At
the risk of oversimplification, it can be said that liberal communitarians
are eager to affirm individual rights but are reluctant to protect or advance
such rights through foreign intervention.[18]

Cosmopolitanism, by contrast, is concerned mainly with the well-being
of persons. Cosmopolitan thinkers argue that states have a moral obligation to defend and protect basic rights and that when they fail to do so they
lose their moral standing within international society. Because cosmopolitanists view nation-states as legitimate political actors only to the extent
that they protect and secure human rights, state boundaries are not morally
significant.[19] While affirming the legal principle of nonintervention, *cosmopolitan justice* assumes that the existing structures and rules of international society should not be used to protect injustice within states. Thus,
when gross human rights abuses occur, foreign intervention, whether individual or collective, is not only permissible but also, in exceptional circumstances, morally obligatory. Accordingly, when states are unable or
unwilling to secure citizens' rights and, more important, when they intentionally violate universally accepted human rights norms, they lose their

moral standing in the international society of states. In short, sovereignty is subordinated to human rights.

These two conceptions of political justice provide alternative approaches to the pursuit of world order and the protection of human rights. Because the communitarian approach emphasizes the role and legitimacy of states, it is more likely to foster international stability. The cosmopolitan approach, by contrast, focuses on individual welfare and thus is more likely to encourage the protection of human rights. Moreover, because the quest for global order and the protection of human rights are not complementary processes, the pursuit of order will often come at the expense of human rights and vice versa. If the pursuit of world order is primary, honoring state autonomy may require tolerating domestic injustices. However, if human rights claims are primary, sovereignty might have to be compromised through humanitarian intervention to halt the gross violation of human rights. Thus, because the pursuit of international justice frequently involves a trade-off between sovereignty and human rights, between autonomy and suffering, the quest for a just international order can be realized only imperfectly, most often by giving precedence to either a cosmopolitan or a communitarian perspective.

On the basis of the concepts and approaches developed previously, I next examine the ethics of foreign aid, seeking to illuminate some of the important dilemmas and issues involved in foreign economic assistance.

CASE NO. 8–2
THE ETHICS OF FOREIGN AID

Do rich societies have a moral obligation to provide economic assistance to poor countries? If it is assumed that developed nations have a moral duty to alleviate hunger, human suffering, and poverty, how much economic aid should states provide, and to whom should the aid be given—to people directly (through NGOs) or to their governments? Before examining such moral dimensions of economic assistance, I briefly sketch the origins and development of modern foreign aid.

Background

The modern foreign aid regime began in 1949, when the United States inaugurated a foreign economic assistance program to foster economic growth and development in the developing nations of Asia, Africa, and Latin America. In launching the U.S. foreign aid program (called Point Four), President Harry S. Truman noted that, because more than half the world was living in conditions of hunger, disease, and misery, the United States "should make available to peace-loving peoples the benefits of our store of technical knowledge in order to help them realize their aspirations for a better life." As Truman asserted, "Greater production is the key to prosperity and peace. And the key to greater production is a wider and more vigorous application of modern scientific and technical knowledge. Only by helping the least fortunate of its members can the human family achieve the decent, satisfying life that is the right of all people."[20] Although the Point Four program was modest in its inception, U.S. economic assistance expanded greatly throughout the 1950s and 1960s. Moreover, beginning in the late 1950s, other developed democratic states joined the United States in providing development assistance to the poor nations. Although their contributions were modest at first, they increased both absolutely and relatively throughout the 1970s and 1980s. Whereas the United States provided more than half of all development aid in the 1950s and 1960s, by 1975 it had declined to 30 percent and by 1989 to only 16 percent.[21]

Foreign aid, generally referred to as official development assistance (ODA), involves loans and grants provided bilaterally and multilaterally to assist the economic development of poor countries. It has been estimated that developed democratic countries have given more than $1.1 trillion (constant 1988 dollars) in ODA during the Cold War era. Because ODA includes only the official financial transfers from Western governments to the Third World and does not include foreign direct investment, commercial loans, or nongovernment financial transfers and humanitarian relief, it greatly understates the net transfer of financial resources from Western societies to developing nations. For example, although OECD estimated that in 1982 $18 billion of ODA was given for relief and development, the total net transfer of financial resources from the rich to the poor countries was estimated at almost $80 billion, or more than four times the size of ODA.[22] Assuming that total net financial transfers have been roughly three times the size of ODA, it would be reasonable to assume that during the 1950–90 period total net financial transfers (official and commercial, governmental and nongovernmental) from the West to the Third World were at least $3 trillion, or about three times the estimated $1.1 trillion ODA.

Although numerous justifications have been given for granting foreign aid, David Lumsdaine argues convincingly that humanitarian concerns have provided the major impetus for economic assistance to the Third World. After examining Western economic assistance during the 1949–89 period, Lumsdaine concludes that donor countries' "sense of justice and compassion" provided the major reason for giving aid. He writes, "Support for aid was a response to world poverty which arose mainly from ethical and humane concerns and secondarily, from the belief that long-term peace and prosperity was possible only in a generous and just international order where all could prosper."[23]

It is one thing to claim with Lumsdaine and others that foreign aid has been given for moral reasons, but has such aid resulted in improved living conditions for Third World peoples and contributed to global economic justice? Moreover, has foreign economic assistance fostered distributive justice within global society by reducing international economic inequalities among states? Critics of foreign aid, such as economist P.T. Bauer, have argued that development assistance has been counterproductive because it has exacerbated the politicization of Third World regimes, reinforced irresponsible behavior, and fostered economic dependency. Thus, rather than contributing to the economic development of the poor countries, foreign aid has created distortions that have impaired job creation.[24]

In chapter 2, I observed that an ethical foreign policy was one whose intentions, means, and results were moral. Noble goals might inspire the human spirit but they are not enough to ensure global justice. Although humanitarian intentions (e.g., relieving Third World poverty) are necessary in developing an ethical foreign economic policy, they will not alone ensure an ethical foreign economic policy. What is equally important is that meeting short-term human needs should not impair a country's long-term prospects for economic growth.

Morality, Justice, and Foreign Aid

Political philosophers generally differentiate between those motivations that involve universal, binding obligations and those that do not. According to Brian Opeskin, aid given as charity or benevolence is provided to help relieve hunger and suffering but does not involve a moral duty to do so.[25] Peoples and societies that do not transfer resources to those in need are not morally blameworthy, because such "supererogatory" acts are not morally obligatory and are expected only of saints and other moral exemplars, not of average human beings. According to the charity thesis, rich societies should provide economic assistance to poor nations to reduce extreme poverty and make the world a more humane environment. Seeking to improve the living standards of poor peoples is a worthy, noble goal, but there is no moral obligation to do so. Western foreign aid has been inspired and justified largely by this ethical perspective.

An alternative approach to foreign economic assistance is one that regards aid as morally obligatory. Political philosophers typically justify such moral duties on the basis of either claims of justice or claims of humanity. Following Aristotle, Opeskin argues that justice imposes two types of international obligations: corrective claims and distributive claims.[26] Because corrective, or restitutive, justice involves reparations for past wrongs, such justice requires that the prior injustices be clearly delineated before appropriate action can be taken. Claims of distributive justice, on the other hand, are rooted in the conviction that social and economic goods within a community should be distributed equitably. Although there is widespread support for the notion that the state has a moral obligation to ensure distributive justice within domestic society, there is much less support for the idea that distributive justice should be applied within the fragile international community.[27] As noted in the following, the more prevalent analyses of distributive justice involve the application of communitarian versus cosmopolitan claims.

Another major ethical basis for foreign aid is the moral claims of humanity. According to this thesis, because human beings are moral agents, they are entitled to universal protection regardless of proximity, ethnicity, nationality, or citizenship. When people suffer from hunger, disease, malnutrition, and other calamities, their fundamental worth as moral agents is compromised. In an influential essay written in response to the massive famine in Bangladesh, Peter Singer illustrates this approach by arguing that the societies with resources have a moral obligation to relieve human suffering regardless of where it is found. According to this argument, if people have the ability to prevent something bad from happening without sacrificing anything of comparable moral importance, they also have a moral obligation to help relieve suffering.[28]

In sum, foreign aid can be morally justified through claims of charity, justice, or humanity. Whereas charity encourages voluntary financial transfers to relieve suffering, justice and humanity impose moral obligations on the transfer of financial and material resources. Such aid can be justified either on the basis of rectifying past wrongs or to ensure a just distribution of the world's social and economic goods.

I noted previously that justice in global society can be defined either from the perspective of states (communitarian justice) or from the perspective of persons (cosmopolitan justice). From a communitarian perspective, rich states have a moral obligation to assist the economic development of poor countries to relieve poverty and human suffering in those lands. However, to whom is this moral duty owed—to poor states, to peoples in poor lands, or to both? Moderate communitarianism assumes that developed states have a moral obligation to both peoples and states in meeting immediate humanitarian needs as well as in fostering the economic development which alone can provide the basis for long-term improvement in living conditions. Although nongovernment actors can facilitate the distribution of short-term aid and contribute to long-term job creation, the development of infrastructure and the establishment of structures and policies conducive to job creation are essential in stimulating national economic expansion. As a result, communitarians strongly support government-to-government financial transfers. Because Western economic aid has been rooted in this moderate communitarian approach, most ODA has been given directly to governments.

The alternative approach of radical communitarianism assumes that states have a moral obligation to ensure distributive economic justice. From this perspective, rich states have a duty to assist low-income states to help reduce international economic inequalities. The NIEO, a proposal developed and proclaimed by the developing nations during the 1970s and early 1980s, was essentially a plan rooted in this "radical" communitarian vision. Essentially, the NIEO sought to reduce the economic gap between the rich and poor countries by calling for increased financial and technological transfers to the developing nations and for increased Third World participation and influence in the structures of the global economy itself. Although the NIEO was a relatively modest proposal, the underlying premises were rooted in the radical claim that the existing international economic system was morally bankrupt because of excessive and continually expanding international economic inequalities. By the late 1980s, however, the NIEO had lost much of its appeal, in great part because of the significant economic growth of some Third World countries and the growing support for economic liberalism, the prevailing ideology of the global economic order.

Of course, the most extreme approach to economic assistance is the cosmopolitan perspective. Because cosmopolitanism regards human welfare within global society as the principal determinant of justice, state and non-state actors have a moral obligation to relieve hunger and poverty wherever it occurs. Because state boundaries are not morally significant, foreign economic assistance should be provided until basic needs of all human beings have been met. Some thinkers, following the logic of cosmopolitanism, have argued that the welfare policies of modern democratic states should be applied to global society. However, political leaders have not seriously considered such speculative notions because governments from both poor and rich countries have remained staunchly committed to the system of sovereign states.

Moral Reflections

This case study suggests a number of critical issues.

- Because the international community is a global society of many different nations, are the rich, industrial states morally obligated to assist the poor countries?
- If a moral obligation exists, to whom should the aid be given—the people directly, NGOs, or governments?
- What should be the aim of foreign aid—to reduce global economic inequalities, foster national economic development, or meet basic human needs?

The Individual and Global Society

Historically, liberal political thought has been concerned mainly with defining the rights and duties of citizens within the boundaries of states. From the perspective of political liberalism, theorists have consistently asserted that just as citizens have the rights of freedom of speech or freedom of assembly, they have a right to freedom of movement within territorial boundaries. However, classical thinkers did not extend this argument to international society. Although international law has provided some regulatory principles governing emigration and immigration, transnational migration was left largely to the discretion of states. At the same time it is important to emphasize that the classical perspective did not assert unbridled nationalism. It did not claim, as Garrett Hardin has, that nations are like "lifeboats," each with a limited carrying capacity that requires that states impose strict limits on immigration.[29] All that the traditionalist perspective asserted was that states should take into consideration national and international claims when establishing rules for governing migration.

However, as global interdependence has increased the ease of transnational migration, the traditional view of absolute control over borders has been increasingly challenged. Some theorists, such as Joseph Carens and Peter Singer, have argued that international justice requires an open admissions policy.[30] They have suggested that, because birth and citizenship are entirely a matter of chance, there is no moral justification for distributing economic, social, and political benefits through states. Following the cosmopolitan perspective, these thinkers have argued that the rights of persons must take moral precedence over the political claims of national autonomy. More particularly, they have suggested that citizens' economic, social, political, and cultural claims must be subordinated to the basic needs of foreigners and especially to the fundamental human rights claims of migrants.

The Ethics of Migration

Are the territorial subdivisions of the international community morally important? More particularly, are the rights and interests of states morally significant, as communitarians suggest, or must national interests be subordinated to the claims of individuals, as cosmopolitanists suggest? How should the needs of migrants be morally reconciled with the claims of national autonomy?

From the perspective of international political morality, individuals have an inherent right to leave their homeland. This right, which has become increasingly accepted as a fundamental human right in the contemporary international system, is defined in categorical and unqualified terms by the Universal Declaration of Human Rights (Article 13): "Everyone has the right to leave any country, including his own." The moral basis of the right of emigration is rooted in the voluntary character of democratic societies. Alan Dowty explains the priority of the right to emigrate as follows:

> The right to leave thus gets at the very essence of government by consent—a concept that has achieved near universal acceptance in principles, even amongst states that rarely abide by it. Since government by consent holds that citizenship is a voluntary act, the right to leave a country implicitly serves to ratify the contract between an individual and society. If a person who has the right to leave chooses to stay, he has signaled his voluntary acceptance of the social contract. From this follows his obligation to society. But if he does not have the option of leaving, then society's hold on him is based only on coercion.[31]

Dowty argues that the character of a regime is revealed by the respect that it accords to personal self-determination and, in particular, to the right of emigration. As Dowty's statement at the beginning of this chapter suggests, the degree of personal autonomy is a measure of a country's "overall social health."

Individuals also have a right of emigration from an international legal perspective. Although some European states extended the doctrine of sovereignty in the seventeenth and eighteenth centuries to prohibit emigration (to increase their population base), it is clear that contemporary international law provides states with no such right.[32] From an international legal perspective, persons have the right to leave their homeland or country of residence. Thus, when East Germany erected the Berlin Wall to keep its people from migrating to West Berlin, this action was considered morally and legally reprehensible. Similarly, when the government of the Soviet Union refused exit visas to Soviet Jews, this action was widely condemned as an affront to international human rights. Fundamentally, then, individuals, not governments, have the right to decide whether and when they will leave their country of residence. Moreover, although states have the legal and moral right to expel illegal aliens (i.e., foreign persons whose entry into a country was not legally approved), it is legally and morally impermissible for governments to deport their own people.

Although individuals have a right to emigrate, they do not necessarily have a right of immigration. This is because governments, not international organizations or migrants themselves, determine admission into sovereign countries.[33] Although the Universal Declaration of Human Rights (Article 15.1) affirms the right to a nationality, this claim does not entitle a person to reside in a country of his or her choice. As Brian Barry has noted, "It is a general characteristic of associations that people are free to leave them but not free to join them."[34] Thus, emigration and immigration are morally and legally asymmetrical. The moral asymmetry between exit and entry, departure and arrival, is illustrated in everyday social and economic life. For example, workers have a right to leave their place of employment but are not entitled to another job of their own choosing. Employers, not prospective employees, determine employment. Similarly, students may withdraw from colleges and universities at any time, but their desire to continue their studies at another academic institution depends wholly on their admittance to that institution.

Michael Walzer has set forth one of the most powerful arguments about the ethics of border regulation. He argues that regulating membership through admission and exclusion is essential in preserving "communities of character," that is, "historically stable, ongoing associations of men and women with some special commitment to one another and some special sense of their common life."[35] Walzer explains the necessity of regulating migration as follows:

> The distinctiveness of cultures and groups depends upon closure and cannot be conceived as a stable feature of human life without it. If this distinctiveness is a value . . . then closure must be permitted somewhere. At some level of political organization something like the sovereign state must take shape and claim the authority to make its own admissions policy, to control and sometimes restrain the flow of immigrants.[36]

Walzer illustrates the nature and importance of membership by comparing political communities with neighborhoods, clubs, and families. States, he suggests, are like neighborhoods in that national cohesion depends significantly on common cultural, social, and ethnic bonds. Just as neighborhood unity is rooted in shared values and customs, national cohesion similarly derives from common cultural and political norms and widely shared communal aspirations. States are also like clubs in that membership is entirely up to the members themselves to decide. Admissions policies, like immigration laws, are a significant feature of communal life because they contribute to the maintenance of cohesion and a sense of shared purpose. Finally, states resemble families in that they can help meet the human needs of nonmembers. Although family commitments are generally directed toward next of kin, families also provide periodically for the well-being of strangers; similarly, states frequently extend refuge to persons in need even when there is no religious, ethnic, or political bond between the refugees and the state's citizens.

Walzer's analysis suggests that political communities have the right to protect their distinctive cultural, social, and political features and to seek to perpetuate those distinctive qualities through immigration controls. At the same time, political communities, he suggests, have a moral obligation to strangers, especially those who suffer persecution and destitution. Walzer's arguments are significant because they provide moral justification for the contemporary immigration regime based on widely shared rules and procedures governing migration flows. Myron Weiner characterizes this emerging consensus as follows:

> . . . that no government is obligated to admit migrants, that migration is a matter of individual national policy, that most governments need more effective control over their borders, that more forceful measures are needed to halt illegal migration and the growth of worldwide migrant smuggling, that improved procedures are needed to distinguish genuine asylum seekers and refugees suffering from persecution and violence from individuals who use these procedures to migrate, that "temporary" guestworker policies do not work.[37]

One of the most difficult moral issues in immigration politics is the determination of how many immigrants should be admitted annually and what criteria should govern the selection process. Such concerns have become especially salient in the late twentieth century in western European countries and the United States because of the large number of immigrants and refugees seeking admission into developed countries. Immigration pressures, which are much greater than at any time in either the nineteenth or the twentieth century, are a result of several developments. First, as international economic inequalities have increased, people suffering from poverty have tried to escape their relative economic deprivation by seeking entry into more economically prosperous countries. The phenomenon of "boat people"—citizens seeking to escape poverty and oppression by sea travel—is a dramatic illustration of this development. Second, the growth in ethnic and ideological conflicts has resulted in many bitter civil wars that have undermined government authority and have led to the collapse of states. The collapse of public authority has, in turn, encouraged people to flee the bondage and instability of their homeland. Third, the growing global interdependence has provided the information and transportation networks that make mass migration more feasible. As a result of these and other developments, the number of refugees fleeing war, oppression, and persecution has increased dramatically—from a level of less than 5 million refugees in the 1970s to more than 15 million in the 1990s.

The Ethics of Asylum

Among the many moral challenges posed by migration politics, none is more complex and morally vexing than the issue of refugees or "forced migrants," that is, people displaced from their political home.[38] Several factors make the plight of refugees especially challenging legally and morally. First, because refugees fall, as Louis Henkin has noted, "in the interstices of state boundaries," they suffer from the lack of protection from authoritative institutions.[39] To be sure, humanitarian organizations, such as the Office of the UN High Commissioner for Refugees (UNHCR), play a major role in caring for refugees, but it is governments that determine whether refugees return to their homeland, remain in the country of first asylum or are accepted for permanent resettlement in a third state.

Second, determining which peoples are entitled to refugee status is difficult. Although there is broad consensus that a refugee is any person living outside his or her homeland because of a "well-founded fear of persecution,"[40] governments have applied widely different admission criteria for asylum seekers. Determining which asylum seekers have legitimate claims is frequently complicated by the large number of refugees making claims on particular states as well as by the rising number of claims regarded as unwarranted and unfounded. Because western European countries, especially Germany, have historically maintained generous asylum policies, it is not surprising that tens of thousands of persons sought protection in these states in the wake of increasing civil strife and economic turmoil in Yugoslavia and former Soviet-dominated countries. It has been estimated that from 1988 to 1992, the number of refugees in western Europe increased from 230,000 to 660,000, resulting in a major migration crisis.[41] This was especially the case in Germany, the country with the largest number of refugees. Because government officials considered many of the refugees' claims to be unfounded, governments, led by Germany, established more restrictive refugee policies to manage and reduce the number of asylum seekers.[42]

Third, because the number of persons seeking asylum has greatly exceeded the supply of authorized visas, governments have established preferential criteria for determining refugee admissions. For example, during the last half of the Cold War the United States gave preferential treatment to political refugees (persons fleeing tyrannical regimes, especially communist countries) over economic refugees (persons fleeing desperately poor nations).

Although scholars and public officials generally concur that states bear a moral obligation to care for foreigners in need, there is little agreement on the nature and scope of humanitarian assistance that should be provided, especially to refugees. Cosmopolitanists, for example, argue that refugee resettlement should be greatly increased,[43] whereas nationalists would prefer to limit such practices in the belief that significant refugee flows undermine national economic, social, and cultural well-being. Communitarians, holding to an intermediary position, assume that states have a moral obligation to provide humanitarian assistance but not necessarily an obligation to accept refugees. Human suffering requires that states care for strangers but not that they grant membership. Myron Weiner has described the intermediary position as follows: "If someone is in urgent need and the risks and cost of giving aid are low, we ought to help the injured stranger—not on the basis of justice but on the basis of charity."[44]

Although the Universal Declaration of Human Rights enshrines the right of return (repatriation), the ability and willingness of people to avail themselves of this right depends largely on local political conditions. Normally, repatriation is difficult because the political instability, oppression, and enmity that originally forced people to flee are seldom remedied in the short term. As a result, refugee protection generally depends on the humanitarian concern of foreign governments, especially neighboring states, and more generally on international organizations such as the UNHCR.

In addressing the needs of refugees, it is generally acknowledged that for communal reasons the most desirable long-term solution for refugees is repatriation back to the home country. It is also generally recognized that third-country resettlement is the least desirable solution, in part because of the great cultural, social, and economic challenges that refugees themselves must overcome in becoming fully integrated into the new society. Repatriation is most easily accomplished when refugees have found temporary relief in refugee camps in neighboring states. It is most difficult when refugees have been resettled in far-away lands in modern states. Thus, Vietnamese refugees in the United States or Rwandan refugees in Sweden are unlikely to return to their homeland unless they are forced to do so.

Although international migration pressures are being faced by many developed states, they are especially acute in the United States, a country that has historically maintained one of the most liberal immigration and refugee policies in the world. I next illustrate some of the moral dilemmas involved in migration policies by exploring U.S. immigration practices.

CASE NO. 8–3
THE ETHICS OF U.S. IMMIGRATION POLICY

Background

Historically, the United States has been a nation of immigrants. The growth and early development of the country are closely bound to immigration. From 1820 to 1860, nearly five million immigrants came to the United States. During the next twenty years, another five million foreigners arrived, principally from England, Ireland, and German states. The growth of immigration culminated in the 1900–20 period, when more than 14.5 million persons, principally from southern and eastern Europe, settled in the United States. This mass migration was facilitated in part by the relatively modest regulations governing immigration. However, this open and largely unregulated approach changed abruptly in the aftermath of World War I, when Congress turned inward by first passing temporary immigration restrictions in 1921 (the Temporary Quota Act) and then adopting the Immigration Act of 1924. The 1921 law established strict national immigration controls for the first time, reducing total annual immigration and creating a national origins quota system to maintain the country's ethnic and cultural distribution. The new law set the annual immigration quota at 3 percent of a given nationality residing in the United States in 1910; the 1924 Immigration Act reduced the quota to 2 percent and moved back the target year to 1890. Because these laws sought to maintain the ethnic and cultural status quo, they favored the early immigrant peoples of northern and western Europe and discriminated against newcomers, such as Italians, Spaniards, and Russians and especially Asians, Africans, and Latin Americans.

In time, the national quota system was perceived as politically and morally unacceptable. As a result, Congress passed the 1965 Immigration and Nationality Act, replacing nationality with family reunification and employment-based immigration criteria. In addition to giving priority to relatives of citizens or permanent residents and to immigrants who possessed skills needed in the American economy, the law granted preferences to refugees, who were brought within the general immigration system for the first time. As expected, the new legislation resulted in major changes in immigration patterns, including a significant rise in the number of non-Europeans. At the same time, illegal immigration began to grow, especially from Mexico and other Central American countries. To reduce the growing number of undocumented aliens, Congress passed the 1986 Immigration Reform and Control Act (IRCA), which required employers to verify the legal status of workers. At the same time, IRCA granted amnesty to all undocumented aliens who could prove that they had been living in the United States prior to January 1, 1982—a development that resulted in some 2.7 million illegal aliens gaining citizenship eligibility.[45]

The basic statutory guidelines for admitting refugees were first established in the Refugee Act of 1980. This legislation is significant because it greatly expanded refugee admissions and established greater order in refugee resettlement. The latter was achieved by requiring annual executive-legislative consultation to establish the maximum number and geographical distribution of refugees to be admitted in a given year.[46] The Refugee Act also authorized the Immigration and Naturalization Service, the federal agency responsible for implementing immigration and refugee policies, to annually grant asylum to some 10,000 eligible asylees.

The most recent changes in U.S. immigration policy are defined in the 1990 Immigration Act (IMMACT), which increased total annual immigration levels to roughly 700,000 and modified the immigration criteria, granting 80 percent of total immigration for family reunification and 20 percent for desired employment.[47] In addition, IMMACT defined groups that are to receive special humanitarian consideration, including Amerasians (children of American fathers and Vietnamese mothers), refugees (persons suffering from persecution who request entry from outside of the receiving state), and asylees (refugees who seek permission to remain in the receiving state after they have arrived). In the early 1990s, the United States was annually accepting about 120,000 refugees for permanent resettlement and granting admission to about 10,000 asylees.

Morality and U.S. Immigration Policy

During the late 1980s and early 1990s, the United States admitted about 800,000 persons annually. Of the total legal admissions, about 15 percent were classified as refugees, with most immigrants being admitted on the basis of family reunification (65 percent) and skill-based preferences (19 percent). From an ethical perspective, are such admissions distributions morally justified? Do U.S. immigration policies provide sufficient protection to refugees? Is the preferential treatment accorded aliens with close family ties to a U.S. citizen or those with needed job skills morally justifiable? Clearly, there are no "right" moral answers to such questions, because they depend on prudential judgments rooted in a variety of competing and conflicting claims, especially between the claims of nationals and those of migrants. Moreover, the admissions policies will involve moral ambiguity because of the inevitable trade-off between the moral claim of compassion and the legitimate responsibility to protect communal rights and interests.

I have argued that the existing international system gives sovereign states the legal and moral right to regulate immigration. It follows that governments are entitled to establish immigration ceilings and to implement preferential treatment that they believe will contribute to the social, political, economic, and cultural development of nations. Ethical traditions and moral values are essential in developing admissions policies because they provide the normative structure for defining and assessing the means and goals of government action. However, although morality is important in developing a prudent admissions policy, it is not alone sufficient. Indeed, because moral considerations are but one element of a multidimensional process, migration and refugee issues cannot be defined solely in terms of morality.[48]

From a moral perspective, the persons with the strongest claim to admission in the United States are likely to be refugees. Because such individuals have fled their homeland to avoid persecution, there is a general consensus that such persons are entitled to special protection. However, their need of refuge does not entitle them to admission into the United States (or, for that matter, any other state), because admission in the contemporary international system is normally regarded as a humanitarian act, not a binding moral obligation. This is the underlying principle of the 1980 Refugee Act, which views refugee admissions as "an exceptional *ex gratia* act provided by the United States in furthering foreign and humanitarian policies."[49]

Although refugee claims should receive special moral consideration, in practice the granting of refuge is a difficult task that is made all the more challenging by excessive immigration demand and by the growing range of abuses and human sufferings that are used to justify refugee status. Because of the large number of peoples seeking admission into the United States, millions of aliens, especially from Caribbean and Central American countries, have sought illegal entry into the United States. Moreover, because migration is governed by statutory limitations and regulations, hundreds of thousands of undocumented aliens have entered illegally into the United States, hoping to bypass immigration laws and seeking legal status through judicial review proceedings. The great demand for entry into the United States is evidenced by the fact that U.S. officials apprehended more than 8.3 million deportable aliens in the 1980s.[50] Nonetheless, hundreds of thousands of persons have succeeded in entering the country illegally. Although estimates of the number of undocumented aliens vary significantly, a conservative estimate suggests that as of 1992 there were 3.4 million illegal aliens, of whom 1.3 million (roughly 40 percent) were from Mexico.[51]

Equally problematic is the broadening interpretation of refugee entitlement. Although the United States follows international law in defining refugees as those persons who have fled their homeland because of "a well-founded fear of persecution," the circumstances justifying refugee status have expanded in light of growing admissions pressures. During the Cold War, the United States granted refugee claims largely on the basis of political oppression, but in the post-Cold War era, other factors, such as religion, ethnicity, and cultural mores, have been accepted as legitimate justifications for persecution. For example, a young Muslim woman successfully claimed refugee status because female circumcision was required of all young women in her homeland.[52] Because refugee admissions are governed by geographical and preferential criteria, the changing application of refugee status has resulted in different admissions policies that have modified but not necessarily increased refugee admissions.

The difficulty in responding to refugee claims is illustrated by the moral challenge posed by the tens of thousands of Haitians who have sought to enter the United States illegally since the early 1980s. Throughout the 1970s, a growing number of Haitians migrated to the United States, most of them legally. However, in the 1980s, a large number of Haitians sought to flee their homeland not only because of its abject poverty, civil unrest, and political oppression but also because of the desire to find refuge in a developed country. The number of Haitian "boat people" increased dramatically in the early 1980s, in part because of growing leniency toward Haitian asylees (Haitian refugees in the United States) and because of the success of some 125,000 Cubans fleeing their homeland in the 1980 Mariel boatlift.[53] To stem the tide of Haitian illegal immigration, the Reagan administration made an agreement in 1981 with Haiti's dictator, Jean-Claude Duvalier, permitting the U.S. Coast Guard to interdict Haitian vessels and screen refugees at sea. In addition, U.S. officials began a large-scale detention of Haitian asylees with the hope that such action would deter illegal immigration. As a result of these and other initiatives, Haitian illegal migration declined significantly.

However, following the 1991 military coup that overthrew the elected government of President Jean-Bertrand Aristide, the number of Haitian refugees increased once again, especially after the international community's economic sanctions began to inflict significant hardship. Indeed, the number of Haitians being interdicted was so high by late 1991 that the United States established a temporary processing center in Guantanamo Bay, Cuba, that was filled to capacity by mid-1992. Because of the overwhelming flow of refugees, President George Bush issued an executive order authorizing the U.S. Coast Guard to halt all Haitian boat people and return them, as well as those held in Guantanamo Bay, to Haiti.[54] Although Bill Clinton criticized the Bush administration's policy of repatriating Haitian refugees, he followed a similar policy after he assumed office, and when the flow of Haitian boat people increased again in 1994, the United States forced the removal of the military government and the reinstatement of President Aristide. This development contributed greatly to the reduction in Haitian illegal immigration.

The moral assessment of U.S. immigration policy will depend in great measure on what ethical traditions and methodologies are utilized. For example, since cosmopolitanism regards state boundaries as morally insignificant, cosmopolitan thinkers are likely to conclude that U.S. immigration statutes are of dubious moral validity because they subordinate refugee claims to the national interest. On the other hand, nationalists (amoral realists) will similarly disapprove of American immigration policies, but for opposite reasons, namely, because citizens' claims are unnecessarily subordinated to those of immigrants and refugees. Only principled realists, that is, those who seek to reconcile national claims with global needs, power, and morality, are likely to endorse the American approach to immigration because it seeks to protect the legitimate interests of domestic society while also providing humanitarian care.

However, because principled realists hold a wide variety of conceptions of the nature, role, and priority of political morality, their ethical perspectives on American immigration policy differ as well. For example, some principled realists, such as Walzer, have justified the American communal approach by claiming that states are entitled to regulate migrant and refugee admissions and that no person, even a refugee, is morally entitled to admission in a foreign state. Walzer suggests that although political communities, following the principle of "mutual aid," should provide humanitarian aid as the need arises and as resources permit, refugees have no right to expect admission.[55] Other principled realists, such as Weiner, have sought to defend regulatory immigration policies while deemphasizing morality. Although Weiner recognizes that migration and refugee issues involve both moral and political considerations, he emphasizes the prudential nature of public policies, arguing that immigration policies are "not a matter of general moral principles but of politically defined national interests and values, that is, in the broadest sense, national sovereignty."[56]

Moral Reflections

This brief examination of U.S. immigration policy raises a number of critical moral issues about migration politics.

- Do individuals have a basic right to emigrate?
- What are states' moral obligations toward migrants and especially refugees? Do these moral obligations toward foreigners depend on the size, wealth, or population density of a country?
- Is U.S. immigration policy consistent with international morality? In light of the U.S. admission of about 800,000 migrants and refugees annually, does U.S. policy adequately protect the communal solidarity of the American nation while also adequately caring for the needs of immigrants?
- Is the U.S. policy of granting preferential treatment to families and, to a lesser degree, to workers with particular job skills morally justified?
- What policy should the United States pursue toward illegal aliens?

Should such aliens be deported? Should they be accorded similar social, economic, and civil benefits as legal migrants? What policies should be adopted to reduce illegal immigration?

Summary

The quest for international justice in global society is elusive not only because governments fail to formulate and implement policies that advance the common good but also because analysts and public officials hold different and frequently conflicting conceptions of global justice. For example, policies based on procedural justice will differ from those based on distributive justice, and policies based on communitarian values will differ from those based on cosmopolitanism. Because of competing conceptions of international justice, foreign policies must frequently choose between strategies that promote states' rights and those that focus directly on human dignity, recognizing that the pursuit of the latter will not necessarily enhance the sovereignty, economic development, and national well-being of countries. Indeed, as the analyses of foreign aid and international migration suggest, the claims of sovereignty are frequently in conflict with the legitimate claims of citizens. Thus, in formulating a moral foreign policy, governments must weigh the claims of foreign states and their people against legitimate domestic interests.

CHAPTER NINE

ETHICS MATTER

> Politics will, to the end of history, be an arena where con-
> science and power meet, where the ethical and coercive fac-
> tors of human life will interpenetrate and work out their ten-
> tative and uneasy compromises.
>
> Reinhold Niebuhr[1]

Ethics matter. Although most international relations are carried out by complex entities called states, these political communities bear moral responsibilities domestically and internationally. Domestically, states are just and legitimate to the extent that they fulfill widely accepted international moral obligations, such as the protection of human rights and the promotion of the social and economic well-being of persons; internationally, states are morally legitimate to the extent that they fulfill their legal and ethical responsibilities as members of global society, including such duties as honoring the sovereignty and territorial integrity of other states, the pursuit of peaceful foreign relations, the promotion of international stability and global justice, and the protection of the global environment.

The realist tradition has commonly regarded international relations as an arena dominated by the quest for security and by the instruments of power and force. Although security is a core national interest, survival is not the only goal of states. Indeed, most global politics involves the pursuit of many different individual and collective interests through a variety of means other than power. Because the conceptualization of national interests and the development and implementation of policies are based on moral values and ethical judgments, political decision making is of necessity a moral enterprise—a truth that is regularly confirmed by contemporary international events. For example, after India and Pakistan carried out nuclear tests in mid-1998, thereby confirming their status as nuclear powers, the U.S. government was faced with the challenge of responding to this dangerous development. Political calculations were involved in determining how the U.S. government should confront India and Pakistan in their violation of the nonproliferation regime. However, moral reasoning was also involved as decision makers pondered the short- and long-term implications of these developments. The U.S. government's decisions to provide famine relief to North Korea in 1997 and 1998 and to continue comprehensive economic sanctions against Iraq in the aftermath of the Persian Gulf War were similarly rooted in moral judgments. Clearly, the claim of moral skeptics that power and necessity alone dictate international politics is unpersuasive.

As Reinhold Niebuhr's statement at the beginning of this chapter suggests, political decision making is a domain in which morality and power coalesce. This study has sought to defend the Niebuhrian claim by exploring the nature and role of moral values in international relations. The aim has not been to provide "moral" solutions to major international issues. Rather, the goal has been to define concepts, strategies, and ethical traditions that facilitate moral reflection about international relations and to illustrate the role of political morality in global politics with case studies in five major problem areas: human rights, force, intervention, economic sanctions, and global issues.

As noted throughout this study, moral values are essential in developing a sound foreign policy and creating norms and structures that are conducive to a more peaceful and just global society. As ancient philosophers long ago observed, the good life (summum bonum) is based on individual and communal justice. A major aim of international ethics is to foster political justice within and among states by illuminating relevant moral norms and structuring moral reasoning. This task is especially daunting because global society is comprised of many states, each with its own cultural norms and conceptions of morality. However, the existence of cultural pluralism does not invalidate either the quest for international justice or the legitimacy of political morality. Rather, the reality of competing cultures and moral traditions provides an environment for encouraging a deeper, more reflective political morality and a more self-critical application of such morality to international affairs.

One of the reasons for scholars' and decision makers' limited concern with international ethics is the belief that politics and moral reasoning are two distinct realms that should not be integrated: Politics is a domain of power and community-wide decision making, whereas ethics, as a branch of philosophy, is a domain of speculative reasoning. It is commonly assumed that whereas the task of the moral philosopher is to explore the nature of morality and the basis of moral obligation, the task of the statesman is to foster global order, facilitate transnational cooperation, and promote peaceful conflict resolution. These two tasks, it is sometimes argued, should not be combined if analysis and decision making are to remain logical and internally consistent. However, applied ethics, by definition, seeks to develop moral reasoning in specific areas of public and private life. Thus, international ethics is concerned with the interrelationship of moral values and foreign policy, ethics and international politics.

Of course, not all issues, claims, and arguments in international relations are concerned with ethics. As noted in chapter 1, ethics involves the identification, critique, and application of moral values to human life. International ethics is thus concerned solely with the normative realm, that is, with choices and actions involving right and wrong, good and evil. Nonmoral concerns—such as historical facts about territorial boundary claims or the international law of the sea or empirical facts about the balance of trade, weapons development programs, or environmental protection rules—are not a central focus of international ethics because descriptive issues do not involve normative judgments. Thus, in bringing moral reasoning to bear on international affairs, it is important to distinguish between the empirical and normative realms and then to identify and apply political morality to particular foreign policy issues or global concerns.

The challenge of differentiating between the empirical and normative realms is illustrated by the phenomenon of global warming, a development brought about partly by human-made greenhouse gases that trap solar heat. Knowledge about the nature, causes, and potential effects of global warming is based on science and thus is not subject to moral judgment. By contrast, defining the nature and extent of states' responsibilities for global warming is a normative issue because the individual and collective behaviors of states are partly responsible for the earth's climate. In view of the effects of greenhouse emissions on the earth's temperature, continued industrialization is likely to encourage further climate change. Thus, the potential adverse effects of increased global warming pose significant moral issues about states' individual and collective responsibility for past greenhouse emissions and for curbing future pollution.

In fostering moral reasoning and ethical decision making, statesmen and moralists employ a variety of approaches that rely on different methodologies, strategies, and ethical traditions. In classifying moral decision making, it is helpful to distinguish between those approaches that apply political morality deductively and those that do so inductively. The first approach is essentially a "top-down" methodology, bringing first principles to bear on specific issues and problems. Fundamentally, it is based on a rule-based strategy and is characterized by a highly structured decision-making process, relying heavily on moral theories. This approach is deductive because it begins with core norms and then applies them to particular issues and problems.

The application of the just-war tradition to issues of war and peace illustrates this approach. As one of the most sophisticated and comprehensive moral theories in international relations, the just-war tradition defines norms by which to assess when and how states may employ force in pursuing political justice. As a moral theory of decision making, the just-war tradition provides an understanding of statecraft in which the use of force in the service of justice is "both permitted and restrained."[2] Because the just-war doctrine is based on the quest for interstate justice, the doctrine's concepts and propositions are useful in assessing not only issues of war and peace but also other international relations concerns, such as economic sanctions and humanitarian intervention.[3]

The second approach to ethical decision making is inductive and informal, relying on a variety of concepts and strategies. It is a "bottom-up" methodology that applies morality flexibly to the goals, means, and results of decisions, relying mainly on the ends-based and tridimensional strategies described in chapter 2. Because this approach is eclectic, it is less structured than the deductive application of moral principles. Moreover, unlike the deductive method, this approach does not seek to apply rules and norms directly to issues but instead relies on prudence, allowing decision makers to define and select actions in light of potential alternatives. According to Robert Kagan, this inductive, prudential approach to decision making is politically and morally superior to an approach based on a priori guidelines because it permits flexibility in addressing the dynamic, ever-changing events of global society.

Both the deductive and the inductive decision-making models are ideal types, representing extremes along a continuum. Because most moral reasoning and decision making in international affairs involve elements from both models, most international ethical analysis will be found in the middle of the continuum. In implementing eclectic decision making rooted in deductive and inductive approaches, it is desirable to adhere to procedural rules that ensure moral accountability. As noted in chapter 2, a flexible, inductive approach can quickly lead to consequentialism if the integrity of decision making is not protected.

Regardless of which decision-making approaches and ethical traditions are applied to international affairs, it is clear that virtually all important foreign policy issues and global concerns involve moral values. Although politically salient issues such as disarmament, Third World poverty, gross human rights abuses, air and water pollution, and war clearly involve political morality, even technical problems and politically neutral issues might involve moral judgments. Indeed, because political life is based on human choices, few national and international concerns can bypass normative judgments. Moreover, in bringing political morality to bear on public policies, decision makers must judge moral action not only in terms of outcomes, as is commonly the case, but also in terms of the intended goals and methods used. Thus, developing a moral foreign policy is challenging precisely because few issues are likely to comply completely with all the demands of the tridimensional model of political ethics sketched in chapter 2.

Given the complexity of most global issues, ethical reasoning in international affairs seldom results in simple moral verdicts. Indeed, the explicit integration of political morality with the development and implementation of foreign policies rarely results in consensus among public officials and citizens. However, this lack of agreement does not imply (as some cynics have suggested) that moral standards do not exist in global politics, that moral reflection is unnecessary in foreign affairs, or that ethical decision making is a wholly subjective, relativistic enterprise. To be sure, the absence of agreement in international ethics is sometimes due to the underdeveloped nature of global morality. However, the lack of consensus in international ethics is often based on conflicts and disagreements over facts and interests, not moral values. As a result, what appears to be a dispute over political ethics might in reality be a conflict over different interpretation of facts or different assessments of political strategies.

For example, the mid-1980s global debate over the moral appropriateness of economic sanctions against South Africa was rooted mainly in different views of the political effectiveness of such statecraft, not in different perspectives on apartheid. Some apartheid critics favored sanctions in the belief that they would hasten democratic reform in South Africa; others opposed sanctions because they believed that isolating South Africa would only delay political change. Similarly, the failure of the United States and other major Western powers to respond to ethnic cleansing in the Bosnian war was partly due to strategic calculations about the costs, feasibility, and likely consequences of military intervention and partly due to a lack of moral courage to act on behalf of the common good. However, the international community's inaction toward the Bosnian genocide was also influenced by the widely disparate interpretations about the nature and causes of the war and the nature, sources, and scope of ethnic violence. Some viewed ethnic cleansing mainly as a Serb strategy to destroy the Muslim people and their culture; others viewed ethnic violence as part of a war among Croats, Muslims, and Serbs over whether and how to construct a multiethnic Bosnian state.[4] Although most Western observers viewed Serbs as the major perpetrators of Bosnian violence, by 1995 it was evident that Croats and Muslims had also carried out significant ethnic killing. Thus, the reticence and ineffectiveness of the United Nations in halting Bosnian violence was based in part on the perceived complexity and ambiguity of the conflict itself.

Although lack of knowledge might inhibit people from confronting gross evil in global society, the main obstacle to a vigorous application of international political ethics is behavioral, not intellectual. It is not the absence of empirical and moral knowledge that contributes to injustice and instability in global society; rather, leaders themselves fail to fulfill perceived moral obligations. One scholar has observed that in moral life "ignorance isn't all that common; dishonesty is far more so."[5] Thus, in developing a more humane and just global society, the great challenge is to develop both moral knowledge and personal character that leads to the fulfillment of foundational moral obligations. Applying international ethics will require knowledge of relevant concepts, strategies, and theories of international political morality. However, it will also involve the cultivation of moral character and human virtue that are essential in the moral life. If international ethics is to contribute to a more humane and just world order, citizens and leaders must possess both the wisdom to define international justice and the moral courage to fulfill moral duties.

CHAPTER NOTES

Introduction (pages xi to xvi)

1. George F. Kennan, "Morality and Foreign Policy," *Foreign Affairs* 64 (Winter 1985/1986): 206.

2. Arnold Wolfers, *Discord and Collaboration: Essays on International Politics* (Baltimore: Johns Hopkins University Press, 1962), 58.

3. The Dayton Peace Accord was a U.S.-brokered agreement among Muslim, Serb, and Croat leaders that brought an end to the fighting in Bosnia. The agreement, signed in November 1995, calls for a federal Bosnian state comprised of two government entities, one Serb and the other Muslim-Croat. To maintain order during a transitional phase, a 65,000-member NATO military force, led by the United States, was introduced to keep the belligerents apart and to ensure compliance with the accord's electoral and political provisions.

4. Although states are entitled under the norms of the international community to develop military capabilities to ensure their national security, the nonproliferation regime prohibits nonnuclear states from developing or acquiring nuclear arms.

Chapter One (pages 1 to 25)

1. Arnold Wolfers, *Discord and Collaboration: Essays on International Politics* (Baltimore: Johns Hopkins University Press, 1962), 58.

2. James Q. Wilson, "What Is Moral and How Do We Know It?" *Commentary* (June 1993): 43.

3. Sir Harold Nicolson, *Diplomacy*, 3rd ed. (New York: Oxford University Press, 1973), 147.

4. Dean Acheson, "Ethics in International Relations Today: Our Standard of Conduct," *Vital Speeches of the Day* 31 (February 1, 1965): 227.

5. Thomas Donaldson, "Kant's Global Rationalism," in *Traditions of International Ethics*, ed. Terry Nardin and David R. Mapel (Cambridge: Cambridge University Press, 1992), 137.

6. R. M. Hare, *Freedom and Reason* (Oxford: Oxford University Press, 1963), 15.

7. John Rawls, *A Theory of Justice* (Cambridge: Harvard University Press, 1971). For a further elaboration of Rawls's conceptualization of morality, see "The Nature and Bases of Political Morality" in this chapter.

8. Lord Moulton of Bank, "Law and Manners," quoted in Rushworth M. Kidder, *How Good People Make Tough Choices* (New York: Morrow, 1995), 67.

9. For a discussion of the distinction between moral and nonmoral decision-making realms, see William Frankena, *Ethics*, 2nd ed. (Englewood Cliffs, N.J.: Prentice Hall, 1973).

10. Lea Brilmayer, *American Hegemony: Political Morality in a One-Superpower World* (New Haven, Conn.: Yale University Press, 1994), 25.

11. It is interesting to note that a major aim of normative political theory has been to define the nature, scope, methods, duties, and constraints involved in just or legitimate political rule. Political thinkers have given many different justifications for political hierarchies, including knowledge, power, consent, social class, and religious fidelity.

12. Michael Walzer, *Just and Unjust Wars: A Moral Argument with Historical Illustrations* (New York: Basic Books, 1977).

13. Charles Beitz, *Political Theory and International Relations* (Princeton, N.J.: Princeton University Press, 1979).

14. George Kennan, *Realities of American Foreign Policy* (New York: Norton, 1966), 48.

15. John Rawls, "The Law of Peoples," in *On Human Rights: The Oxford Amnesty Lectures, 1993*, ed. Stephen Shute and Susan Hurley (New York: Basic Books, 1993), 41–82. For a penetrating critique of Rawls's argument, see Stanley Hoffmann, "Dreams of a Just World," *New York Review of Books,* November 2, 1995, 52–56.

16. Rawls, "The Law of Peoples," 55.

17. See, for example, David Gauthier, *Morals by Agreement* (Oxford: Oxford University Press, 1986).

18. Terry Nardin, "Ethical Traditions in International Affairs," in Nardin and Mapel, eds., *Traditions,* 12–13.

19. Dorothy V. Jones, *Code of Peace: Ethics and Security in the World of Warlord States* (Chicago: University of Chicago Press, 1992).

20. Michael Walzer, *Thick and Thin: Moral Argument at Home and Abroad* (Notre Dame, Ind.: University of Notre Dame Press, 1994), 1–19.

21. Ibid., 8.

22. Francis V. Harbour, "Basic Moral Values: A Shared Core," *Ethics and International Affairs* 9 (1995): 155–70.

23. A. J. M. Milne, "Human Rights and the Diversity of Morals: A Philosophical Analysis of Rights and Obligations in the Global System," in *Rights and Obligations in North-South Relations: Ethical Dimensions of Global Problems,* ed. Moorehead Wright (New York: St. Martin's Press, 1986), 21.

24. Walzer, *Just and Unjust Wars,* 19.

25. Thomas Donaldson, *The Ethics of International Business* (New York: Oxford University Press, 1989), 1.

26. John C. Bennett, *Foreign Policy in Christian Perspective* (New York: Scribner's, 1966), 36.

27. David Halloran Lumsdaine, *Moral Vision in International Politics: The Foreign Aid Regime, 1949–1989* (Princeton, N.J.: Princeton University Press, 1993), 283.

28. Ibid., 287.

29. Robert W. McElroy, *Morality and American Foreign Policy* (Princeton, N.J.: Princeton University Press, 1992), 30.

30. William Wilberforce labored for nearly fifteen years in the House of Commons before the slave trade was outlawed in 1807; he then devoted his remaining eighteen years in Parliament to the emancipation of slaves within the British Empire. On July 29, 1833, eight years after Wilberforce retired from Parliament, the House of Commons passed a bill abolishing slavery.

31. Robert Kennedy, *Thirteen Days* (New York: Norton, 1968), 27.

32. Arthur Schlesinger, Jr., "The Necessary Amorality of Foreign Affairs," *Harper's Magazine*, August 1971, 73.

33. Stanley Hoffmann, *Duties beyond Borders* (Syracuse, N.Y.: Syracuse University Press, 1981), 33.

34. Hannah Arendt, *The Human Condition* (Chicago: University of Chicago Press, 1958), 238–40.

35. Patrick Glynn, "Toward a New Peace: Forgiveness as Politics," *Current*, March/April 1995, 19.

36. For an illuminating study of the potential role of forgiveness in politics, see Donald W. Shriver, Jr., *An Ethic for Enemies: Forgiveness in Politics* (New York: Oxford University Press, 1995).

37. Elie Wiesel, "Remarks of Elie Wiesel at Ceremony for Jewish Heritage Week," in *Bitburg: In Moral and Political Perspective,* ed. Geoffrey Hartman, (Bloomington: Indiana University Press, 1986), 243.

38. Lance Morrow, "Forgiveness to the Injured Doeth Belong," *Time*, May 20, 1985, 90.

39. Wiesel, "Remarks," 242.

40. Ibid., 243–44.

41. "Interview of President Reagan by Representatives of Foreign Radio and Television," in Hartman, ed., *Bitburg,* 250–51.

42. William Safire, " 'I Am a Jew . . .' " in Hartman, ed., *Bitburg*, 214.

43. Quoted in Shriver, *An Ethic for Enemies,* 110.

Chapter Two (pages 27 to 46)

1. Peter Berger, "Moral Judgment and Political Action," *Vital Speeches of the Day* 54 (December 1, 1987): 179.

2. Stanley Hoffmann, *Duties beyond Borders: On the Limits and Possibilities of Ethical International Relations* (Syracuse, N.Y.: Syracuse University Press, 1981), 143–44.

3. Jeremy Bentham, *Principles of Morals and Legislation,* in *Great Political*

Thinkers: Plato to the Present, 4th ed., ed. William Ebenstein (Hinsdale, Ill.: Dryden Press, 1969), 515.

4. Jonathan Schell, *The Fate of the Earth* (New York: Avon Books), 152.

5. Bernard Brodie, "Implications for Military Policy," in *The Absolute Weapon: Atomic Power and World Order,* ed. Bernard Brodie (New York: Harcourt Brace, 1946), 76.

6. Henry Kissinger, *The Necessity for Choice: Prospects of American Foreign Policy* (Garden City, N.Y.: Doubleday, 1962), 12.

7. George F. Kennan, *The Nuclear Delusion* (New York: Pantheon, 1982), 202.

8. Michael Walzer, *Just and Unjust Wars: A Moral Argument with Historical Illustrations* (New York: Basic Books, 1977), 282.

9. Such conditions can involve norms for going to war (e.g., pursuit of a just cause, limited wartime goals, and exhaustion of alternatives before resorting to war) and norms for conducting the war (e.g., the use of proportional violence and the protection of civilians).

10. Michael Mandelbaum, *The Nuclear Revolution* (Cambridge: Cambridge University Press, 1981), 4.

11. National Conference of Catholic Bishops, *The Challenge of Peace: God's Peace and Our Response* (Washington, D.C.: United States Catholic Conference, 1983), 41–42.

12. The concept of firebreak, used by firefighters to denote land that is cleared to prevent the escalation of forest fires, refers to the physical and psychological area of demarcation between conventional and nuclear arms.

13. During the 1970s and 1980s, U.S. military strategists debated the relative merits of limited, nuclear war-fighting threats versus massive assured destruction threats. The first strategy, known as counterforce, or nuclear utilization theory (NUT), emphasized the actions that would be taken in the event of a failure in deterrence; the other strategy, known as countervalue, or MADvocy, emphasized the prevention of nuclear conflict altogether by emphasizing the unacceptability of nuclear conflict and by opposing nuclear war-fighting options that made retaliation more credible.

14. John Mearsheimer, "Why We Will Soon Miss the Cold War," *The Atlantic Monthly,* August 1990, 37.

15. Thomas Schelling, "What Went Wrong with Arms Control," *Foreign Affairs* 64 (Winter 1985/1986): 233.

16. Walzer, *Just and Unjust Wars,* 382.

17. National Conference of Catholic Bishops, *The Challenge of Peace,* 54–55.

18. John Lewis Gaddis, *The United States and the End of the Cold War* (New York: Oxford University Press, 1992), chap. 10.

19. Schelling, "What Went Wrong with Arms Control," 233.

20. See, for example, John Mueller, "The Essential Irrelevance of Nuclear Weapons: Stability in the Postwar World," *International Security* 13 (Fall 1988): 55–79; and John A. Vasquez, "The Deterrence Myth: Nuclear Weapons and the Prevention of Nuclear War," in *The Long Postwar Peace: Contending Explanations and Projections,* ed. Charles W. Kegley, Jr. (New York: HarperCollins, 1991), 205–23.

21. Thomas Donaldson, "Kant's Global Rationalism," in *Traditions of International Ethics,* ed. Terry Nardin and David R. Mapel (Cambridge: Cambridge University Press, 1992), 137–38.

22. David Halloran Lumsdaine, *Moral Vision in International Politics: The Foreign Aid Regime, 1949–1989* (New Haven, Conn.: Yale University Press, 1993), 283.

23. Frederick Lewis Schuman, *American Policy toward Russia since 1917* (New York: International Publishers, 1928), 277.

24. Thomas A. Bailey, *America Faces Russia: Russian-American Relations from Early Times to Our Day* (Ithaca, N.Y.: Cornell University Press, 1950), 253.

25. For an analysis of Herbert Hoover's role in the Russian famine relief, see Benjamin M. Weissman, *Herbert Hoover and Famine Relief to Soviet Russia: 1921–1923* (Stanford, Calif.: Hoover Institution Press, 1974).

26. Schuman, *American Policy toward Russia,* 204.

27. Weissman, *Herbert Hoover and Famine Relief,* 199.

28. Robert W. McElroy, *Morality and American Foreign Policy* (Princeton, N.J.: Princeton University Press, 1992), 86.

29. George F. Kennan, *Russia and the West under Lenin and Stalin* (Boston: Little, Brown, 1960), 180.

30. Hoffmann, *Duties beyond Borders,* 190–91.

31. Alberto R. Coll, "Normative Prudence as a Tradition of Statecraft," *Ethics & International Affairs* 5 (1991): 33.

32. Joseph S. Nye, Jr., *Nuclear Ethics* (New York: Free Press, 1986), 22.

33. Ronald Reagan, "Launching the SDI," in *Promise or Peril: The Strategic Defense Initiative,* ed. Zbigniew Brzezinski (Washington, D.C.: Ethics and Public Policy Center, 1986), 49.

34. William E. Burrows, "Ballistic Missile Defense: The Illusion of Security," *Foreign Affairs* 62 (Spring 1984): 844.

35. McGeorge Bundy, George F. Kennan, Robert S. McNamara, and Gerard Smith, "The President's Choice: Star Wars or Arms Control," *Foreign Affairs* 63 (Winter 1984/1985): 265.

36. Leon Wieseltier, "The Ungrand Compromise," *The New Republic,* November 16, 1986, 31.

Chapter Three (pages 47 to 68)

1. Charles R. Beitz, "The Reagan Doctrine in Nicaragua" in *Problems of International Justice,* ed. Steven Luper-Foy (Boulder, Colo.: Westview Press, 1988), 194.

2. Peter Berger, "Moral Judgment and Political Action," *Vital Speeches of the Day* 56 (December 1, 1987): 120.

3. Gordon A. Craig and Alexander L. George, *Force and Statecraft: Diplomatic Problems of Our Time,* 2nd ed. (New York: Oxford University Press, 1990), 275–88.

4. Terry Nardin, "Ethical Traditions in International Affairs," in *Traditions of*

International Ethics, ed. Terry Nardin and David R. Mapel (Cambridge: Cambridge University Press, 1992), 6.

5. Ibid.

6. Ibid. Interestingly, the tradition of prudence, rooted in the political thought of Aristotle and Aquinas and developed subsequently by Edmund Burke and others, is omitted in this study.

7. David A. Welch, "Can We Think Systematically about Ethics and Statecraft?" *Ethics & International Affairs* 8 (1994): 26–27.

8. Ibid., 33.

9. See J. L. Mackie, *Ethics: Inventing Right and Wrong* (New York: Penguin, 1977), 64.

10. Hans J. Morgenthau, *Politics among Nations: The Struggle for Power and Peace*, 5th ed., rev. (New York: Random House, 1978).

11. Ibid., 5.

12. Kenneth Waltz, *Theory of International Politics* (Reading, Pa.: Addison-Wesley, 1979), 118.

13. Steven Forde, "Classical Realism," in Nardin and Mapel, eds., *Traditions of International Ethics*, 63.

14. Jack Donnelly, "Twentieth-Century Realism," in Nardin and Mapel, eds., *Traditions of International Ethics*, 93.

15. George F. Kennan, "Morality and Foreign Policy," *Foreign Affairs* 64 (Winter 1985/1986): 206.

16. Morgenthau, *Politics among Nations*, 12.

17. Thucydides, *History of the Peloponnesian War*, trans. Rex Warner (Harmondsworth: Penguin, 1972), 23.

18. Donald Kagan, *On the Origins of War* (New York: Doubleday, 1995), 57, 69.

19. Robert Gilpin, *War and Change in World Politics* (Cambridge: Cambridge University Press, 1981), 227–28.

20. Thucydides, *History of the Peloponnesian War*, 402.

21. For an alternative assessment of idealism, see Michael W. Doyle, *Ways of War and Peace: Realism, Liberalism, and Socialism* (New York: Norton, 1997), pt. 2. Doyle differentiates among three types of liberalism in international relations thought: first, institutionalists, such as Locke and Bentham, who emphasize the role of human nature and the necessity of institutions to constrain human passions; second, commercial pacifists, such as Adam Smith and Joseph Schumpeter, who believe that trade is conducive to peace; and third, internationalists, such as Kant and Hume, who emphasize the pacific nature of international relations among constitutional regimes.

22. Ibid., 230–31.

23. For a discussion of Kant's system, see Doyle, *Ways of Peace and War,* 252–58.

24. Joseph M. Grieco, "Anarchy and the Limits of Cooperation: A Realist Critique of the Newest Liberal Institutionalism," in *Controversies in International Relations Theory: Realism and the Neoliberal Challenge,* ed. Charles W. Kegley, Jr. (New York: St. Martin's Press, 1995), 153–54.

25. John J. Mearsheimer, "The False Promise of International Institutions," *International Security* 19 (Winter 1994/95): 15.

26. For a discussion of political idealism in international affairs, see Michael Joseph Smith, "Liberalism and International Reform," in Nardin and Mapel, eds., *Traditions of International Ethics*, 201–24.

27. Ibid., 203.

28. E. H. Carr, *The Twenty Years' Crisis, 1919–1939: An Introduction to the Study of International Relations* (New York: Harper Torchbooks, 1964), 41–60.

29. Zbigniew Brzezinski, *Power and Principle: Memoirs of the National Security Adviser, 1977–1981* (New York: Farrar, Straus & Giroux), 49.

30. R. J. Vincent, "The Response of Europe and the Third World to United States Human Rights Diplomacy," in *The Diplomacy of Human Rights*, ed. David D. Newsom (Lanham, Md.: University Press of America, 1986), 36.

31. For a description and assessment of congressional human rights initiatives throughout the 1970s, see John P. Salzberg, "A View from the Hill: U.S. Legislation and Human Rights," in Newsom, ed., *The Diplomacy of Human Rights*, 13–20.

32. Jimmy Carter, "Power for Humane Purposes," in *Morality and Foreign Policy: A Symposium on President Carter's Stance,* ed. Ernest Lefever (Washington, D.C.: Ethics and Public Policy Center, 1977), 4–5.

33. Hendrik Hertzberg, quoted in Joshua Muravchik, *The Uncertain Crusade: Jimmy Carter and the Dilemmas of Human Rights Policy* (New York: Hamilton Press, 1986), 1.

34. The increased importance of the report is partly evident by its expanded breadth and depth, growing from about 137 pages in 1977 to more than 1,100 pages in 1981.

35. Quoted in Muravchik, *The Uncertain Crusade,* 24.

36. Irving Kristol, "Morality, Liberalism, and Foreign Policy," in Lefever, ed., *Morality and Foreign Policy*, 69.

37. Brzezinski, *Power and Principle,* 126.

38. Ibid., 528.

39. See Muravchik, *The Uncertain Crusade,* 53–73.

40. Jeane Kirkpatrick, "Human Rights and American Foreign Policy: A Symposium," *Commentary,* November 1981, 43.

Chapter Four (pages 69 to 92)

1. R. J. Vincent, "The Idea of Rights in International Ethics," in *Traditions of International Ethics,* ed. Terry Nardin and David R. Mapel (Cambridge: Cambridge University Press, 1992), 267.

2. Charles Krauthammer, "Morality and the Reagan Doctrine," *The New Republic*, September 8, 1986, 20.

3. For further discussion of this distinction, see Maurice Cranston, *What Are Human Rights?* (New York: Basic Books, 1962), 8–12.

4. Alan Gewirth, "Common Morality and the Community of Rights," in *Pros-*

pects for a Common Morality, ed. Gene Outka and John P. Reeder, Jr. (Princeton, N.J.: Princeton University Press, 1993), 30–31.

5. Ibid.

6. Rhoda E. Howard and Jack Donnelly, "Human Dignity, Human Rights, and Political Regimes," *American Political Science Review* 80 (September 1986): 802.

7. Ibid., 804.

8. R. J. Vincent, *Human Rights and International Relations* (Cambridge: Cambridge University Press, 1986), 21.

9. For a contrary view, see Arthur Schlesinger, Jr., "Human Rights and the American Tradition," *Foreign Affairs* 57, no. 3 (1979): 504. Schlesinger argues that because religion had traditionally rejected the notion that people were entitled to earthly happiness, Christianity had little to do with the rise of the idea of human rights.

10. Eugene Kamenka, "The Anatomy of an Idea," in *Human Rights*, ed. Eugene Kamenka and Alice Erh-Soon Tay (London: Edward Arnold, 1978), 5–6. See also Jack Donnelly, *Universal Human Rights in Theory and Practice* (Ithaca, N.Y.: Cornell University Press, 1989), 50.

11. The transcendent moral order applicable to political society has historically been defined as natural law. To simplify my argument, I avoid using this concept altogether, although it is clear that the foundation of classical human rights was the notion of natural law.

12. For an excellent overview of the meaning of the human rights doctrine, see Donnelly, *Universal Human Rights*, 9–27.

13. Vincent, *Human Rights and International Relations*, 7.

14. According to the philosophy of utilitarianism, decisions should seek to maximize "utility" by making choices that provide "the greatest good for the greatest number."

15. Christian Bay, "Self-Respect as a Human Right: Thoughts on the Dialectics of Wants and Needs in the Struggle for Human Community," *Human Rights Quarterly* 4 (February 1982): 53–75.

16. Charles R. Beitz, "Human Rights and Social Justice," in *Human Rights and U. S. Foreign Policy*, ed. Peter G. Brown and Douglas MacLean (Lexington, Mass.: Lexington Books, 1979), 45–63.

17. Henry Shue, *Basic Rights: Subsistence, Affluence, and U.S. Foreign Policy* (Princeton, N.J.: Princeton University Press, 1980), 13–34.

18. A. J. M. Milne, "Human Rights and the Diversity of Morals: A Philosophical Analysis of Rights and Obligations in the Global System," in *Rights and Obligations in North-South Relations,* ed. Moorehead Wright (New York: St. Martin's Press, 1986), 21.

19. Vincent, *Human Rights and International Relations*, 54–55.

20. Donnelly, *Universal Human Rights in Theory and Practice*, 112–14.

21. James Finn, ed., *Freedom in the World: The Annual Survey of Political Rights and Civil Liberties, 1994–1995* (New York: Freedom House, 1995), 505–8.

22. Michael Elliott, "The Caning Debate: Should America Be More Like Singapore?" *Newsweek*, April 18, 1994, 22.

23. Kishore Mahbubani, "The United States: 'Go East, Young Man,' " *The Washington Quarterly* 17 (Spring 1994): 11.

24. Ibid., 21.

25. Jack Donnelly, *International Human Rights* (Boulder, Colo.: Westview Press, 1993), 7.

26. Louis Henkin, *The Age of Rights* (New York: Columbia University Press, 1990), 19.

27. Other important international human rights agreements include the International Convention on the Prevention and Punishment of the Crime of Genocide (1948); the International Convention on the Elimination of All Forms of Racial Discrimination (1965); the Convention against Torture and Other Cruel, Inhuman or Degrading Treatment or Punishment (1984); and the Convention on the Rights of the Children (1989).

28. The right to development became an official part of the UN lexicon in 1986 when the General Assembly adopted the Declaration on the Right to Development. Among other things, the statement proclaims that "[t]he right to development is an inalienable human right by virtue of which every human person and all peoples are entitled to participate in, contribute to, and enjoy economic, social, cultural and political development, in which all human rights and fundamental freedoms can be fully realized."

29. Charles J. Brown, "In the Trenches: The Battle over Rights," *Freedom Review,* September-October 1993, 9.

30. Since the Vienna meeting, several other conferences have reinforced the growing cultural and political pluralism in the international community. The three most important were the International Conference on Population and Development in Cairo (1994), the World Summit on Social Development in Copenhagen (1995), and the Fourth International Conference on Women in Beijing (1995).

31. Vincent, *Human Rights and International Relations*, 142.

32. George F. Kennan, "Ethics and Foreign Policy: An Approach to the Problem," in *Foreign Policy and Morality: Framework for a Moral Audit*, ed. Theodore M. Hesburgh and Louis J. Halle (New York: Council on Religion and International Affairs, 1979), 44.

33. Stanley Hoffmann, "Reaching for the Most Difficult: Human Rights as a Foreign Policy Goal," *Daedalus* 112 (Fall 1983): 33.

34. Ibid., 28.

35. R. J. Rummel, *Death by Government* (New Brunswick, N.J.: Transaction Publishers, 1994), 15.

36. Ibid., 4.

37. For a detailed examination of these and other developments prior to the genocide, see Gérard Prunier, *The Rwanda Crisis: History of a Genocide* (New York: Columbia University Press, 1995), esp. 159–92.

38. The ineffectiveness of UNAMIR after the genocide began was also due to the fact that the original mission was limited to being an observer force. Even after evidence became available that a major genocide was underway, the UN Security Council refused to increased the size of UNAMIR or to expand its mandate.

39. David Rieff, "The Age of Genocide," *The New Republic,* January 26, 1996, 31.

40. The most complete and dispassionate account of the genocide is Prunier, *The Rwanda Crisis.*

41. Rieff, "The Age of Genocide," 31.

42. Milton Leitenberg, "Anatomy of a Massacre," *New York Times*, July 31, 1994, sec. 4, 15.

43. Ibid.

44. Robert Goldwin, "Human Rights and American Policy, Part IV—Arguments and Afterwords," *The Center Magazine*, July-August 1984, 59.

45. For a criticism of the Carter administration's human rights policy, see Joshua Muravchik, *The Uncertain Crusade: Jimmy Carter and the Dilemmas of Human Rights Policy* (New York: Hamilton Press, 1986).

46. William H. Gleysteen, Jr., "Korea: A Special Target of American Concern," in *The Diplomacy of Human Rights,* ed. David D. Newsom (Lanham, Md.: University Press of America, 1986), 99.

47. George F. Kennan, *The Cloud of Danger: Current Realities of American Foreign Policy* (Boston: Little, Brown, 1977), 43.

48. Herbert Butterfield, *History and Human Relations* (London: Collins, 1951), 110.

Chapter Five (pages 93 to 117)

1. Arthur Schlesinger, Jr., "The Necessary Amorality of Foreign Affairs," *Harper's Magazine*, August 1971, 72.

2. Carl von Clausewitz, *On War*, trans. Michael Howard and Peter Paret (Princeton, N.J.: Princeton University Press, 1976), 370.

3. Stanley Hoffmann, *Duties beyond Borders: On the Limits and Possibilities of Ethical International Politics* (Syracuse, N.Y.: Syracuse University Press, 1981), 81.

4. Quoted in James Turner Johnson, "Threats, Values, and Defense: Does the Defense of Values by Force Remain a Moral Possibility?" in *The Nuclear Dilemma and the Just War Tradition,* ed. William V. O'Brien and John Langan (Lexington, Ky.: Lexington Books, 1986), 36.

5. John Howard Yoder, *The Politics of Jesus* (Grand Rapids, Mich.: Eerdmans, 1972).

6. Cited in Roland H. Bainton, *Christian Attitudes toward War and Peace: A Historical Survey and Critical Re-evaluation* (New York: Abingdon Press, 1960), 153.

7. James Turner Johnson argues that although first-century Christians avoided military service, they did so not out of convictions about the evil of violence but because they held themselves "aloof from the kingdom of Caesar in expectation of the imminent coming of the kingdom of Christ." See James Turner Johnson, *The Quest for Peace: Three Moral Traditions in Western Cultural History* (Princeton, N.J.: Princeton University Press, 1987), 42.

8. Ibid., xiii–xv.

9. Ibid., 267–75.

10. Thucydides, *The Peloponnesian War,* trans. Rex Warner (New York: Penguin, 1954), 402.

11. Bernard Lewis, *The Political Language of Islam* (Chicago: University of Chicago Press, 1988), 73.

12. Bernard Lewis, "The Roots of Muslim Rage," *The Atlantic Monthly*, September 1990, 49.

13. See, for example, John Kelsay, *Islam and War: The Gulf War and Beyond* (Louisville, Ky.: John Knox Press, 1993), chap. 4.

14. Ibid., 148.

15. Bainton, *Christian Attitudes*, 45.

16. Will and Ariel Durant, *The Story of Civilization: Part III. The Age of Louis XIV* (New York: Simon and Schuster, 1963), 195.

17. For a comprehensive account of this theory, see Paul Ramsey, *The Just War: Force and Political Responsibility* (New York: Scribner's, 1968). For a historical account of the origins and development of this theory, see James Turner Johnson, *Ideology, Reason, and the Limitation of War: Religious and Secular Concepts, 1200–1740* (Princeton, N.J.: Princeton University Press, 1975); and James Turner Johnson, *Just War Tradition and the Restraint of War: A Moral and Historical Inquiry* (Princeton, N.J.: Princeton University Press, 1981).

18. James Turner Johnson, "The Concept of Just Cause," *American Purpose* 10 (Spring 1996): 4; see also James Turner Johnson, "The Broken Tradition," *The National Interest*, Fall 1996, 27–30.

19. William V. O'Brien, *The Conduct of Just and Limited War* (New York: Praeger, 1981).

20. Robert W. Tucker, "Justice and the War," *The National Interest*, Fall 1991, 111.

21. Because war frequently results in massive collateral destruction, scholars have developed the corollary principle of *double effect* to define the problem of civilian casualties. According to this norm, civilian casualties are morally permissible only when they are an unintentional by-product of the intentional targeting of military forces.

22. James Turner Johnson, "The Just War Tradition and the American Military," in *Just War and the Gulf War*, ed. James Turner Johnson and George Weigel (Washington, D.C.: Ethics and Public Policy Center, 1991), 22.

23. This evil became especially apparent when Iraq used civilians as protective shields during the air war, dumped large quantities of petroleum into the Persian Gulf, and destroyed nearly a thousand Kuwaiti oil fields.

24. Michael Walzer, "Perplexed," *The New Republic*, January 28, 1991, 14.

25. Michael Walzer, "Justice and Injustice in the Gulf War," in *But Was It Just? Reflections on the Morality of the Persian Gulf War*, ed. David E. DeCosse (New York: Doubleday, 1992), 3.

26. Quoted in George Weigel, "The Churches and War in the Gulf," *First Things* 11 (March 1990): 39.

27. "Message from Thirty-Two Church Leaders to President Bush," in Johnson and Wiegel, eds., *Just War and the Gulf War,* 137.

28. Walzer, "Perplexed," 13.

29. See, for example, Walzer, "Justice and Injustice," 12–13.

30. Robert W. Tucker, "Justice and the War," *The National Interest*, Fall 1991, 111–12.

31. Jean Bethke Elshtain, "Just War and American Politics," *The Christian Century*, January 15, 1992, 43.

32. Francis X. Winters, "Justice and the Gulf War," *The National Interest*, Winter 1991/92, 104.

33. Kalevi J. Holsti, *The State, War, and the State of War* (Cambridge: Cambridge University Press, 1996), 22.

34. Michael T. Klare, "Low-Intensity Conflict," *Christianity and Crisis*, February 1, 1988, 11–14.

35. Michael Walzer, *Just and Unjust Wars: A Moral Argument with Historical Illustrations* (New York: Basic Books, 1977), 179–96.

36. Charles Krauthammer, "Morality and the Reagan Doctrine," *The New Republic*, September 8, 1986, 23.

37. Charles Krauthammer, "The Reagan Doctrine," *Time*, April 1, 1985, 54–55. For a more extensive elaboration of the doctrine, see Charles Krauthammer, "The Poverty of Realism," *The New Republic*, February 17, 1986, 14–22.

38. Robert Kagan, *A Twilight Struggle: American Power and Nicaragua, 1977–1990* (New York: The Free Press, 1996), 209.

39. Ibid., 211.

40. For an illuminating moral assessment of optimistic and pessimistic worldviews, see Reinhold Niebuhr, *The Children of Light and the Children of Darkness: A Vindication of Democracy and a Critique of Its Traditional Defense* (New York: Scribner's, 1944).

41. James M. Scott, *Deciding to Intervene: The Reagan Doctrine and American Foreign Policy* (Durham, N.C.: Duke University Press, 1996), 20–21.

42. Ibid., 223.

43. Krauthammer, "The Reagan Doctrine," 54.

44. Robert H. Johnson, "Misguided Morality: Ethics and the Reagan Doctrine," *Political Science Quarterly* 103 (Fall 1988): 512.

45. Krauthammer, "Morality and the Reagan Doctrine," 19–20.

46. Johnson, "Misguided Morality," 520.

47. Ibid., 512.

48. Krauthammer, "Morality and the Reagan Doctrine," 20.

49. Charles R. Beitz, "The Reagan Doctrine in Nicaragua," in *Problems of International Justice*, ed. Steven Luper-Foy (Boulder, Colo.: Westview Press, 1988), 189.

50. Robert A. Pastor, *Whirlpool: U.S. Foreign Policy toward Latin America and the Caribbean* (Princeton, N.J.: Princeton University Press, 1992), 82.

51. Krauthammer, "Morality and the Reagan Doctrine," 23.

52. Scott, *Deciding to Intervene*, 79.

53. Indeed, the Afghanistan guerrillas received more ($500 million) in 1986 than the Nicaraguan Contras received from 1981 to 1988, the period of U.S. assistance.

54. Kagan, *A Twilight Struggle*, 722.

55. Ibid., 723.

56. George Shultz, *Turmoil and Triumph: My Years as Secretary of State* (New York: Scribner's, 1993), 1129.

57. Although this view is contested, it is the conclusion of numerous scholars and public officials. See, for example, Jack F. Matlock, Jr., *Autopsy on an Empire: The American Ambassador's Account of the Collapse of the Soviet Union* (New York: Random House, 1995), 668–70. For a contrary view, see Raymond L. Garthoff, *The Great Transition: American-Soviet Relations and the End of the Cold War* (Washington, D.C.: The Brookings Institution, 1994), 754–55.

Chapter Six (pages 119 to 143)

1. Lea Brilmayer, *American Hegemony: Political Morality in a One-Superpower World* (New Haven, Conn.: Yale University Press, 1994), 154.
2. Charles Krauthammer, "Morality and the Reagan Doctrine," *The New Republic*, September 8, 1986, 21.
3. Quoted in Drew Christiansen and Gerard F. Powers, "The Duty to Intervene: Ethics and the Varieties of Humanitarian Intervention," in *Close Calls: Intervention, Terrorism, Missile Defense, and "Just War" Today*, ed. Elliott Abrams (Washington, D.C.: Ethics and Public Policy Center, 1998), 183.
4. Quoted in Kelly Kate Pease and David P. Forsythe, "Human Rights, Humanitarian Intervention, and World Politics," *Human Rights Quarterly* 15 (1993): 292.
5. According to Chapter VII, the Security Council can take whatever political and military actions it designates to respond to "a threat to peace, breach of the peace or act of aggression." In effect, the United Nations can, when the Security Council so decides, intervene against the wishes of a member state. Such action was undertaken in 1992 when the United Nations authorized U.S. military intervention in Somalia.
6. Michael Mandelbaum, "The Reluctance to Intervene," *Foreign Policy*, no. 95 (Summer 1994): 14.
7. Ibid., 15.
8. For an informative collection of essays on emerging norms governing international boundaries, see Laura W. Reed and Carl Kaysen, eds., *Emerging Norms of Justified Intervention* (Cambridge, Mass.: Committee on International Security Studies, American Academy of Arts and Sciences, 1993).
9. Michael Walzer calls this approach the "domestic analogy." For a discussion of this argument, see Michael Walzer, *Just and Unjust Wars: A Moral Argument with Historical Illustrations* (New York: Basic Books, 1977), 58.
10. Ibid., 101.
11. Ibid., 88.
12. Michael Walzer, "The Moral Standing of States: A Response to Four Critics," *Philosophy & Public Affairs* 9, no. 3 (Spring 1980): 214.
13. Walzer, *Just and Unjust Wars*, 54.
14. Jefferson McMahan, "The Ethics of International Intervention," in *Political Realism and International Morality: Ethics in the Nuclear Age*, ed. Kenneth Kipnis and Diana T. Meyers (Boulder, Colo.: Westview Press, 1987), 82–83.
15. Ibid., 85.
16. Stanley Hoffmann, *Duties beyond Borders: On the Limits and Possibilities*

of Ethical International Politics (Syracuse, N.Y.: Syracuse University Press, 1981), 58.

17. Dorothy Jones, *Code of Peace: Ethics and Security in the World of Warlord States* (Chicago: University of Chicago Press, 1992).

18. Ibid., xii, 163–64.

19. Ibid., 61–63.

20. Ibid., 90–108. A number of scholars have challenged Walzer's international relations paradigm as being too statist and insufficiently sensitive to the injustices that arise within states. For a critique of Walzer's argument, see Gerald Doppelt, "Walzer's Theory of Morality in International Relations," *Philosophy & Public Affairs* 8, no. 1 (1978): 2–26; Charles R. Beitz, "Bounded Morality: Justice and the State in World Politics," *International Organization* 33 (Summer 1979): 405–24; and David Luban, "Just War and Human Rights," *Philosophy & Public Affairs* 9, no. 2 (1979): 161–81. For Walzer's response to his critics, see Michael Walzer, "The Moral Standing of States: A Response to Four Critics," *Philosophy & Public Affairs* 9, no. 3 (1980): 209–29.

21. Mandelbaum, "The Reluctance to Intervene," 8.

22. Stanley Hoffmann, "Delusions of World Order," *New York Review of Books,* May 28, 1992, 37–43.

23. Charles Krauthammer, "When to Intervene," *The New Republic*, May 6, 1985, 11.

24. For a discussion of the role of relevance of the just-war doctrine to military intervention, see Kenneth R. Himes, "Just War, Pacifism and Humanitarian Intervention," *America*, August 14, 1993, 15, 28–29.

25. For a clear articulation of these three justifications, see U.S. Department of State, Bureau of Public Affairs, "The Decision to Assist Grenada," January 24, 1984. In this statement, Langhorne Motley, the Assistant Secretary of State for Inter-American Affairs, explains to the House Armed Services Committee why the United States intervened in Grenada.

26. Terry Nardin and Kathleen D. Pritchard, "Ethics and Intervention: The United States in Grenada, 1983," *Case Studies in Ethics and International Affairs, No. 2* (New York: Carnegie Council on Ethics and International Affairs, 1990), 16.

27. See, for example, John Norton Moore, "Grenada and the International Double Standard," *American Journal of International Law* 78 (January 1984): 153–59.

28. See, for example, Christopher C. Joyner, "The United States Action in Grenada," *American Journal of International Law* 78 (January 1984): 131–44; and Francis A. Boyle et al. "International Lawlessness in Grenada," *American Journal of International Law* 78 (January 1984): 172–75.

29. Moore, "Grenada and the International Double Standard," 148–49.

30. Alberto R. Coll, "Why Grenada Was Important," *Naval War College Review* 40 (Summer 1987): 4–13.

31. Nardin and Pritchard, "Ethics and Intervention," 7.

32. Coll, "Why Grenada Was Important," 7–8.

33. Michael W. Doyle, *Ways of War and Peace: Realism, Liberalism, and Socialism* (New York: Norton, 1997), 415.

34. Ibid., 413.

35. Ibid., 411.

36. Jack Donnelly, "Human Rights, Humanitarian Intervention and American Foreign Policy: Law, Morality and Politics," *Journal of International Affairs* 37 (Winter 1984): 313.

37. For an excellent discussion of the U.S. military and diplomatic operation in Somalia, see John L. Hirsch and Robert B. Oakley, *Somalia and Operation Restore Hope: Reflections on Peacemaking and Peacekeeping* (Washington, D.C.: U.S. Institute of Peace Press, 1995).

38. Hirsch and Oakley, *Somalia and Operation Restore Hope,* 145.

39. It is important to emphasize that the Security Council authorized this action in great part because of the total breakdown of government authority. Because there was no effective government in Somalia, the UN Charter's prohibitions against UN intervention in the domestic affairs of states (Article 2.7) were not applicable.

40. Alberto R. Coll, "Somalia and the Problems of Doing Good: A Perspective from the Defense Department," in Abrams, ed., *Close Calls,* 177–81.

41. John R. Bolton, "Somalia and the Problems of Doing Good: A Perspective from the Department of State," in Abrams, ed., *Close Calls,* 157.

42. Coll, "Somalia and the Problem of Doing Good," 179.

43. Chester Crocker, "The Lessons of Somalia," *Foreign Affairs* 74 (May/June 1995): 7.

Chapter Seven (pages 145 to 165)

1. Quoted in Barry E. Carter, *International Economic Sanctions: Improving the Haphazard U.S. Legal Regime* (Cambridge: Cambridge University Press, 1988), 9.

2. Margaret P. Doxey, *International Sanctions in Contemporary Perspective* (New York: St. Martin's Press, 1987), 145.

3. Quoted in Richard E. Sincere, Jr., *The Politics of Sentiment: Churches and Foreign Investment in South Africa* (Washington, D.C.: Ethics and Public Policy Center, 1984), v.

4. David A. Baldwin, *Economic Statecraft* (Princeton, N.J.: Princeton University Press, 1985).

5. See, for example, Roger Fisher, *Conflict for Beginners* (New York: Harper & Row, 1969).

6. James M. Lindsay, "Trade Sanctions as Policy Instruments: A Re-examination," *International Studies Quarterly,* no. 30 (June 1986): 155–56.

7. Kim Richard Nossal, "International Sanctions as International Punishment," *International Organization* 43 (Spring 1989): 313–14.

8. National Association of Manufacturers, *A Catalog of New U.S. Unilateral Economic Sanctions for Foreign Policy Purposes, 1993–96* (Washington, D.C.: National Association of Manufacturers, 1997), 1–4.

9. Charles Kindleberger, *Power and Money: The Economics of International*

Politics and the Politics of International Economics (New York: Basic Books, 1970), 97.

10. Margaret P. Doxey, *Economic Sanctions and International Enforcement* (New York: Oxford University Press, 1971), 139.

11. Baldwin, *Economic Statecraft*, 57.

12. M. S. Daoudi and J. S. Dajani, *Economic Sanctions: Ideals and Experience* (London: Routledge & Kegan Paul, 1983).

13. Donald L. Losman, *International Economic Sanctions: The Cases of Cuba, Israel and Rhodesia* (Albuquerque: University of New Mexico Press, 1979), 1, 124.

14. Gary C. Hufbauer, Jeffrey J. Schott, and Kimberly Ann Elliott, *Economic Sanctions Reconsidered: History and Current Policy*, 2nd ed. (Washington, D.C.: Institute for International Economics, 1990), 49–73.

15. For a discussion of the relationship between private and public actors, see Kenneth A. Rodman, "Public and Private Sanctions against South Africa," *Political Science Quarterly* 109 (Summer 1994): 313–34.

16. Hufbauer, Schott, and Elliott, *Economic Sanctions Reconsidered*.

17. Robert A. Pape, "Why Economic Sanctions Do Not Work," *International Security* 22 (Fall 1997): 90–136.

18. Franklin L. Lavin, "Asphyxiation or Oxygen? The Sanctions Dilemma," *Foreign Policy* 104 (Fall 1996): 153.

19. Kimberly Ann Elliott, "Factors Affecting the Success of Sanctions," in *Economic Sanctions: Panacea or Peacebuilding in a Post-Cold War World?*, ed. David Cortright and George A. Lopez (Boulder, Colo.: Westview Press, 1995), 53.

20. The MFN principle, the most basic norm of the world economy, requires that trade be carried out in a reciprocal and nondiscriminatory manner, so that any trade preferences must be extended to all member states.

21. The Jackson-Vanik amendment (to the Trade Act) was adopted to encourage the Soviet Union to allow greater freedom of Jewish emigration. Although the amendment's sponsors assumed that the threat of economic penalties would encourage greater emigration liberalization, in actual fact the law had the direct opposite effect, resulting in a significant decline in the number of emigrants.

22. James Lilley, "Freedom through Trade," *Foreign Policy* 94 (Spring 1994): 40.

23. According to the order, the improvement in human rights had to be realized in seven areas, two of them mandatory. The two mandatory areas were emigration of dissidents' family members and termination of prison-made exports to the United States. The five other areas were (1) allowing Voice of America broadcasts to China, (2) accounting for political prisoners, (3) improving prison conditions, (4) easing political repression in Tibet, and (5) providing better treatment of religious minorities.

24. Richard Dicker, "The US Business Community and Human Rights in China," *Current History,* September 1994, 253.

25. Lavin, "Asphyxiation or Oxygen?" 140.

26. In the end, the United States intervened militarily in December 1989 to oust the Noriega government and to capture and bring the dictator to trial.

27. Hufbauer, Schott, and Elliott, *Economic Sanctions Reconsidered,* 53–54.

28. Baldwin, *Economic Statecraft*, 96–114.

29. Lisa Martin, *Coercive Cooperation: Explaining Multilateral Economic Sanctions* (Princeton, N.J.: Princeton University Press, 1992).

30. William Kaempfer and Anton Lowenberg, *International Economic Sanctions: A Public Choice Perspective* (Boulder, Colo.: Westview Press, 1992), 133.

31. For a discussion of this point with reference to selective cases (the Megarian decree, the League of Nations sanctions against Italy, and the trans-Siberian pipeline sanctions), see Stefanie Ann Lenway, "Between War and Commerce: Economic Sanctions as a Tool of Statecraft," *International Organization* 42 (Spring 1988): 409–19.

32. Baldwin, *Economic Statecraft*, 359. See also Patrick Clawson, "Sanctions as Punishment, Enforcement, and Prelude to Further Action," *Ethics & International Affairs* 7 (1993): 17–37; Lori Fisler Damrosch, "The Collective Enforcement of International Norms through Economic Sanctions," *Ethics & International Affairs* 8 (1994): 73–74; and Albert C. Pierce, "Just War Principles and Economic Sanctions," *Ethics & International Affairs* 10 (1996): 99–113.

33. Drew Christiansen and Gerard F. Powers, "Economic Sanctions and the Just-War Doctrine," in Cortright and Lopez, eds., *Economic Sanctions*, 102.

34. See, for example, Pierce, "Just War Principles and Economic Sanctions."

35. Rodman, "Public and Private Sanctions."

36. The principle of double effect provides that civilians may be killed in war but only if their death is the by-product of the destruction and violence directly intended against military targets.

37. Pierce, "Just War Principles and Economic Sanctions," 100–101.

38. Michael Walzer, *Just and Unjust Wars: A Moral Argument with Historical Illustrations*, 2nd ed. (New York: Basic Books, 1992), 146.

39. Lori Fisler Damrosch, "The Civilian Impact of Economic Sanctions," in *Enforcing Restraint: Collective Intervention in International Conflicts,* ed. Lori Fisler Damrosch (New York: Council on Foreign Relations Press, 1993), 279.

40. Drew Christiansen and Gerard F. Powers, "Sanctions: Unintended Consequences," *The Bulletin of the Atomic Scientists*, November 1993, 43.

41. Michael Walzer, "Justice and Injustice in the Gulf War," in *But Was It Just? Reflections on the Morality of the Persian Gulf War,* ed. David DeCosse (New York: Doubleday, 1992), 3.

42. Christiansen and Powers, "Economic Sanctions and the Just-War Doctrine," 102.

43. William H. Kaempfer, James A. Lehman, and Anton D. Lowenberg, "Divestment, Investment Sanctions, and Disinvestment: An Evaluation of Anti-Apartheid Policy Instruments," *International Organization* 41 (Summer 1987): 461.

44. Jennifer Davis, "Sanctions and Apartheid: The Economic Challenge to Discrimination," in Cortright and Lopez, eds., *Economic Sanctions,* 178.

45. Kenneth A. Rodman, "Public and Private Sanctions against South Africa," *Political Science Quarterly* 109 (Summer 1994): 323.

46. Thomas W. Hazlett, "Did Sanctions Matter?" *New York Times,* July 22, 1991, sec. A, 5.

47. Helen Suzman, "Sanctions Won't End Apartheid," *New York Times*, October 4, 1987, sec. IV, 23.

48. Alan Paton, *Cry, the Beloved Country* (Cape Town: Hans Strydom Publishers, 1987), 7.

49. Federated Chamber of Industries, *The Effect of Sanctions on Unemployment and Production in South Africa* (Pretoria: FCI Information Services, 1986).

50. Neta C. Crawford, "The Humanitarian Consequences of Sanctioning South Africa: A Preliminary Assessment," in *Political Gain and Civilian Pain: Humanitarian Impacts of Economic Sanctions,* ed. Thomas G. Weiss et al. (Lanham, Md.: Rowman & Littlefield, 1997), 77.

51. The Anglo-American Corporation paid about 20 percent less than the value of traded stock, and it did so with undervalued South African currency (rand).

52. Merle Lipton*, Sanctions and South Africa: The Dynamics of Economic Isolation,* Special Report No. 1119 (London: The Economist Intelligence Unit, January 1988), 92.

53. Crawford, "The Humanitarian Consequences of Sanctioning South Africa," 73.

54. Ibid., 77.

55. F.W. de Klerk, "The Bull in the Garden," *Civilization* 5 (April/May 1998): 61.

Chapter Eight (pages 167 to 196)

1. Charles R. Beitz, *Political Theory and International Relations* (Princeton, N.J.: Princeton University Press, 1979), 151.

2. Stanley Hoffmann, *Duties beyond Borders: On the Limits and Possibilities of Ethical International Politics* (Syracuse, N.Y.: Syracuse University Press, 1981), 19.

3. Alan Dowty, *Closed Borders: The Contemporary Assault on Freedom of Movement* (New Haven, Conn.: Yale University Press, 1987), 226.

4. For a mid-twentieth-century application of Lloyd's metaphor, see Garrett Hardin, "The Tragedy of the Commons," *Science,* December 13, 1968, 1243–48.

5. For a discussion of the regulation of the earth's collective goods, see Per Magnus Wijkman, "Managing the Global Commons," *International Organization* 36 (Summer 1982): 511–36.

6. Sharon Begley, "Too Much Hot Air," *Newsweek,* October 20, 1997, 50.

7. Henry D. Jacoby, Ronald G. Prinn, and Richard Schmalensee, "Kyoto's Unfinished Business," *Foreign Affairs* 77 (July/August 1998): 60.

8. For a moral assessment of "emission rights," see Michael J. Sandel, "It's Immoral to Buy the Right to Pollute," *New York Times*, December 15, 1997, sec. A, 15.

9. Brian Tucker, "Science Friction: The Politics of Global Warming," *The National Interest,* Fall 1997, 84.

10. Hoffmann, *Duties beyond Borders,* 164–65.

11. For a review of contemporary analyses of international justice from a proce-

dural perspective, see Chris Brown, *International Relations Theory: New Normative Approaches* (New York: Columbia University Press, 1992), 170–88.

12. Terry Nardin, *Law, Morality and the Relations of States* (Princeton, N.J.: Princeton University Press, 1983), 267–68.

13. Stanley Hoffmann, "The Crisis of Liberal Internationalism," *Foreign Policy*, no. 98 (Spring 1995): 160.

14. The domestic analogy is based on the comparison of international society to domestic order. The a priori rights and duties of states are viewed as comparable to the rights and duties of citizens in prepolitical society, that is, the state of nature.

15. Examples of communitarian thinkers include seventeenth-century German international lawyer Samuel Pufendorf, eighteenth-century Swiss jurist Emmerich de Vattel, nineteenth-century British political theorist John Stuart Mill, and contemporary political philosopher Michael Walzer. For a recent normative justification of the existing international system, see Mervyn Frost, *Ethics in International Relations: A Constitutive Theory* (Cambridge: Cambridge University Press, 1996). Frost's "constitutive theory" provides a normative justification for the communitarian perspective.

16. Examples of cosmopolitan thinkers include sixteenth-century Spanish theologian Francisco Suarez, nineteenth-century German philosopher Immanuel Kant, and contemporary political philosopher Henry Shue. One of the most influential expositions of this perspective is Charles Beitz, *Political Theory and International Relations* (Princeton, N.J.: Princeton University Press, 1979).

17. For a comparative assessment of cosmopolitan and communitarian perspectives, see Chris Brown, *International Relations Theory: New Normative Approaches* (New York: Columbia University Press, 1992).

18. Ibid., 110.

19. For a full exposition of this position, see Beitz, *Political Theory and International Relations*, which applies John Rawls's theory of justice to international affairs.

20. Quoted in David Halloran Lumsdaine, *Moral Vision in International Politics: The Foreign Aid Regime, 1949–1989* (Princeton, N.J.: Princeton University Press, 1993), 221–22.

21. Ibid., 257.

22. Nick Eberstadt, "Famine, Development and Foreign Aid," *Commentary*, March 1985, 28.

23. Lumsdaine, *Moral Vision in International Politics*, 3.

24. P. T. Bauer, *Reality and Rhetoric* (Cambridge: Harvard University Press, 1984), 38–62. See also P. T. Bauer, *Equality, the Third World, and Economic Delusion* (Cambridge: Harvard University Press, 1981).

25. For a discussion of this point, see Brian R. Opeskin, "The Moral Foundations of Foreign Aid," *World Development* 43 (January 1996): 21–44.

26. Ibid., 26–30.

27. In his study *Basic Rights*, Henry Shue illustrates the role of the distributive justice idea to the meeting of human needs. Shue argues that people are entitled to fundamental rights, including the right to subsistence, and justifies this claim on the basis of the notion of distributive justice, not on the basis of the essential worth

and dignity of the human person. Henry Shue, *Basic Rights: Subsistence, Affluence, and U.S. Foreign Policy* (Princeton, N.J.: Princeton University Press, 1980).

28. Peter Singer, "Famine, Affluence, and Morality," *Philosophy and Public Affairs* 1 (Spring 1972): 229–43.

29. See Garrett Hardin, *Living within Limits: Ecology, Economics and Population Taboos* (New York: Oxford University Press, 1993), esp. 276–93.

30. See, for example, Joseph H. Carens, "Aliens and Citizens: The Case for Open Borders," *The Review of Politics* 49 (Spring 1987): 251–73; Carens, "Migration and Morality: A Liberal Egalitarian Perspective, in *Free Movement: Ethical Issues in the Transnational Migration of People and of Money,* ed. Brian Barry and Robert E. Goodin (University Park: Pennsylvania State University Press, 1992), 25–47; and Peter and Renata Singer, "The Ethics of Refugee Policy," in *Open Borders? Closed Societies? The Ethical and Political Issues*, ed. Mark Gibney (New York: Greenwood Press, 1988), 111–30.

31. Dowty, *Closed Borders*, 15.

32. For a discussion of the role of the right of emigration in traditional international law, see David C. Hendrickson, "Migration in Law and Ethics: A Realist Perspective," in Barry and Goodin, eds., *Free Movement,* 223–27.

33. The right of return is a delimited claim for admission. The right of return applies mainly to peoples seeking to return to their nation's homeland on the basis of historic ties of prior membership. For a discussion of how this right applies to Palestinian and Jewish people within Israel, see W. Gunther Plaut, *Asylum: A Moral Dilemma* (Westport, Conn.: Praeger, 1995), 82–88.

34. Brian Barry, "The Quest for Consistency: A Skeptical View," in Barry and Goodin, eds., *Free Movement,* 284.

35. Michael Walzer, *Spheres of Justice: A Defense of Pluralism and Equality* (New York: Basic Books, 1983), 62.

36. Ibid., 9–10.

37. Myron Weiner, "Ethics, National Sovereignty and the Control of Immigration," *International Migration Review* 30 (Spring 1996): 192.

38. For an illuminating account of the international community's responsibility to the growth in refugees in the late twentieth century, see Gil Loescher, *Beyond Charity: International Cooperation and the Global Refugee Crisis* (New York: Oxford University Press, 1993).

39. Louis Henkin, *The Age of Rights* (New York: Columbia University Press, 1990), 48.

40. According to the 1951 UN Convention on the Status of Refugees, a refugee is "a person who owing to well-founded fear of being persecuted for reasons of race, religion, nationality, membership of a particular social group or political opinion, is outside the country of his nationality and is unable or, owing to such fear, is unwilling to avail himself of the protection of that country."

41. Myron Weiner, *The Global Migration Crisis: Challenge to States and to Human Rights* (New York: HarperCollins, 1995), 56.

42. For example, Germany's 1993 asylum law permits the government to immediately deport refugees from a country free of persecution. In addition, the law states that any person who travels through a "safe country" can be deemed to have found protection there and thus may be returned to that state.

43. For example, Peter and Renata Singer, following the principle of "equal consideration of interests," argue for greatly increasing the number of refugees resettled in rich countries. See Peter and Renata Singer, "The Ethics of Refugee Policy," in Gibney, ed., *Open Borders?* 122–28.

44. Weiner, "Ethics, National Sovereignty and the Control of Immigration," 175.

45. U.S. Commission on Immigration Reform, *U.S. Immigration Policy: Restoring Credibility* (Washington, D.C.: U.S. Government Printing Office, September 1994), 230.

46. For example, the 1995 proposed refugee admissions called for a ceiling of 110,000 refugees, distributed as follows: Africa, 7,000; East Asia, 40,000; former Soviet Union/Eastern Europe, 48,000; Latin America and the Caribbean, 8,000; and Near East, 5,000.

47. Family-sponsored immigration is governed by the four following preferences, listed in priority: (1) unmarried sons and daughters of U.S. citizens, (2) spouses and unmarried sons and daughters of permanent resident aliens, (3) married sons and daughters of U.S. citizens, and (4) brothers and sisters of U.S. citizens who are at least twenty-one years old. Employment-based immigration is governed by five preferences, listed in priority: (1) priority workers, who have demonstrated extraordinary professional abilities, (2) professionals with advanced degrees, (3) skilled workers with baccalaureate degrees and some unskilled workers, (4) special immigrants, such as religious ministers; and (5) investors.

48. Weiner, "Ethics, National Sovereignty and the Control of Immigration," 195.

49. Singer, "The Ethics of Refugee Policy," 116.

50. "Immigration Today: Current Policy and Statistics," *Congressional Digest*, May 1996, 135.

51. Ibid., 136.

52. *New York Times*, June 14, 1996, sec. A, 1, 13.

53. The Mariel boatlift occurred in the spring of 1980 after Fidel Castro announced that anyone wishing to leave Cuba could do so. As a result, some 125,000 Cubans, with the help of more than a thousand Florida boats, migrated to the United States during a two-month period. Because U.S. law would not allow such a large number of immigrants or refugees, the U.S. government classified such persons as "special entrants."

54. This decision was contested in court. Human rights advocates filed a legal suit arguing that the executive decision was unconstitutional because it violated the 1951 Convention on Refugees. A district court affirmed the decision, and a federal appeals court overturned the lower court ruling. The Justice Department immediately filed an appeal with the U.S. Supreme Court. After granting the Bush administration temporary authority to continue forced repatriation, the high court ruled that the original executive order was not unconstitutional.

55. Walzer, *Spheres of Justice*, 18–21.

56. Weiner, "Ethics, National Sovereignty and the Control of Immigration," 179.

Chapter Nine (pages 197 to 202)

1. Quoted in Michael W. Doyle, *Ways of War and Peace: Realism, Liberalism, and Socialism* (New York: W.W. Norton, 1997), 383.

2. James Turner Johnson, "Just Cause Revisited," in *Close Calls: Intervention, Terrorism, Missile Defense, and 'Just War' Today,* ed. Elliot Abrams (Washington, D.C.: Ethics and Public Policy Center, 1998), 38.

3. Drew Christiansen and Gerard F. Powers, "The Duty to Intervene: Ethics and the Varieties of Humanitarian Intervention," in Abrams, ed., *Close Calls,* 183–208.

4. G. Scott Davis, "Interpreting Contemporary Conflicts," in *Religion and Justice in the War over Bosnia,* ed. G. Scott Davis (New York: Routledge, 1996), 4–5. See also Michael Sells, "Religion, History, and Genocide in Bosnia-Herzegovina," in Davis, ed., *Religion and Justice in the War over Bosnia,* 25–28.

5. Michael Walzer, *Just and Unjust Wars: A Moral Argument with Historical Illustrations* (New York: Basic Books, 1977), 19.

INDEX

ABOUT THE AUTHOR

Mark R. Amstutz is professor of political science at Wheaton College (Illinois), where he teaches courses in international relations and Third World politics. He is author of *International Conflict and Cooperation: An Introduction to World Politics,* 2nd ed. (McGraw-Hill, 1998) and *Christian Ethics and U.S. Foreign Policy* (Zondervan, 1987). He is currently doing research on the potential role of forgiveness in international relations.